In the Company of Scholars

In the Company of Scholars

The Struggle for the Soul of Higher Education

• JULIUS GETMAN •

University of Texas Press, Austin

Requests for permission to reproduce material from this work should be sent to
Permissions, University of Texas Press, Box 7819, Austin, TX 78713-7819.

⊗ The paper used in this publication meets the minimum requirements of
American National Standard for Information Sciences—Permanence of Paper
for Printed Library Materials, ANSI Z39.48-1984.

Library of Congress Cataloging-in-Publication Data

Getman, Julius G.
  In the company of scholars : the struggle for the soul of higher education /
Julius Getman.
     p.   cm.
  Includes bibliographical references.
  ISBN 0-292-72755-0
  1. Education, Higher—United States—Philosophy.   2. Education, Higher—
Political aspects—United States.   3. Education, Humanistic—United
States.   4. Elites (Social sciences)—United States.
  I. Title.
  LA227.G48   1992
  378.73—dc20   92-20150
                                                                       CIP

To the memory of my father, Samuel Getman, 1900–1959, and to my mother, Charlotte Getman, from whom I learned that pleasure in ideas, intelligence, curiosity about people, love of music, art, and literature do not require formal education.

Contents

Preface

This book has taken a long time to write. I began working on it about a decade ago when I was teaching at Yale Law School. The original plan was to describe and discuss a series of academic issues from a personal and liberal perspective. Although I did not have a conscious theme, certain themes began to emerge during the long period of writing.

I concluded that almost all of us enter academic life seeking a mix of four goals—meaning, prestige, community, and time to devote to study and reflection. The goals are worthy but for most of us are far more difficult to achieve than we had anticipated, and they often are in conflict with each other. My own experiences are in many ways typical.

I entered the academic world because I believed that, if one were a law professor, status was automatically achieved and thereafter ceased to be a source of concern, that achievement would be meaningful and recognizable, and that success was based on merit. I thought that universities provided an opportunity for caring relations, a sense of community, an atmosphere in which ideas were shared and refined, an egalitarian ethic, and a style of life that would permit time for family, friends, and self-expression. The reality, as I discovered, was quite different. The academic world is hierarchical and competitive; achievement is generally ephemeral and difficult to measure. Much that is done in the name of scholarship or teaching makes little contribution because it is removed from reality and the concerns of humanity. Rather than feeling an automatic sense of community, I have often felt alienated. In particular, the desire for success and status has often conflicted with other goals of meaning, community, study, and reflection.

My experiences have been far from unique. Many academics, even those whose lives seem tranquil and successful, are unhappy and disappointed. Some feel cheated, some wonder if what they have experienced is really all there is to the life that once seemed so full of promise, and others become caught up pursuing goals of success, recognition, and meaning that seem just out of reach. The more I tried to explain why the good academic life is so difficult to achieve, the more the answer seemed to reside in the ubiquitous conflict between the egalitarian and elitist aspects of higher education. Within colleges and universities, this conflict is regularly manifested in the discussion and resolution of academic issues. It also resonates internally for almost all of us who devote major parts of our lives to teaching or scholarship. Once again, I believe my experiences to be typical. My background has made me receptive to both the lure of elitism and the appeal of egalitarianism.

When I first entered academic life right after a stint as a teaching fellow and graduate student at the Harvard University Law School, I was committed to a conventional and elitist vision of academic excellence. I was convinced that grades and intelligence were powerfully correlated, that analytical rigor was the highest form of intellectual achievement, and that good teaching and careful scholarship were inevitably meaningful and rewarding. That point of view changed dramatically and permanently during the late 1960s and 1970s. In part, change came with the times, but it also came from an unconscious reevaluation of my own background. I became increasingly aware of sins committed in the name of academic excellence. I began to wince when people spoke reverentially of the need to maintain academic standards, and I started to seriously question the widely shared assumption of my colleagues that professors at elite institutions were smarter and more thoughtful than other people. Eventually I came to revel in my differences with my colleagues, much as I once reveled in my Harvard degree. But that too has gradually changed, and I have become more tolerant of academic elitism and less comfortable with its populist critics. Today, years after I first entered the academy, I find myself almost as critical of academic liberals as I am of its traditionalists.

I realized while writing this book that widespread insecurity is inevitable among professors because some kind of failure is an almost certain aspect of academic life, even (or, perhaps, especially) for its most creative scholars and ambitious teachers. Able academics are inevitably seekers after discovery and enlightenment, and these goals are far more difficult to achieve than success in many other fields or success as a student, which is the experience most likely to lead people into academic life.

Because this book utilizes actual experiences, mostly my own, to illustrate many of its major themes, it may be argued that its conclusions should not be considered valid for higher education in general. I recognize that my teaching has been limited to professional schools associated with major universities and that I have no firsthand experience with small liberal arts, religious, or junior colleges. However, because of my long-time involvement with the American Association of University Professors, I have had the opportunity to work with, represent, and interview faculty members at many different types of schools over a long period of time. I also have conducted a series of interviews of academics with a variety of different backgrounds in conjunction with the writing of this book. As a result, I am confident that the basic tensions, conflicts, ambitions, and satisfactions that I describe are common throughout academic life. The search for meaning, the desire to impart one's ideas, the wish to be recognized as an authority, and the need to choose the topics and issues with which one deals are all ubiquitous. At every level of academic life, success is difficult to achieve and failure of one sort or another is always lurking.

Those from far different backgrounds who have read part or all of the book have almost invariably recognized in the stories their own experiences, attitudes, and feelings. I write often of teachers or scholars disappointed by and alienated from academic life, yet I have come to an increasing appreciation of the great number of committed and successful scholars and teachers who are to be found at every academic institution.

The following names are pseudonyms: Randy Baker, Harold Benjamin, Dick Brimmer, Mike Bradford, Mike Broderick, Jim Bruce, Mike Castellano, Bob Costa, Scott Daily, Jim Eads, Pru Eads, Bob Earl, Gregg Forrest, Terry James, Henry Jonathan, Barbara Kennedy, Jim Kerry, Aaron Levine, Jerry Markowitz, Allen Miller, Anthony Mosca, Dan O'Neill, Sanita Porter, Bill Randolph, Frank Richards, Bob Sanders, Rod Smith, and Tom Weller.

Acknowledgments

This book has been helped by many people. Some helped by reading and criticizing, some by encouraging, some by sharing their stories, some by contributing ideas, and some by examples of their own careers.

I thank Steve Wizner, Boris Bitker, Harry Wellington, Peter Schuck, Marcy Schuck, and the late Robert Cover—all members of the Yale community who took the time to edit and comment upon an earlier version. Steve Wizner, over the course of many running conversations, also helped in defining the basic ideas of the book.

In working on the earlier version, I received great support, encouragement, and very good criticism from Professor Carol Simpson Stearn of Northwestern University and her husband Jay Stearn, Professor Mary Ann Glendon of Harvard University Law School, and from Professor Stephen B. Goldberg of Northwestern University Law School. I am grateful to my colleague at the University of Texas Law School, Dick Markovits, who promptly read several chapters in draft and made his usual trenchant suggestions in the margin, some of which were even legible.

My friend and colleague Dr. Terri LeClercq of the University of Texas Law School did a splendid job of editing. She also helped me to transform the earlier, autobiographical version into a more general statement about academic life. My colleague Zipporah Wiseman, a professor at the University of Texas, read several chapters and gave me many good ideas, both substantive and stylistic.

I have had dedicated secretarial help from Barbara Bellamy, Diane Thompson, and Leslie Bordonaro. I appreciate the diligence and creative work of Roberta Jones, my research assistant. I am especially thankful to Theresa May and Vicki Woodruff, my acquisitions editor and copy editor respectively, for their help with this book. It has been a pleasure working with them.

In the Company of Scholars

I thank all of the academics and former academics who answered my questions and those who have trusted me to write a part of their story. I am particularly grateful to Mel Schwartz, my friend of many years, who convinced me by comparative example when we were both students at Bronx High School of Science that physics was not my field, for taking the time to insure the scientific and factual accuracy of the material concerning his career. My thanks go to Janet Lever and Adrienne Birecree for sharing their stories and being available to answer questions.

I thank Charlie Ellinger for his original insights and dogged insistence on his place in academic life.

I am grateful to David Riesman and the late John P. Dawson for giving me a special example of scholarly excellence, Louis L. Jaffe for providing a new, more positive view of intellectuals, and my late colleague, Ralph Follen Fuchs, for providing a wonderful model of what academic life should be like.

Interviews

Note on interviews:

In researching this book, I conducted interviews with the people listed below. Unless otherwise indicated, all references to and quotes from them in the text come from the interviews.

Lee Balliet, director of the Bureau of Labor Studies, Indiana University. April 1991.

Adrienne Birecree, formerly professor of economics, Bucknell University; currently professor of economics, Radford University. June, July, and August 1991.

Linda Brodkey, professor of English, University of Texas. April and May 1991.

Charles R. Ellinger, associate professor of labor studies, Indiana University. May of 1987.

Glenda Hodges, formerly professor of communications, Hampton College; currently attorney, Enforcement Litigation Section, National Labor Relations Board, and adjunct professor of business law, Howard University. March 25 and 27, 1987.

Perry Hodges, writing instructor, Indiana University School of Law, Bloomington. April 1987.

Aaron Konstam, professor of computer science, Trinity University. October 1987.

Janet Lever, formerly professor of sociology, Northwestern University; currently professor of sociology, California State University, Los Angeles. June 1987 and subsequently.

In the Company of Scholars

Bruce Mann, professor of law, University of Pennsylvania. Summer 1987.

Herbert Marks, professor of comparative literature, Indiana University, Bloomington. April 17, 1987.

Robert Nielson, formerly professor of math, University of Maryland; currently special assistant to the director, American Federation of Teachers. Fall 1989.

Melvin Schwartz, Nobel laureate in physics; formerly professor of physics, Stanford University; currently associate director of physics, Brookhaven National Laboratory. June 25, 1987, and subsequently.

Matthew Straud, professor of foreign language, Trinity University. October 1987.

Elizabeth Warren, professor of law, University of Pennsylvania Law School. Fall 1986 and Spring 1987.

Steven Weinberg, Nobel laureate in physics; professor of physics, University of Texas. June 1987.

Lawrence Weinstein, formerly professor of business and marketing, Fairfield University. August 8, 1987.

In addition, less formal interviews that informed the book were conducted with Carol Simpson Stearn of Northwestern University, past president of the American Association of University Professors, and various other members, officers, and employees of the AAUP.

In the Company of Scholars

ONE

The Attraction of Academic Life

Introduction

It was the spring of 1980 and I was seated on the podium of the meeting hall at the New York Bar Association, about to be introduced to the Yale Law School alumni by the dean of the school, Harry Wellington. He was obviously enjoying himself. "About Jack Getman there is this to be said: now that Wellington has left the classroom, he is undoubtedly the best labor law professor in America." His face radiated a well-satisfied sincerity that increased my sense of professional success.

When my turn came, I spoke about my reasons for leaving Stanford University in favor of Yale. I mentioned the challenge of living up to the school's great tradition without arrogance, fear of the past, or unimaginative copying of what had previously been done. I talked of the pride and concern that came with being the colleague of such great scholars and lawyers as Charles Black, Burke Marshall, and Boris Bittker. I ostentatiously exaggerated my awe at teaching Yale students, every one of whom, I noted, had far better credentials than I had as a law student. I pointed out that several students had already published more than most of my colleagues had at Indiana University. I duly noted that the alumni included great lawyers, several presidential candidates, noted authors, and the ablest legal scholars at many other law schools. My audience enjoyed the flattery and recognized its basic sincerity.

Everything about that meeting gratified my ego and made me feel important. In a relatively brief time I had gone from a run-of-the-mill teaching position to a unanimous offer to join the faculty at one of the two great law schools in America. My scholarship had been recognized. My teaching was popular. I was regularly called upon for advice and recommendations from other law schools, and I was general counsel (being considered for the presidency) of the American Association of University

The Attraction of Academic Life

Professors, the oldest and most prestigious faculty association in the country.

However, my self-satisfaction was short-lived. Soon I began to feel less important, inadequately appreciated, and less satisfied with my work. I became uneasy with the Yale Law School, critical of its scholarship, and troubled by its smugness. I began this book to articulate my sense of disappointment and alienation from the status I had fought so hard to achieve.

Initially I thought that my reaction to academic life was unique, but after many interviews with faculty in different disciplines and discussions with colleagues, I realized that my responses are widely shared. Many faculty are disappointed with academic life. Like most academics, I became a professor because academia appeared to offer meaning, status, and a pleasant life-style. These promises turned out to be largely illusory and often in conflict. I also came to realize that the surface calm of academic life obscured a continual struggle between the elitist and egalitarian aspects of higher education. This struggle occurs on many levels, from momentous issues of national educational policy to small questions of status in the most insignificant-seeming aspects of academic life. Finally I came to conclude that the issue is so crucial in academic life because it mirrors internal conflicts present in almost all of us. These internal conflicts arise for many reasons. They reflect divisions within the family and conflicts between background and aspiration, family and community. They also come from the mixed elitist and egalitarian messages that are an inevitable part of American culture and our educational system.

In teaching and research, we identify and articulate values that join together different parts of the society. Education provides a method for social mobility and reduces class distinctions for those who experience it. It made it possible for rail splitters, haberdashers, and peanut farmers to become presidents of the United States and for the children of pushcart peddlers, laundry workers, and farmers to become Nobel laureates. It broadens the group familiar with the achievements of Western culture and it provides the forum for a dialogue in which different groups express their views on important social and political issues.

Education (and, in particular, higher education) also divides. It separates those who have experienced it from those who have not, in terms of learning, language, aspirations, and self-perception. It certifies ideas, books, art, and intellectual achievements. By setting standards, it generally announces that certain works, ideas, and people are not entitled to serious attention in the world of ideas.

Introduction

The conflict between elitist and egalitarian experiences has affected every academic I have known at the various universities where I have taught and all of the people I have interviewed for this book.

Melvin Schwartz, Nobel laureate in physics, was a product of the city streets. His family loyalties were working-class socialist and egalitarian. One of his formative early experiences was membership in *Habonim*, a Labor Zionist youth group that preaches the importance of physical labor and distrust for empty theorizing. He also went to select schools, Bronx High School of Science and Columbia University, where he was encouraged to recognize his own special qualities and where he came to be a part of the intellectual elite. Despite his great success, the conflict of values never ceased. It was one reason that he felt out of place in the academic splendor of the Stanford physics department, which he finally left.

Elizabeth Warren, now a highly regarded law professor at the University of Pennsylvania, thinks of herself as both a poor kid from Oklahoma whose values were shaped by family hardship, alcoholism, and lack of status and a person whose early satisfactions and claim to distinction came from books and learning. As she has progressed in the academic hierarchy from modest to elite schools, she has come increasingly to think of herself as an "Okie." Her academic career has demonstrated the strength of this dual heritage and the conflicts, both internal and external, that it creates.

Herb Marks, now a professor of comparative literature at Indiana University, felt out of place at both public school and Princeton University. He described his first night at Princeton: "I remember the first night. I saw football players . . . throwing iceboxes out of fourth-story windows in a state of drunken stupor then, on the other hand, the Exeter types parading around in their sports jackets. . . . My response was a sense of isolation."

Sociologist Janet Lever's parents encouraged her to see herself as ordinary, to see success in limited, family-oriented terms. She did not consider herself a thinker, student, or scholar until later in life, when she realized that formal study of society could enlarge her vision and make sense of her own world. Her ambition, vision, and dedication brought her remarkable success as a teacher and a scholar, but her failure to conform to academic stereotypes played a big role in her later unsuccessful struggle for tenure—a struggle that has blighted her life.

In my own case, virtually every aspect of my family education and background helped to create internal conflicts between elitist ambition and egalitarian values.

The Attraction of Academic Life

Both of my parents were immigrants without formal education, but their views of education differed greatly. My father thought of education as a process for enriching life and overcoming differences. My mother saw it as part of a system by which people were deprived, by poverty and birth, of opportunities to learn and by which those without academic credentials were made to feel inadequate.

My father was a garment worker who treasured ideas. He started working in the sweatshops of the garment industry when he was eleven, and he learned to read through special classes taught by the International Ladies' Garment Workers' Union and the Hebrew Immigrant Aid Society. Books became an escape from the oppressive reality of his life. He seized upon literature as a chance to understand the world and to come into contact with its greatest thinkers and artists. At night after work, with the help of an English-Yiddish dictionary, he read and reread the great books by the most influential writers of English and Russian literature: Shakespeare, Tolstoy, Dickens, and Conrad. All his life he regretted his lack of education, his poor handwriting, and his uncultured immigrant accent.

His greatest pleasure was talking about books, music, and politics with his friends who, like him, were immigrant workers and intellectuals. They argued with great passion but without rancor about socialism, unions, Zionism, and the nature of American society. They illustrated what my later experience confirmed: that ideas are not the special province of the academically certified.

My father was sure that with greater education he could have had a more rewarding life. He wanted me to be a professional and live the kind of life he would have desired for himself if he had had a choice. Our greatest argument came when I graduated from high school and proposed going to live on a kibbutz rather than going on to college.

My mother was suspicious of intellectuals and jealous of the educated. She devoted much of her formidable intelligence to criticism of those she envied. She often ridiculed my teachers, and she constantly compared the American school system unfavorably to the Russian *gymnasia* of her youth—a system that she knew only by reputation. She insisted over and over again, to my father's annoyance, that higher education was overrated and rarely prepared people for life. I recall vividly her one-way conversations, responding to authors, movie characters, and radio commentators. "A lot you know," she would say contemptuously, or, "You think you can fool the public with that stuff, but, believe me, you're only fooling yourself." When a point was repeated more than once by a news commentator, she was certain to blurt out, "Enough, enough already. I'm bored. Say something new."

There was something positive, however, in her attitude toward those she called "regular people." She would strike up conversations with nondescript-looking strangers, whose history and ambitions she would learn and whose virtues she would thereafter extol. They were a varied group: a housewife whose children studied music in Iowa, a teenage girl hoping to be a rodeo rider, a shoemaker recently arrived from Italy. Her descriptions of them were colorful and her stories fascinating. I learned from her that people cannot be judged easily by station, background, or accomplishment—a lesson I have had to relearn periodically.

I never wanted to think of myself as an intellectual. Intellectuals were personified by Aaron Levine, who lived next door, a soft-looking boy who never got dirty and rarely laughed. He was an excellent student whose report cards, adorned with special commendatory comments, were prominently displayed in the living room by his adoring parents. He read Shakespeare when he was ten and memorized long passages, which he loved to recite. He wrote poems, claimed to understand Einstein, and talked knowledgeably about philosophic theory. He couldn't throw a ball twenty yards.

To this day, I reflect both my father's respect for ideas and education and my mother's suspicion of intellectuals. Their example has also helped me to appreciate that many people of great intelligence and creativity do not easily demonstrate their talents through traditional measures of achievement or ability.

The Role of Education

There are many people like me in the academic world: children of working-class immigrants with little or no formal education. That we have become professors is an indication of the strength of the system of public education in this country.

Public education in New York City has always provided special opportunities for the intellectually promising children of the working class. I attended the Bronx High School of Science and City College of New York before going on to the Harvard University Law School, where much of my tuition was paid by the G.I. bill. In going to these schools, I was a beneficiary of the long-standing national commitment to provide quality education even to those who cannot afford to pay its costs.

Admission to Bronx High School of Science was a surprise. It certified that because I did well on an objective test I had academic promise, something that my performance in school often put in doubt. Most educators I have talked to in other parts of the country have had similar experiences. They were almost invariably placed on a track that permitted them to think of themselves as special.

Bronx Science was a fine institution. There were many superb students, including three future Nobel laureates, in the student body while I was a student there. I recall an English class that summed up most of what was best about Bronx Science: its focus on critical thinking and questioning conventional wisdom. We were studying *The Old Curiosity Shop*. The teacher read aloud to the class with great emotion the passage describing the death of Little Nell. He then asked us to comment on it. We fell all over ourselves to praise it. I remember commenting, "It goes beyond literature. It sings like great music." Other students made similar points. The teacher said nothing. A black student who often seemed out of place among our noisily intellectual classmates and who rarely spoke in class raised his hand and said, in a voice rich with contempt for us all, "I don't care who wrote this. Nobody talks like that or acts like that when they are dying."

"At last," said the teacher. "Someone who is actually paying attention to the material. He is thinking and not just responding to the fact that it's Dickens and he knows it's a classic." The teacher then reread the passage; as he did so, I felt acutely embarrassed. Its flaws were obvious and, had I not known that it was written by Dickens, I would have recognized this instantly. The message of the lesson was profoundly egalitarian. All great thinkers are subject to criticism, even from nonprofessionals. I determined never to get caught like that again. And to this day, when I begin to feel myself persuaded by someone's eloquence, reputation, or title, that moment comes back to me and I wonder whether I am again repressing my critical judgment because of the person's status.

My parents did not have the money to send me to college. Nevertheless, I was able to attend CCNY, a school with a splendid faculty and bright, well-motivated students. CCNY is like many schools in different parts of the country that provide free or inexpensive education to students who indicate academic promise in one way or another. Its former students include a great number of distinguished writers, academics, and politicians. During the time I was there, the atmosphere was charged with intellectual excitement.[1] At any time in the cafeteria, one could hear political discussion, academic debate, folk music, or personal conversation, all being conducted simultaneously with little attention to manners, decibel level, or traditional notions of eloquence. When I left CCNY, I did not think of myself as part of an educated elite. I did, however, feel capable of dealing with and evaluating ideas.

The Crucial Academic Experience: Graduate School

The Vision of Status Based on Merit

It is at graduate school that future professors learn the basic structure of their disciplines; acquire models for scholarship, pedagogy, and intellectual style; meet colleagues; experience the joys of scholarship; and learn of the pressure, anxiety, and frequent frustration that generally accompany academic ambition.

All graduate schools convey the message that their students are select, will be specially trained, and will be made part of the intellectual elite. Within graduate schools, considerable variation in status and much concern about ranking exists. In some fields, such as physics, admission to a top graduate school automatically establishes one's status as a scientist. Graduate students at the University of Chicago often work closely with Nobel laureates. Mel Schwartz, once he entered the graduate program at Columbia, began doing original research in collaboration with top scientists. On the other end of the spectrum are professional students at non-prestigious schools. Sally Sharp, now a professor at the University of North Carolina, told me that when she attended law school at Memphis State University, the understanding was that if she finished at the top of her class she would be hired by a good local firm or perhaps one in Nashville. That she would be preparing for an academic career was unthinkable. She eventually had to get another degree from Yale to become academically acceptable.

My own graduate career fell between these extremes. I attended Harvard Law School in the mid-1950s. The understanding was that most of the top students would have careers on Wall Street and that a handful, those who made law review and clerked for federal judges, would be eligible to teach.

Harvard Law School, at that time, reflected both the best and worst aspects of American graduate education. It was exciting, challenging, intellectually diverse, and committed to evaluation based on merit. It was also unnecessarily competitive, hierarchical, smug, snobbish, and pretentious.

My law school career began when the entire class met in a huge auditorium to listen to Dean Erwin Griswold. He spoke in a deep, resonant voice that announced his importance and the greatness of the institution. His manner was serious, his language elegant, his message impressive. He told us that we were the most highly select group of students in the world and the most fortunate. He reminded us of the achievements of the Harvard Law School since its founding by Justice Joseph Story in colonial times. He stressed its ancient lineage, its legendary alumni, and its incomparable faculty. He described our class with evident pride. Among us were several people with Ph.D.'s, two people with M.D.'s, and more than twenty people with master's degrees. Included were writers, dancers, and Olympic athletes. Most of us were undergraduates at Ivy League colleges, and from our ranks would come important judges, professors, and leaders. Our individual futures were to be determined largely by our performance at law school.

As he spoke, my heart pounded. I felt alternately inspired and inadequate: proud to be part of so illustrious a group and fearful that I did not belong. I seemed to be the only person out of place. My classmates in gray suits and prep-school ties seemed entirely at ease, familiar with professional elegance and certain of success. I have since learned that almost all of us were frightened: some, like me, felt out of place, some had the burden of generations of Harvard-trained lawyers to live up to, and some feared that their records of academic achievement were based on their abilities to fool their teachers—a deception soon to be revealed. The feeling of intellectual inadequacy at the start of graduate school is common.

The Pleasure of Intellectual Transformation

All graduate schools transform. English majors who enter graduate schools because they love literature learn to criticize and deconstruct it. Law students who begin their studies concerned with justice and rules are trained to value analytic rigor and technical competence. This was particularly true during the 1950s, when I attended Harvard Law School. We read edited opinions and then answered questions posed by our professors about their meaning. What was most noticeable about the first classes was the tremendous sense of tension that came from 150 ambitious students trying to take each other's measure. We sat in terraced rows radiating out from the podium, where our professors stood like gladiators waiting to do battle with our misconceptions, complacency, and intellectual fuzziness. At first, I expected the professors to tell us which part of the decisions we were expected to know, but instead they limited themselves to asking questions. Each class was like a morality play in which professorial rigor did battle with student misconception in the cause of sophistication.

A typical class would begin with the professor calling on a student to state the case that we all had read. The dialogue would follow a fairly fixed pattern:

"Mr. Little, will you state the facts in *Groves v. Wonder*."

"This case involves the lease of land from the plaintiff to the defendant. The defendant agreed to remove the sand and gravel on the land and to leave the property 'at a uniform grade, substantially the same as the grade now exists.' The defendant removed sand and gravel but did not regrade the land. To do so would have cost $60,000 and the land would only have been worth $12,150. The trial court awarded the plaintiff $12,150 for breach of the contract, but the Supreme Court of Minnesota reversed and awarded the plaintiff the $60,000 that would have been required to complete the contract."

"What is the rule that supports the result?"

Usually the student would be ready for that question and could either read it verbatim or paraphrase the rule as stated by the court that decided the case. "In reckoning damages for breach of a building or construction contract, the law aims to give the disappointed party, so far as money will do it, what he was promised."

"What was the plaintiff promised?"

"A regraded parcel of land."

"What would be the value of such a promise?"

"The court values it as $60,000."

"Do you agree?"

"Yes." (The great majority of us when called upon tried to justify the court's conclusion.)

"What would the plaintiff have had if the defendant performed?" the professor might ask, as though confused.

"A graded piece of property."

"Worth?"

"$12,150."

"What you're telling me, then, is that to vindicate the value of a promise worth at most $12,150, the law awards the plaintiff $60,000."

The student at this point would feel foolish, perhaps misled by the court's opinion. He would wonder why he had not seen something so obvious. "Well, the court declared that to be the value of the plaintiff's promise."

"Sir, at the Harvard Law School, the fact that nonsense has been uttered by a judge does not make it any less nonsense." Such a statement would inevitably be greeted by laughter and applause from the class. We reveled in the message that no judge was beyond criticism from the Harvard Law School and delighted in the fact that our professors could always demonstrate an important flaw in opinions that when first read seemed ineluctably correct. I often wondered whether professors at lesser schools taught in this same wonderful, critical way. For many of us, each class was a mixture of high theater, personal challenge, and constant inward competition with classmates.

Classes were exciting in part because of the intellectual challenge of the material and in part because I was being transformed in my thinking, speech, and manner from a person whose immigrant, working-class background was obvious into one worthy of mingling with the country's professional, intellectual, political, and social elite. I was awed by my classmates—by their backgrounds, training, and achievements; they were the people I had always envied. I was elated by the opportunity to know such people and perhaps to become accepted by them. I amused myself by fantasies in which I casually told my working-class friends and schoolyard adversaries the pedigrees of those with whom I swapped casual conversation.

I learned that justice was more complicated than I had imagined. One could not resolve legal issues simply by favoring the poor or the oppressed: one had to understand the procedural posture, the applicable precedent, and the problems that might be created by change. My early legal heroes, Justices Hugo Black and William O. Douglas, turned out to be woefully deficient in all of these technical, professional ways. I was pleased to realize that my standards for evaluating legal decisions had become technical and professional rather than emotional. I was learning a new way to evaluate reality. Every event had a legal dimension that permitted me to analyze it professionally. I was certain that I had been taught an analytic scheme far superior to that which laypeople or lawyers from lesser schools possessed. For the first time in my life, I began to think of myself as part of the intellectual elite, those who could analyze problems of any sort rigorously and unemotionally.

The transformation of graduate education almost always involves narrowing focus and merging one's identity with that of the institution. That was certainly true for most of us who attended Harvard Law School in the mid-1950s. We talked law but even more about the law school. We analyzed classes as though they were theatrical events. We ranked our teachers for pedagogical style, brilliance, wit, and eloquence. We told stories about their academic exploits and their professional triumphs. We repeated ancient gossip about former students who had become successful lawyers or judges. We compared Justice Brandeis to Justice Frankfurter in terms of their classroom performance and grades in law school. We spent hours evaluating our classmates. Some were considered brilliant and others confused. We graded each other for eloquence and performance. We criticized unmercifully those who talked too much, fell apart under professorial questioning, or asked stupid questions. Almost all of our discussions either directly or implicitly underlined the importance of grades. Grades measured intelligence, predicted future success, signified achievement, and ranked us in terms of comparative ability to each other and to the long, illustrious list of Harvard Law School graduates. What I did not realize was how narrow my world had become and how simplistic my evaluations of people were, even as I reveled in my new sophistication. In this, too, I was replicating the experience of countless generations of graduate students and learning habits of thought that continue to harm the process of education.

The Role of Anxiety

It is common for graduate students to have their ambitions thwarted by anxiety they do not understand. Invariably students who experience this are confused by and feel guilty about it. The graduate student nightmare is common to all disciplines: the students dream they are called on in a class and realize they do not have any knowledge of the subject—it sounds like a foreign language. Or, a variant: they are in an examination setting, receive the test, and it covers material they've never seen. Science majors report this dream—and so do fine arts majors and those in library science.

At the point during my first year when learning should have been the most enjoyable and intense, I began to have difficulty studying. I would set out from home determined to work in the library, but I would end up gossiping, compulsively reading newspapers from cover to cover, or going for beer and sports conversations at a nearby bar. I felt guilty, foolish, and completely frustrated, as though my ambitions were held down by a powerful, invisible force. The buildings and classrooms became my enemies. I particularly came to hate the library, with its atmosphere of intense concentration, the endless conversations outside in the halls about law, and the special, central role of the law review editors.

By mid-spring, I found it a burden to enter the building. I was more and more confused in class, certain that I would do very poorly in my exams, perhaps even flunk out entirely.

At that time I was sure that my experiences were unique, but I have since discovered that many of my students have had almost identical experiences. In part, this phenomenon is a product of the great emotional intensity and anxiety that mark graduate study. None of the more obviously pressure-laden experiences in my career, trying cases, negotiating labor disputes under threat of strike, or facing a hall full of angry state troopers, was nearly as anxiety-laden as the first year at Harvard Law School.

Because such feelings of anxiety in graduate school are common and because graduate school identifies and trains the great majority of future academics, faculties are filled with people who perform well in the face of anxiety and therefore trust it as a pedagogic tool. Indeed, many successful academics have all their lives lived with anxiety related to academic performance and ranking. That is why the picture of tranquility that appears so often in plays and films about academic life is generally so far from the mark.

Anxiety is compounded by issues of identity and by the ubiquitous conflict between elitist and egalitarian standards. I now realize that some part of me was battling the Harvard Law School, resisting the values and standards that it promoted and the life of a successful corporate lawyer that so much at the school indicated was the natural culmination of success.

The Twin Lures, Status and Achievement

I was most influenced by The Federal Courts and the Federal System, a course that inspired generations of future academics and profoundly influenced legal scholarship for many years. Professor Henry Hart, who taught the course, seemed to personify academic excellence in manner, appearance, and expression. He was the coauthor of our casebook, a work of massive original scholarship. Responding adequately to the questions posed in it required technical competence, careful reading, and rigorous analysis. Grappling with them forced me to constantly confront the limits of my understanding of the legal system.

I felt certain that in only a few law schools were such issues considered, and only at Harvard were they dealt with in so profound a fashion. This sudden awareness of the majesty and elegance of an area of thought is one of the reasons people enter academic life. The positive aspects of such inspiration are obvious, but such experiences also contain the seeds of intellectual snobbery by conveying the sense that true understanding is limited to those with a special academic background.

By the time I had graduated from law school, I had significantly changed my way of using language, my self-image, my reasoning ability, and my view of education. Although many of the changes induced by law school were positive and some necessary, I remain appalled and angry at the Harvard Law School of my day: its arrogant assumption of intellectual superiority; its social, intellectual, and professional rating systems; its limited focus; its overemphasis on professional competence; its failure to provide an opportunity to express other aspects of our intellectual ability, such as creativity, empathy, and understanding; and most of all its presumption in setting intellectual limits for people prematurely. It announced which of us had a right to think of ourselves as brilliant, which were worthy of respect by the most demanding of intellectuals, and which were entitled to consider ourselves superior only to those not intelligent enough to qualify for Harvard Law School. This failing—the claim to be able to determine students' intellectual potential—is not limited to Harvard Law School but is an aspect of every prestigious school with which I am familiar.

It took many years and a long process of self-discovery before I came to value those aspects of myself that were most out of place in the Harvard Law School when I was a student there. I blush now to recall that I felt ashamed of my working-class, immigrant background; that my parents had never been formally educated; that I had a public school education and went to CCNY rather than to an Ivy League college; that I did odd jobs, served as an enlisted man, and put in long hours playing basketball at the schoolyard. My difficulties in dealing with Harvard were far from unique. Similar feelings of alienation are common among students from working-class or minority communities who attend prestigious schools. For many of us, this has turned out to be an advantage both in teaching and research because it has helped to make us doubtful of accepted academic wisdom.

At the time I decided to enter teaching, I was not conscious of my anger. I was aware only that I greatly admired my teachers and thought that they lived the best lives possible. Professors had high prestige. They influenced, trained, and continued to be in contact with powerful people. They had the opportunity to interact with the best minds in different generations. They were honored and given the opportunity to do important tasks outside the academy whenever they wanted.

The path by which I entered law teaching was inevitably idiosyncratic, but the basic decision not to enter the field for which I was trained is one made by everyone who chooses teaching over a professional career. We reject the lives we are preparing our students to live. Embedded in this simple fact is an awful irony. We seek meaning by preparing students for a life we do not find meaningful. For me, hidden in this irony (which I did not appreciate) was another conclusion that I would have totally rejected—blinded as I was by hopes for status—namely, that the abler and better equipped were the students I taught, the less meaningful would be my role.

The Basic Academic Processes and the Search for Meaning: The Conflict between Elitist and Egalitarian Values

Teaching

The Inspiration of Great Teaching

The desire to instruct, demonstrate, explain, or justify is ubiquitous. Many people would like to be teachers. They envy those of us who teach full time at the college level because the time commitments seem slight in comparison with most other jobs, the end product of our efforts is valuable, the work is interesting, and the potential rewards are significant. But teaching as a fantasy or as a casual part of another occupation is far different from the experience of those who do it over a long period of time on a regular basis. For most who attempt it, the teaching process turns out to be more complex, difficult, demanding, and frustrating than they ever anticipated. The process often becomes contaminated by elitist values and sometimes by egalitarian pretense. As a result, great teaching is rare and great teachers who can sustain their interest, enthusiasm, and commitment over a long period of time are even rarer.

Great teaching inevitably has both elitist and egalitarian aspects. It also requires a special combination of learning, dedication, and imagination. An example is contained in the portrait of Siddie Joe Johnson by Elizabeth Forsythe Hailey that appears in *An Apple for My Teacher*:

> I cannot imagine a more sympathetic audience. She listened as if each one of us was a poet laureate. "Now who has brought something to share with the class?" she asked expectantly. The boy sitting next to me raised his hand. "I want to get this over with," he said apologetically, then plunged into a poem about a boy who'd broken his leg playing baseball . . . I remember feeling uncomfortable at how much he was revealing. It didn't even sound like poetry—full of slang and awkward rhymes.

When he finished, I waited nervously to hear what Miss J. would say. I hoped she wouldn't be too hard on him. . . . But to my amazement she applauded and said he'd made the best possible use of poetry—to transform experience. "How'd you really break your leg?" she then asked with a smile. He blushed and mumbled something about tripping over a hoe in the back yard. She assured him it was all right and said you didn't have to be true to facts when you wrote a story or poem, you just had to be true to your own feelings.

I was glad he'd gone first because the next person to read convinced me I was in the presence of a professional. She was a tall, thin girl with intricate French braids that I couldn't help studying as I listened to her recite. Her rhyme scheme was as complicated as her hairdo. I was sure Miss J. would offer to send the poem straight off to her own publisher, and it would be printed in a book. What was I doing in that class?

"I think you must have liked that poem by Wordsworth we read last week very much," Miss J. began, oh so gently. Then she went over the parallels between the two poems, never accusing the girl of anything but trying to imitate something she admired. No one ever left one of Miss J.'s classes feeling like a failure.

The next week on the way to class I met Miss J. outside the library. As we crossed the street, the wind whipping our coats about our legs, she turned to me and said with a smile, as if we were speaking our own special language, "This wind's like a whetted knife." I was astonished to hear that phrase from the poem she had read the week before translated into something I could feel on my skin. At that moment I began to see the possibility of poetry in my own experience. Perhaps sensing I was at a turning point, Miss J. began the class that day with her own definitions of poetry: "Poetry is washing dishes—and hoping you will see a rainbow in the suds. Poetry is seeing the whole sky in a single drop of dew. Poetry is what happens every day to everybody." . . .

For Christmas that year, instead of buying a present for my parents as I usually did, I copied out my poems, bound them with cardboard, tied them with ribbons—and dared believe they were a gift worth giving.[1]

Read carefully, this story suggests the combination of skill, daring, insight, and knowledge that is required for great teaching. Siddie Joe Johnson is subtle ("You must have liked that poem by Wordsworth"); tough in her constant insistence that literature and life cannot be separated; insightful ("How did you really break your leg?"); elegant in the simplicity of language ("Poetry is seeing the whole sky in a single drop of dew"); and loving in her careful listening and willingness to treat students as equals. She is also inspired: at just the right moment, she addresses

Teaching

Elizabeth Forsythe Hailey in poetry, conveying that it is their "own special language." After teaching for thirty years, I can only marvel at the special quality of mind that permitted her to seize that opportunity so splendidly.

The proof of her success is that she made her students feel capable when they had previously felt inadequate. She also permanently changed their standards for judging. They learned that literature is not merely erudite imitation. It requires an honest dealing with one's experience, even if done in "slang and awkward rhymes." This is the type of success many of us strive for but few ever achieve.

Routine encouragement is not equivalent to good teaching. Indeed, it is surprising how many people recall with pleasure a teacher who, by pushing, forced them to surpass their best previous work. I had such a teacher, Theodore Goodman, who taught creative writing at CCNY. Comparing him with Siddie Joe Johnson suggests what is common among great teachers and the ways in which great teachers, like successful parents, differ.

Goodman was a martinet. His writing class was run according to a series of precise rules that he insisted we follow without deviation. No one was to be admitted after the bell, nor could we leave before he dismissed us. Stories not handed in on time were automatically graded F. If a student received two F grades on stories, he or she flunked the course. We were to avoid showing off either our toughness or our sensitivity. The most important rule of all was that we were to write only about things we knew. The most serious transgression of Goodman's rules was "derivative writing." Stories based on what we had read rather than on what we had experienced, no matter how well written, received an F. When I tried to challenge him about this rule during the first class, he cut me short, ridiculed my understanding of literature, and then announced to the class, "This is an age when anyone who can belch considers himself a critic."

Goodman made clear that we were not to think of ourselves as his equals, and he would react with ridicule when he thought either our writing or criticisms pretentious.

His insistence on originality was ferocious. "It's bad enough when Hemingway imitates Hemingway. It's ludicrous when Schwartz imitates Hemingway," he once told a student. He described a paper as "hash, made out of hash." But when a student used a personal experience honestly, Goodman responded with such enthusiasm that the student felt awe and delight at the achievement. One student, Artie Pomerantz, wrote about a son teaching his illiterate father to read. The father's behavior throughout the story is childish and petulant. The son feels stifled and unappreciated. He confronts the father, who only dimly understands his annoyance. Finally the bewildered father says, "I give you a lot of trouble, don't I?" Goodman was delighted with the choice of topic and with the pathos of the ending. "You can't make up a line like that. It comes out of reality," he said. Pomerantz beamed with pleasure, but Goodman compared him to a man who stepped into a puddle and came out with a five-dollar bill stuck to his shoe.

Under Goodman's relentless pressure and occasional praise, we began to search our experiences for similar revealing incidents as the term went on. The stories became less overtly dramatic but more emotionally honest. The best writing was about family relations, like Anthony Mosca's story about his feeling of pride watching his father do construction work and his desolation when his father was crippled in an accident. Goodman called him "a younger brother to our greatest writers." He told another student he liked one of his stories so much that he lowered his grade because no one with such talent should have handed in his earlier work. He convinced us that the raw material for literature was present in our lives if we had the wit to see it and the skill to capture it.

I looked forward to Goodman's class as I did to athletic competition, with a sense of great excitement tinged with anxiety. I constantly regaled my friends with stories about the class, and when I read a book I wondered what he would think of it. I felt little resentment toward this vain, tyrannical man whose pronouncements were stated with such certainty, whose rules were inflexible, and whose humor was often barbed. What he offered was intense personal engagement, intelligence, high standards, and a passionate desire that we break through the limits imposed by culture and class. He treated our work seriously even as he ridiculed it. In Goodman's class I began for the first time to appreciate the capacity of teaching to touch people's lives, alter their values, and permanently change their perceptions of themselves.

Goodman's encouragement was not based on the assumption that literary achievement was easily available for anyone. He constantly emphasized the way in which our writing fell short of the standards by which first-rate critics judged writing. He told us who the great writers were, explained why they were great and why our own work was inadequate— sometimes laughably, sometimes pathetically, sometimes infuriatingly so in comparison. The course was elitist in ranking writers and even in differentiating among serious and casual readers, but its message was profoundly egalitarian in insisting that our experiences contained the ingredients of literature and that we, whatever our backgrounds or educational pedigrees, could aspire to the calling of writers.

Goodman opened the world of literature to ordinary, working-class college students. He made me realize that if I wasn't capable of writing first-rate stories, it was because of my lack of vision and failure to understand the subtlety of language, not because of the absence of drama in my life. Most of us began the class thinking that the only parts of our backgrounds that might be interesting to anyone were our sexual experiences. I now realize that this is why he refused to let us write about sex. He invited us to write about it on our own and "bore the hell out of each other," but he insisted that the real drama lay in our relations with parents and friends. He reinforced my mother's insistence that there are no uninteresting people.

Several students wrote better stories for Goodman than they thought they were capable of when they began, and most of us left the class with an elevated sense of our potential—a gift common to great teachers. Professor Elizabeth Warren said of one of her favorite teachers: "He would help you and let you flesh it out, and, before you knew it, you had done the entire Empire State Building."

Siddie Joe Johnson's emphasis on originality and the connection of literature and life were the same as Professor Goodman's. He was obviously tough and masked his caring, while she was obviously caring and masked her toughness. Each insisted that literature be tied to life and each provided for the students a model of scholarly and artistic integrity. Each ultimately altered the students' vision of themselves. This combination of toughness and caring is almost always present in student recollections of great teachers. As Lawrence Weinstein, now a business school professor, recalls: "I felt that Mrs. Spanning was a wonderful influence on me because she was the first person I really met who did not simply take what I had written and accept it, grade it and forget it. She kept handing it back saying, 'You can do better. You are not working up to your potential. Try harder.'"

Teaching as a Craft

Successful teaching is inevitably related to personality. Teaching is also, in part, a craft that may be learned through instruction or experience. Yet, for most who teach at the college level, the opportunity to learn much about the process before beginning is rare. Many have never taught at all. Others may have had the experience of working as a teaching assistant to a senior professor, but this rarely involves any training, apprenticeship, or formal consideration of the teaching process. Most teaching assistants grade papers and meet on occasion with small groups, where their task is to answer questions arising from the formal professorial lectures. As Max Wise reports, teaching assistants "get little help from senior faculty members on the teaching problems they encounter." He also notes that "they report feeling that they are treated as individuals of low status employed to do work that no one else wishes to do." Wise also points out that "in most programs of study the graduate student develops very limited perspectives of teaching." The final result is that "having uncritically assimilated limited perspectives of teaching, the typical young teacher is prepared to spend his professional life replicating these experiences."[2] Although this discussion was written some time ago, it is more true today because more emphasis is placed on research and less on teaching at most schools now than was the case in the late 1960s and early 1970s, when the student movement, for a period, made concern with teaching fashionable.

There are always schools that are experimenting with new programs designed to give teaching assistants and young professors training. Unfortunately, these programs are, for the most part, short-lived and rarely live up to their designers' hopes. They tend to be expensive, the results are typically mixed, and the senior faculty involved quickly lose interest. Such programs are nevertheless usually valuable for those who take part. In addition, if an aspiring teacher is lucky he or she may become involved as an assistant with a senior professor who feels an obligation to instruct about pedagogy. I had the good fortune to be a teaching associate for Harvard's famous sociologist, David Riesman. He would meet with us regularly to discuss how to conduct small group meetings. This was done at his home over dinner and often with other leading scholars brought in to participate. Those who served as his assistants invariably felt fortunate and often inspired.

Sometimes a young professor will find a teaching mentor. Elizabeth Warren, now a highly successful teacher, reports that "John Mixon at the University of Houston taught me how to teach." She describes their meetings after each class as "sort of like psychotherapy . . . calming and loving and yet very serious about teaching." Such mentoring with respect to teaching is increasingly rare as institutions begin to place a greater emphasis on research.

I had the opportunity to learn how to teach through a special teaching-fellow program at Harvard. The only reason that I had this chance was that my record as a student was not good enough to permit me to begin immediately as an assistant professor, which was the typical first appointment in law then as it is now. Being a teaching fellow, even at Harvard, was starting near the bottom of the teaching hierarchy in law. Our function was not to teach law but to make the first year a little easier for the students. In our program, by dictate of the regular faculty, no grades were given and attendance was not mandatory. During the first few weeks, we taught the students rudimentary skills of case reading.

Before my first class, my students were asked to read and abstract a case in which a woman sued a manufacturer for a faulty product which had injured her. The product had been purchased by someone else. The New York court held that there was no liability because of the "absence of privity." Privity is an ancient legal concept of vague origins and meaning that refers generally to direct dealing between the parties. I prepared hypotheticals designed to show that the court's reasoning was confusing and foolish.

We met in a small seminar room. I was at one end of a large oak table wearing my charcoal gray suit and striped tie. About me sat twenty first-year law students; their faces were serious, almost grim, their eyes focused on me quizzically as though trying to ascertain where I fit into the majestic scheme of the Harvard Law School. I began by explaining that my purpose was to help them with their regular courses and that the key to law school was learning how to read cases. I asked for a volunteer to state the case. For a long while no one moved, and I wondered what I should do if they refused to cooperate. Finally, after what seemed like hours, a hand was raised tentatively. I quickly asked the student his name. "Harold Benjamin," he replied. He was a dark-haired young man with deep-set brown eyes magnified by the thick lenses of his glasses. He stated the case competently, but when I asked whether he agreed with the opinion he looked bored and said he wasn't sure.

"I suppose you think it was nice enough of you to state the case and that I should quit while I'm ahead," I said. A faint smile seemed to curl the edge of his mouth, but it quickly disappeared.

"Does anyone disagree with the opinion?" No one raised a hand. "How many agree?" Again, nothing. "Does anyone give a damn?" A few smiles and one or two giggles indicated promise of involvement. I decided suddenly to depart from my lesson plan and pursue the point I had raised inadvertently as a joke. "Mr. Benjamin, is there a reason why anyone should care after almost fifty years whether Judge Hitchcock's opinion makes any sense?" Benjamin looked confused, but I noticed a flicker of interest. "Why do judges write opinions anyway?" I asked.

"So the losing side will know why they lost," Benjamin suggested.

"A good thought." I paused to give Benjamin the sense that he had said something insightful. I meant to use this moment to demonstrate that I was no one to trifle with. "Can you imagine the scene, Mr. Benjamin? The plaintiff reads the opinion and comes to the most critical language: 'the suit must fail for want of privity.' 'Aha,' she says, 'no wonder I lost.' What a wonderful legal system we have." This got a big laugh from the class. The students felt challenged and suddenly hands were in the air all over the room, a wonderful sight for any teacher. I called on a student who seemed excited.

"It's not for the parties. It's for other judges."

"Why do they care?"

Someone referred to the doctrine of *stare decisis*, by which judges are bound to follow their "holding" of previous cases. This permitted me to shift to what had been one of the original purposes. "What do you mean by holding?"

"That part of the opinion which is necessary to the decision," someone answered. I asked the person to read aloud the appropriate language. He tried, but I was able to produce a hypothetical in which a court was likely to ignore the quoted language. I did the same with several subsequent efforts, until someone, in a flash of insight, realized that the concept of holding was a vague one: that the crucial language in a particular opinion was difficult to locate and even more difficult to understand. Someone else added that perhaps the persuasiveness of an opinion would affect how broad later judges declared the holding to be. This was a far better answer than I expected. The students remained animated until the hour and a half ended. I felt exultant. I had changed the students' thinking, gotten them excited, provoked them, and started them on the way to legal sophistication. This small triumph in my first teaching effort was a precursor of my later positive experiences, almost all of which involved using a serendipitous discovery of an interesting idea and encouraging students to think about an issue not obviously presented by the material. Some teachers are at their best when they know precisely how the class will be structured. My best classes tend to involve sudden departures from a carefully prepared plan. Battling with the students in their interests has also been a regularly repeated theme.

During my first weeks as a teaching fellow, I discovered that I learned far more about law as a teacher than I ever had as a student, or even as a practicing lawyer. I read more carefully and thought far more intensely about the material. In the other situations, I had been looking for answers. When I prepared to teach, I read cases looking for interesting questions. These, I gradually discovered, could be found in the ambiguity concealed

Teaching

in elegant phrasing, in the contradictions often implicit in different parts of a single opinion, in the tension between different opinions, or in the difference between what the court said it was doing and the most likely result of its opinion. I was forced to question what I had previously accepted.

I reveled in the give-and-take of the classroom. In part, my enjoyment stemmed from the feelings of respect, admiration, and even liking from my students. In part, it came from the discovery that I could maintain the upper hand in debate with the highly select students of the Harvard Law School. More than anything, I liked the feeling that I was helping my students to understand. Sometimes when a student would suddenly grasp the point and articulate a sophisticated answer, I would feel my spine tingle with excitement.

My initial euphoria was short-lived, however. On a Monday in the middle of October, I walked into the seminar room in which I held my classes and was startled to find that, instead of the normal buzz of conversation and the rustling of papers, there was an eerie, almost embarrassed, silence. Only four of the twenty-two students in the class were present. When I asked where everyone else was, they told me that most of the others had moot court briefs due that week. This made me feel slightly better, but I was still profoundly insulted. A little while after the class was scheduled to begin, two more students strolled in, and their arrival convinced me to conduct class rather than call it off. It was a poor class. I found it difficult to concentrate on the material and acted angrily toward the few students who had shown up. I felt sorry for myself, certain that I had been unfairly judged by the students who had cut the class.

For the next month the problem persisted. Going to class became a humbling experience. When I passed some of the absentees in the hall, I would respond stiffly to their friendly greetings. One day when I arrived at the appointed hour, only one student was present. I wondered why and how I had failed so profoundly and even briefly considered resigning. My earlier feelings of pleasure and anticipation in preparing for class were replaced by feelings of failure and anger.

During that period, all of the other teaching fellows were going through similar experiences. Our weekly meetings to discuss the class materials became more intense. We listened carefully to each other's ideas, and we addressed such issues as the uses of humor, the importance of encouraging quiet students to speak, the advantages and disadvantages of having detailed lesson plans, and how to deal with students intent on dominating discussion. I began to prepare my classes with new intensity, trying to imagine how they would impress a student dubious about the value of attending. When I did this, my teaching improved and class attendance grew.

One of the most important lessons I learned as a teaching fellow was the importance of developing and communicating a point of view about the assigned material. Most texts are open to many interpretations, and it is up to the teacher to attach meaning to them. I learned this lesson in a traumatic fashion. Toward the end of my first semester as a teaching fellow, our classes were visited by regular faculty members who would use them to evaluate our teaching potential. Because a favorable recommendation from regular faculty members was crucial to my future plans, I would have been anxious even if the first person scheduled to sit in on my class had not been Ben Kaplan, my former first-year civil procedure professor. He was a master Socratic teacher whose rigorous analysis, sophisticated reasoning, and quick humor had awed, frightened, and excited me during my days as a student. I suspected that even my best classes would fall far short of his own high standards.

During the days prior to his visit, I read the class material over and over until it made sense, and carefully prepared questions that demonstrated points that seemed to me significant. When the day came, Kaplan was seated in the back, away from the round oak table at which the students and I sat. His expression was serious and critical. I was sure he remembered me as a mediocre student, and I feared he would find the analysis that I had so carefully prepared shallow and labored. Perhaps he would decide that I had missed the main point of the materials. Instead of the opening remarks that I had prepared, I referred to the case the students had been assigned and asked a particularly able student, "What do you think of the judge's opinion?" The student, who understood the purpose of Kaplan's presence, responded as well as he could to my question, but its vagueness made it difficult to give his answer any focus. I followed up by calling on another of my best students to respond. The two students disagreed somewhat, so I generated a debate between them and made it the focus of the entire class.

I let, or rather made, the students do almost all the work, calling on one after another without pause. I knew that if Kaplan himself had been teaching the material, he would have intervened regularly to add precision to the discussion and correct mistakes, but I felt stifled by an increasing sense of inadequacy. The most I could bring myself to do was to awkwardly restate student positions. Kaplan looked grimmer and grimmer. When the hour and a half ended, my head was pounding and my feeling

Teaching

of failure was overwhelming. Kaplan and I walked out together. "That was fine," he said unconvincingly. "Lots of student participation, but it might have been better if you had controlled the class a little more. My own weakest classes tend to be overcontrolled; you might have a problem in the other direction."

Furious at myself, I told him of the class that I had prepared and discarded. He listened carefully. "That sounds pretty good." He was tentative but not patronizing. I did not realize then that even someone as able as Kaplan would need to read the material carefully to understand and choose from among the possible pedagogic approaches. Desperately I tried to impress him by describing the class I did not teach, but it was futile. He left hurriedly after assuring me that I was too hard on myself and that he could see I had a flair for teaching.

The next week Al Sacks, another noted Socratic teacher, was to visit my class. I had made up my mind that if the class went badly it would not be because I was afraid to reveal my ideas. Paradoxically, because I was prepared to risk failure, I succeeded beyond my expectation. The hour and a half flew by. Students were still talking when Sacks and I left. Instead of evaluating my teaching, he eagerly told me his answer to the problem I had raised.

I felt triumphant but also foolish. Often in my academic career I had failed not for want of ability but for want of courage. Many times since then, the memory of this moment helped persuade me to take a chance in class, to risk exposing my ignorance, to say something I believe to be true.

Academic life is frequently perceived to be a haven for the timid, and there is much to the stereotype. Many of the worst features of academic life—the pedantry, jargon, obscurantism, and removal from reality—have their roots in fear of discovery. Yet meaningful success requires a degree of boldness.

In later years, I realized that many students and young faculty members behave in self-defeating ways, much as I did when Kaplan visited my class. They do not believe that they have anything of value to contribute to a high-level academic debate. Often this feeling prevents people from publishing or teaching effectively and sometimes it makes them pedantic, overly abstract, or unnecessarily elegant in the presentation of their ideas. Sometimes I think that the great majority of young academics fall into two categories: the unnecessarily diffident and the infuriatingly arrogant. In more reflective moments, I realize that the two categories are essentially one. Underneath the arrogance so common among young academics, there is generally fear of being exposed as an intellectual charlatan. The feeling is almost universal. The fear reflects, among other things, that deep down almost all of us are aware of how little we know about the subjects we teach. One of the ablest law professors I have ever known, Charles Black of Yale Law School, told me that whenever he finishes a well-received class, he usually feels one thing: "Well, I fooled them again."

The Emotional Complexity of Classroom Teaching

Teaching can be exhilarating at one moment and profoundly depressing or demeaning the next. A conscientious professor might feel alternately successful and like a failure during a semester. It is difficult to be an effective teacher without careful preparation and difficult to maintain one's level of preparation year after year.

A professor is particularly likely to have powerful emotional responses when he or she begins teaching. I can still remember my first labor law class. My goal was simple: to develop a general framework and to set the stage for future discussion. I began by outlining the development of the various labor statutes and the policies that they reflected. To my surprise, the students wrote intently, as though some penalty would be attached to missing a phrase or omitting a sentence.

At the end of the hour I called for questions and the students asked me about the interrelation of various statutes and about the major techniques employed in their drafting. The questions were neither particularly challenging nor intricate. Nevertheless, finding the right tone for my responses was difficult. I had much to say but didn't want to smother the students' interest by introducing concepts for which they weren't ready. I felt as though I had just begun when the class ended. As soon as I dismissed the class, I was emotionally exhausted.

During the rest of the day, fragments of the class kept returning to my mind. I thought of things I should have said and points I should have raised. I wondered whether I had been too sophisticated or not sophisticated enough. Many of the things I said seemed, in retrospect, inaccurate or misleading, and I vowed to myself to do better the next day.

I was unusually animated and loquacious at coffee and lunch, but before and after my mind was preoccupied with thoughts of pedagogy. Hypothetical problems and illustrations of complex points came to mind unbidden. I read through the material, studied law review articles, and checked over my card catalogue of labor cases. The next day the students and I interacted more. By the third day, the students asked a flurry of technical questions, several of which posed problems I could not solve. I

Teaching

fought the surprisingly strong impulse to make up answers and promised to report back to the students as soon as I could. The students did not seem upset by my ignorance but instead seemed pleased with my effort. During the next weeks, their sense of involvement became more noticeable and their questions more sophisticated. I lived at a high level of excitement during those first few months. I would frequently wake up during the night to relive the day's class or plan the next one. I found that I was so anxious during the half hour before class that I could not read over the materials. I had to go for a walk or pace the halls.

The classroom was where I lived most acutely. It was the place where I defined and expressed myself, where I was the ultimate deliverer of truth and the decider of relevance, the setter of the tone, the center of attention, and the model of professional competence.

When I began teaching, I had no awareness that the process often involves the creation of an artificial personality. Most successful teachers construct an image of themselves that facilitates their teaching. Unsuccessful teachers develop personalities to protect themselves and shift responsibility for their failures to the students or the system. Many attempt to develop a role that suggests that they are too brilliant to be understood by the students they teach. The insecure merely develop a style that suggests greater success, importance, and originality than they feel entitled to. The discontented may, like me, go through a succession of related but distinct characters.

During my first years at Indiana University, I was vaguely aware that I was playing a role—that one important goal of my teaching style was for the students to see me as a brilliant, analytically rigorous, Harvard-trained professor, someone sympathetic but tough, someone who could laugh and tease but who could not be fooled, and someone who took the enterprise seriously. I also tried to convey that I was destined for more important things than being a professor at Indiana University. I did this in a variety of ways: by the complexity of the hypotheticals, by the intricacy of my explanations, by the way I challenged students, by my constant reference to people at Harvard, by the contemptuous way in which I dealt with illogical court and board opinions, and even by the way I paced back and forth during class as though to suggest the speed of my mental processes. Later on I shifted into the far different role of the crafty practitioner, and still later into that of the professorial outsider disdainful of academic theorizing. While each of these reflected my basic attitudes and experiences, in each case there was something made up or put on about the pose.

The creation of teaching personalities inevitably carries over into other relationships. It distorts the personalities of academics and serves to separate them from most of the rest of humanity. This is true in part because the role choices of academics run heavily to the learned, the brilliant, and the idiosyncratic. Second, and more significantly, it means that expression and projection of self replaces communication as the purpose of interaction. Have lunch with a group of steelworkers or cops and the focus will usually be on teasing, exchanging stories, and expressing camaraderie. Have lunch with a group of academics and the focus all too often will be on projection of self-image and ego aggrandizement of one sort or another.

The vast majority of young professors do not know much of the relationship between what they teach and the underlying reality which it purports to describe or upon which it rests. During the first eight years that I taught labor law, the reality of labor relations was almost as much a mystery to me as it was to my students. The same was even more true of contracts, which I also taught. What I substituted for knowledge of reality was mimicry of my professors at Harvard, whose knowledge I simply assumed. As a result, in each area I taught a traditional course, passing on generally accepted truths that I had been taught at Harvard using standard pedagogy. In my pedagogic conservatism, I was like the great majority of young professors everywhere. As Baird W. Whitlock states: "The real traditionalists were young men and women just out of graduate school. They were waving the banners of their disciplines and they felt they would not be able to hold up their heads among their peers at the annual national meetings if they were not teaching the same course in the same way as their colleagues at every other institution. For all their liberal political protestations, they were preservers of their own immediate pasts."[3]

Many professors have even greater limitations to deal with regularly. Many lack the ability to excite, interest or even educate students about the subject matter. They face a professional life marked by daily, tangible failure. This is more ego-battering than what most laborers, craftspeople, or professionals experience. For such professors, teaching becomes a constant trial. This feeling is well brought out in the literature on academic life, along with the jealousy and resentment of great teachers. As one faculty member stated, "I think there are always really super teachers who can teach practically anything to anybody. But I'm not one of them. . . . I have always the sense of failing."

Bruce Mann, who now teaches at the University of Pennsylvania, told me that in his first year, "I was constantly afraid that someone would come into the classroom and arrest me for impersonating a law professor."

Many professors never get over this feeling. A few learn to live, albeit uneasily, with their limitations. Some become hostile toward the students, blaming them for failing to appreciate the subtlety of their teaching. Other faculty members shift their efforts, becoming more involved in research or outside activity that may provide a more positive focus and perhaps even improve the quality of their teaching.

Working With Individual Students

When teaching works, students come to better understand themselves and their values. They are introduced to people they would not otherwise meet and have intellectual experiences they would not otherwise have. The importance of these experiences often creates powerful emotional bonds between students and teacher. In interviews that I conducted with academics, the term "love" kept recurring when professors talked about their favorite or most important teachers. Teachers respond when such emotion is evident and feelings of great intimacy between teachers and students sometimes occur even in a large classroom setting. It is not uncommon for students to have dreams about their professors and for professors to dream about the dynamics of the classroom.

The intimacy and powerful emotion that often accompany and flow from intense teaching mean that teaching can most easily be done in small classes and in informal settings.

An example of this process at its best is contained in Houston A. Baker's description of his relationship to Charles Watkins.[4] Like many of the most successful student-teacher relationships, it began when Watkins' early tough criticism provoked Baker to write a paper on William Blake in which Baker "strained to see every nuance of the *Songs of Innocence*." Emboldened by his first good grade from Professor Watkins, he summoned up "almost enough courage to seek him out during office hours." He went with a friend and stayed for two hours, during which time Watkins talked of himself, his colleagues, and his love of metaphysics. This office visit led to an invitation for dessert a few weeks later:

> There was far more than dessert. His wife was hospitable, witty, attractive—and white. She was the first such person I had met. For partners in interracial marriages were not common in my hometown. . . . The greatest stimulation, however, came when he played the Library of Congress recording of T. S. Eliot reading "The Waste Land." In that moment I became, willy-nilly, a party to "modernism" in its prototypical form. I was

surprised and delighted. I had heard nothing like it before. . . . I spent hours thereafter in the library listening to the sounds of English, French, and American poets.

The result of that evening and his ensuing study of Eliot came later when Baker "stepped into a late fall evening with an entirely new sense of myself and of 'worlds on worlds' rolling ever."

As moving and inspiring as this story is, it is made more problematic by the tension between its elitist and egalitarian aspects, a tension to which Baker is well attuned. He notices that Watkins' manner, language, and life-style are resolutely Ivy League and patrician: "He had crafted an Oxonian mask." Yet, throughout the story, Watkins' black rural roots supply an element of contradiction: "A frayed collar belied his intellectual elegance. His down-at-the-heels shoes were closer to West Virginia than Oxford." These glimpses add individuality, pathos, and tension to the portrait. The result of the struggle is an uneasy balance of forces that has obviously taken its toll on Watkins: "His face was prematurely kneaded and lined. I began to glean the enormous price he had paid."

The final impact on Baker is not clear, but it is certain that Watkins influenced him in ways which made him want to strengthen his connection to intellectuals and separate himself from his other teachers, his fellow students, and his own background. He writes, "I began self-consciously to create a critical vocabulary." This exacerbated his differences from other students and instructors, one of whom wrote at the end of a written assignment: "Are ontological and eschatological the only words you know?"[5] Thus, the story ultimately reveals the separation from others that education often brings. The compensation is that it brings a stronger connection with someone who represents the world of ideas.

During their careers, most professors develop special relationships with individual students. From the professor's point of view, such relationships can be both meaningful and quite satisfying. They are more intimate than relationships with students in large classes, more particular, and generally less anxiety-provoking. Yet the interest in having more individual relationships regularly presents questions of selection, emphasis, time allocation, and favoritism. It occasionally involves dangers of abuse, including sexual liaisons between teachers and students. Like almost every aspect of academic life, individual conferences generally reflect academic hierarchy. The students who come to the professor's office expecting or seeking individual instruction are overwhelmingly those with the best grades. As

Teaching

Houston Baker's story suggests, those who most need help often fear any confrontation and rarely—unless desperate—approach their teachers.

When I first entered law teaching I was, like most of my colleagues, drawn to those students who were quickest, most self-assured, and most contentious. I sought out the class leaders and was flattered when one of them would come to my office.

During the late 1960s, as my approach to teaching changed, I slowly began to make contact with marginal, minority, and alienated students, who, I discovered, included most of the class. This is the group that I have ever since tried to make contact with in one-on-one relationships. When I have succeeded, the results have sometimes been exciting. I recall with particular pleasure a young black woman named Barbara Kennedy. During the fall semester of 1969 when I taught a first-year contracts class, Barbara came to my office looking despondent and on the verge of tears. She told me that she had entered law school despite serious misgivings but was quickly learning that her enrollment had been a mistake. Her writing instructor had just returned her first paper and had told her that it raised doubts about her suitability for the study of law. "Being a good student at Fisk [University] doesn't mean that you are ready to attend a law school. I can see that the teaching fellow is right. I don't have the type of mind to be a lawyer. I'm too emotional and not precise enough." Tears came to her eyes as she finished speaking, and then she burst into sobs.

When I asked to see the paper, she handed it to me like someone giving over a soiled rag. I read it over quickly. It did not seem very different from a typical first-year student effort. When I told her this, she waved her hand dismissively as though to make plain that she knew I was lying. I asked her whether she was enjoying the contracts class, and she said she felt confused. She was particularly distressed by her inability to make sense of the cases dealing with contract remedies. We talked and I realized that she basically understood the cases but was confused because she thought it her role to harmonize the conflicting opinions. I assured her that I couldn't reconcile the cases and neither could the teaching fellow. "The fact is that they are badly reasoned and in conflict. You see this, but somehow you are blaming yourself for the judges' incompetence." She laughed, albeit with much hesitation and no joy.

We met again the following week and then about once a month for a while. Our meetings became less involved with the cases and more focused on the experience of law school. As the semester progressed, she began to act less frightened and more determined. She made it through the first year with Cs, was well above average in her second year, and got outstand-

The Basic Academic Processes and the Search for Meaning

ing grades in her third year, by which time she was poised, articulate, well dressed, and self-confident. She spoke with the precision characteristic of young lawyers. Before graduation, she received an offer from an excellent commercial law firm in Denver, Colorado. She was their first black associate and soon became their first black partner. I got to see her once in Denver. She took me to dinner at a private club located on the top floor of a bank building.

When I was at Yale, she called to let me know that she had been appointed by President Jimmy Carter as general counsel of the Peace Corps, in which capacity she traveled around the world. She became an expert on international development and turned down several law school teaching opportunities. I understand that she is now a partner in a prestigious law firm in Los Angeles.

Gratifying as such experiences are to a teacher, they are also rare. The opportunity to confront students with their own self-image is generally not present and it is patronizing and self-defeating to raise such issues unless the student comes for help. At Indiana, few of us on the faculty ever got to know the struggling white students. They were too polite, diffident, and self-deprecating. They sat quietly in class, laughed politely at our jokes, and passed on silently to the practice of law. Encouraging students to feel comfortable generally requires a great deal of effort. Many times they will begin with a technical question but really want to talk about some personal issue. It is hard and time-consuming work to understand a disguised message and direct a discussion to address a student's underlying concern. When I have been deeply involved in research and writing, I dreaded the tentative knock on my door and the polite, "Are you busy?" that usually preceded an attempt to raise a personal issue. On occasion, personal discussion with particular students has meant that my classes were inadequately prepared; at other times, I have felt that the time with students made me less available to my family. Much time has been spent in not very meaningful and interesting discussions with students with whom real contact was never made.

Most students who came to see me were not seeking profound help. They wanted to make human contact, to get to know a professor in a less formal atmosphere, to try out ideas, or to seek approval. These are all legitimate student desires, but if the professor is writing a book, teaching a heavy load, working on a brief, having problems with children, or going through some personal crises, the competing demands sometimes become overpowering. Sometimes I have ushered students out of my office without finding out what brought them in. Sometimes I have discovered that while they were talking, I was concentrating on some problem of my own, and sometimes I have listened to them talk about something they cared about while wishing they would leave.

The Search for Relevance and Reform

The continuing tension between elitism and egalitarianism ensures that emphasis in teaching will fluctuate regularly from traditional methods stressing the importance of accepted wisdom to experimentation and focus on issues of current relevance. The early 1960s, when I first began teaching, was a period in which traditional values predominated. By the late 1960s, the mood had changed drastically. As the campuses came alive with marches, meetings, and egalitarian rhetoric, many professors were also caught up by the intellectual and emotional fervor. Many teachers made a conscious effort to make common cause with the students and with that great amorphously beckoning entity, "the people." Professors came to look and talk more like students, and many tried to change the focus of their teaching, making it more relevant and democratic.

I joined in the desire to change when I returned to the United States in 1968 after a year in India. I came home shaken by the assassinations of Robert Kennedy and Martin Luther King, convinced that my teaching was too professionally focused on the experiences of labor lawyers and too removed from the important issues of equality and justice with which the society had to deal. I also concluded that my style of teaching, my professional dress, and my professorial style of speaking all served to separate me unnecessarily from my students. I vowed to change. I decided to be less professorial. I stopped wearing a suit, spoke more colloquially, and told the students to call me Jack. I revamped my teaching style, using questioning less often and setting out my views more clearly. In one class, instead of directing the discussion, I had the students ask me questions. I reasoned that it made the class more democratic and it also forced the students to concentrate on discovering what they did not know rather than on figuring out answers. I learned that democracy does not provide an easy road to pedagogic success. My change of pedagogic persona disturbed and offended many of the students, even those who thought of themselves as radicals.

In my course on employment discrimination, the class in which the students did the questioning, a student came to me after he had read one of my articles: "Some people who can teach very well can't write," he said, "but you are obviously the opposite."

This led to a long discussion about my reasons for teaching as I was. He told me that, whatever my goals, I wasn't achieving them. I returned to a more traditional role the next day, and several students came up after class to congratulate me on the improvement in my teaching.

My early unsuccessful efforts at pedagogic reform help to illustrate why meaningful educational change is difficult to achieve. As teaching goals become more sophisticated, they require far more effort and more subtle understanding. Far fewer models are available. And, as my experience suggests, a conservative, elitist streak exists in most students, even (or, perhaps, most especially) in those who see themselves as social activists. As a result, students are frequently resistant to change.

The struggle between elitist values and egalitarian visions emerges in all academic movements, even those committed to change, nurturing, and inclusion. I learned this most powerfully when I spent a semester as a visiting professor at the University of Chicago Law School. Dean Phil Neal, in response to pressure from the Women's Caucus, urged me to teach a course on women's rights. I agreed in large part because teaching a course on the status of women that would focus on law and social change was consistent with the type of professor I wanted to be. I tried to teach the class in a friendly, cooperative manner. At the first meeting I told the students that, although I was not an expert in the area, I looked forward to the class as a joint learning experience. The students responded coldly, disappointed that I was neither a renowned expert nor a dynamic classroom performer.

In one of the first classes, I suggested tentatively that the antiabortion forces had some legitimate arguments that needed to be addressed. This was greeted with anger and derision. On another occasion I listed the goals of the women's movement with the idea of discussing which of them could be achieved by law. I was interrupted by a young woman from New York who commented bitterly, "This movement means a lot to me and I resent your making it a laughingstock through a series of meaningless slogans."

The low point came during a class devoted to constitutional issues, in which the students were barely civil. Afterward, I returned to my office to find Carol Moseley, one of the two young black women in the class, waiting for me.[6] I expected her to register a complaint but she said, instead, "I just wanted you to know there are some of us in the class who can't stand the way these women are treating you. I think you've made some pretty good points in class even if these women ignore you when you try to make them think. They're afraid of the professors here, but since you listen and try to find something positive in what people say, they put you down. They think they're for equality, but they're as bigoted as any group of white racists in the South."

"I really don't understand it," I said. "I've never had this kind of trouble with a class before."

"A lot of this is because they think that Dean Neal is putting the course down by having it taught by a visitor."

A thought suddenly struck me. "Particularly one from Indiana," I said, and she laughed in agreement. "I guess I didn't help when I said I wasn't an expert, did I?"

"No, you sure didn't," she responded. After we talked for a while I realized that, although the Chicago students were political liberals and claimed to reject the school's conservative bias, they were academic snobs who wanted to be taught by great men and who reveled in the status of their professors. As a colleague later said to me, "They are what they claim to despise."

I felt humiliated, angry at the students for their snobbery and at myself for having performed ineffectively, thereby ruining the professional benefits that might otherwise have been derived from teaching at the University of Chicago. My agreeing to visit seemed a great mistake. Perhaps Indiana University marked the limits of my ability to teach successfully. Perhaps I was not learned enough to deal adequately with fundamental constitutional issues. Would I be capable of teaching about such questions effectively at Indiana? Thinking about that question made me realize that I would have taught very differently at Indiana. My dress, language, and approach would all have been less formal; I would have assumed less sophistication on the part of the students; and I would have approached the issue more from the perspective of practicing lawyers than from the lofty heights of a constitutional treatise writer. Much of my pedagogic behavior had been premised on the assumption that what I did at Indiana was unworthy of the students at Chicago. I felt ashamed of myself. I had let the prestige of the institution overwhelm me.

At the time, the class was concerned with sexual equality under the Fourteenth Amendment—the extent to which the Constitution prevents governments from drawing distinctions on the basis of sex. The case law had long recognized the legitimacy of such distinctions.

The Basic Academic Processes and the Search for Meaning

For example, in 1961 the Supreme Court upheld a distinction based on sex when it ruled in *Hoyt v. Florida* that the state could constitutionally eliminate women from jury duty unless they expressly applied for it. The Supreme Court's opinion justified the distinction between men and women in part on the grounds that "despite the enlightened emancipation of women from the restriction and protection of bygone years and their entry into many parts of community life formerly considered to be reserved to men, women are still regarded as the center of home and family life." The defendant had pointed out that the statute's breadth was considerably greater than this justification, but the court said Florida was not required to limit its rules to women with family responsibilities, since such a distinction might not be "administratively feasible."[7]

The soundness of such opinions came under heavy attack during the late 1960s with the reemergence of feminism. The legal arm of the women's movement made a major effort to get the Supreme Court to change its approach to sexual classification. Feminist lawyers felt considerably optimistic when the court agreed to decide *Reed v. Reed*, a case in which a woman challenged the constitutionality of an Idaho statute that gave a preference to men over women in the appointment of administrators.[8] The argument for Sally M. Reed was handled by the American Civil Liberties Union's women's project, which filed a long, eloquent brief on her behalf.[9] The primary effort of the brief, to which 39 of 45 pages were devoted, was to convince the Court that sex should be equated with race and treated as a "suspect classification." If the Court were to adopt this approach, it would mean that any sexual classification in a statute would bear a heavy presumption of invalidity. Heretofore, sexual classification had been dealt with under a much more lenient test that required merely a showing that the statute had a "rational relationship" to a legitimate state purpose.[10] The ACLU brief, which was written by a distinguished group of lawyers, including Ruth Bader Ginsburg (now a federal appeals judge) and the late Pauli Murray, emphasized the pervasiveness of discrimination against women in the law, listing the various ways in which women and men were treated differently.

The Supreme Court, in a very short opinion, held the Idaho statute unconstitutional. The Court did not deal with the issue of suspect classification, which comprised the majority of the ACLU brief. It stated, instead, that the preference for men was "on the basis of criteria wholly unrelated to the objective of the statute." The Court concluded that "the objective of reducing the workload on the probate courts by eliminating one class of contests is not without some legitimacy," but "to give mandatory preference to members of either sex over members of the other merely to accomplish the elimination of hearings on the merits is to make the very kind of arbitrary legislative choice forbidden by the equal protection clause of the Fourteenth Amendment."[11] *Reed v. Reed* was thus the first opinion to invalidate a legislative classification on the basis of sex. Nevertheless, the decision was greeted with considerable disappointment by many feminists who had hoped for a landmark opinion similar to *Brown v. Board of Education*, the decision outlawing racial segregation in public education. In the class prior to my meeting with Carol Moseley, I expressed the view that the decision was in fact quite significant, but my position was received with disdain by the students.

I came to the next class quite early, feeling tense, like a fighter before an important bout, wearing a velour sports shirt instead of a suit. I began by asking the students to assume that a case identical to the jury case, *Hoyt v. Florida*, was now before the Supreme Court and that they were serving as counsel for the defendant, arguing that the different treatment of women and men in the selection of jurors was unconstitutional. I asked them how we would argue the case, which I called *Hoyt II*. No one volunteered. The faces of the students showed a mixture of confusion and amused contempt.

"Is there no argument to be made?" A long pause. "Well, you could always concede and throw yourself on the mercy of the court." There were a few grudging smiles and a few looks of concentration in response to the challenge implied in my ridicule. Another long pause ensued, during which I waited patiently for a volunteer.

Finally, one of the male students raised his hand. "We would have to argue that this is an impermissible sexual distinction." Another pause. I waited. He said nothing.

"Why is it impermissible?" I asked.

A sudden spark of light in his eyes. "Because it is not adequately related to the purposes of the statute."

"And what are the purposes of the statute?"

"The statute involves the selection of jurors, and the distinction between men and women is irrelevant to that distinction," he said, suddenly surprised at the cogency of the argument.

"And what case would you cite for this?"

"*Reed v. Reed*," he said, half a question and half a statement.

"Is there any language in *Reed* that would be particularly useful?"

I could hear the welcome sounds of pages being turned feverishly. Two hands now were in the air. I called on one of the female students. She read from one of the last sentences in the opinion, "By providing dissimilar treatment for men and women who are similarly situated, the challenged section violates the equal protection clause." [12]

I outlined the basic argument on the board. "How would you respond to the following arguments by the state? (1) That the jury duty would be inconsistent with women's primary duties in the home; (2) that the state has the right to assume that men jurors would be more familiar with the questions involved in a trial by virtue of their greater familiarity with worldly affairs; (3) that this method would be administratively easier than making individual decisions." At this point I noticed several hands waving eagerly.

A female student said with excitement, "We could point out that the court in *Reed* could have justified the preference for men on all these bases, but it refused to do so, and then we could quote from the language in the *Reed* case that "to give mandatory preference to members of either sex over members of the other merely to accomplish the elimination of hearings on the merits is to make the very kind of arbitrary legislative choice forbidden by the equal protection clause of the Fourteenth Amendment." [13]

By now the students were impressed with the power of the case that we were able to put together on the basis of *Reed* to the effect that the *Hoyt* decision had been overruled without discussion. I pointed out that, so far in our approach to *Hoyt II*, we had sought a more stringent version of the traditional rational-relationship test. I asked how we could argue for formal adoption of the concept of sex as a suspect classification. Once again there was silence, but this time I could almost feel the concentrated thinking emanating from the students. Then it occurred to me that, as bright as the students at the University of Chicago were, they were not used to thinking in the tactical manner so common to lawyers. I asked them to look at the ACLU's brief dealing with the question of suspect classification, which they did. Then I asked whether the approach struck them as unusual in any way. Again, no answer.

"How does one usually convince a court to adopt a legal doctrine?"

After a pause, Frank Easterbrook, now a judge on the Seventh Circuit Court of Appeals, raised his hand. "By arguing that the doctrine has basically been accepted by earlier opinions."

I could see expressions of agreement and sudden understanding. "Isn't it surprising," I asked, "that the ACLU's brief went out of its way to point out to the court how revolutionary a change it would make to adopt the suspect classification approach?"

I asked the students whether they thought that the brief by the National Association for the Advancement of Colored People in *Brown v. Board of Education* had taken a similar approach. One of the students who had read the brief said that, in fact, it had not; that the brief had instead stressed all of the cases in which the court had struck down racial classification in education. Then I asked if it would have been possible to argue persuasively that sexual classification was by now so inconsistent with the approach of the law that its use should be justified only by a very powerful reason. The students had little trouble in listing the various ways in which the law had come to regard sexual classification as improper: Title VII, the Equal Pay Act, various lower court opinions, and, of course, the *Reed* case. This led to a good discussion between two of the students on the relationship between movement, rhetoric, and legal advocacy, and the incremental and indirect nature of legal change. When the class ended, several students lingered to talk to me and argue with each other.

A series of excellent classes followed, including one in which I urged forcefully that a defense attorney in a rape case might be ethically required to question the victim about her past sexual conduct, a position that most of the students despised. Despite their strong feelings, they listened carefully to the arguments that I made. They responded with passion but without anger or derision. Several came up to compliment me about the class afterward.

I was uncomfortable with the recognition that successful teaching in that class required a battle with my students. But, in fact, my misunderstanding and their snobbery had created an educational barrier which I could not overcome in an easy way.

Much—perhaps all—good teaching at colleges and graduate schools involves some type of struggle between professor and student, whereby internal student barriers to considering new ideas and approaches are overcome. Only rarely can this be achieved by a steady diet of acceptance and encouragement, as it was by Siddie Joe Johnson. Often it requires insistence that the students keep at a problem with which they are bored or confused or one that they think they have explored fully and answered as well as they are able to.

Great teaching is demanding, but most teaching that is demanding is not great. Professors may be demanding to demonstrate their own brilliance rather than to force the students to transcend their own normal limitations. Sometimes professors demand knowledge of minutiae, sometimes of their own pet theories, sometimes of traditional categories. Some demand meaningless work. Insisting that the students perform at an impossibly erudite level is a way of shifting the responsibility for failure to them. A fine line often exists between demanding that the students perform at their best and treating their efforts with contempt or cruelty.

Expertise and Experience

The most subtle way that elitist values confront pedagogic excellence occurs after the professor has taught for a time and has become a recognized expert on the subject. At this point the teacher is in a position to substitute eminence for pedagogy, stressing his or her importance and relying on status and manner to sustain interest. Students who would like to believe that they are being taught by important thinkers often enjoy classes in which this is done. Yet some of the most useful teaching involves demonstrating how much that is fundamental an expert does not know.

This approach is far less ego-gratifying than is playing the great man or woman, and few senior professors have the self-assurance to regularly point out the limits of their expertise. Passing on to the students what one has learned is relatively easy to do and it leaves the professor free for research.

There are many reasons why research comes to dominate the allocation of professional time. Research is less ephemeral than teaching. It usually produces an end product that is permanently visible. By definition, it means involvement with new material and the development of new ideas. Publishing articles brings us gradually into contact with peers around the country. It also has greater payoffs than teaching in terms of prestige, raises, job offers, and promotions. Indeed, its market advantages are now so obvious that we seem to have developed a whole new culture of young academics who enter the university with little commitment to teaching, determined to research, write, and publish while they incidentally meet with their traditionally taught classes.

Continuous pleasure in teaching seems to be most common among those who teach at small liberal arts schools where there is little pressure to publish. A significant number of faculty at such schools find teaching meaningful and academic research silly and pretentious. One told me he thinks that those who focus on teaching "are fighting for the minds, psyches, and souls of their students." He cannot understand professors who try to escape from students or find teaching boring.

Teaching and Failure

Teachers regularly confront failure: its regular presence is one of the factors that leads to academic snobbism, which often serves as an internal defense mechanism in dealing with failure. When I first began teaching, failure meant having a poor class or being unprepared, unclear, or uninteresting. I was sure that failure correlated powerfully with student disapproval.

The first time I recognized that success could not be equated with the reception of my classes came after the completion of my first labor law course, when I graded student exams. The course had been uniformly well received by the students and I looked forward to reading their exam answers. The papers were overwhelmingly disappointing. Questions that seemed to me difficult, but no more so than the hypotheticals I used in class, seemed to confuse a large percentage of the students. Virtually everyone missed some difficult issues that I included for the "A students." After evaluating the common errors in the papers, I realized that my explanations of some technical issues had confused the students more than they had enlightened them. In grading-down students who did poorly on such issues, I had the uncomfortable realization that they were being penalized because of my failures.

I found it extremely difficult to distinguish between those who had developed a system of analysis similar to my own from those who merely told me what they thought I wanted to hear. Reading final exams forced me to reevaluate my success as a teacher. If I had touched, inspired, or altered the students in any significant way, why was so little evidence of it present in their answers? I have since learned that my expectations were unrealistic, that there is often little correlation between what students have learned and what appears on their final exams. Most exams give a tremendous advantage to the self-confident, the well organized, and those who understand whether a particular professor might be looking for technical mastery, glittering generalizations, or informed disagreement. Yet my sense of disappointment correlated with something real. The students had enjoyed the course and had learned some basic labor law concepts, but they left the course as they had entered it, with the same strengths, weaknesses, and biases. It mattered very little, if at all, whether they had me as a teacher or not.

My disappointed reaction was typical. Sit in a faculty lounge during exam period and you are certain to hear vehement feelings of disappointment and anger expressed. Faculty members hate grading partly because, as they will tell you, it is both boring and demanding, but more significantly because it almost always suggests pedagogic failure.

The most profound feeling of failure that I recall came, paradoxically, after a particularly successful first-year contracts class. I taught that class as well as I was capable of teaching. I asked penetrating questions, was witty and unusually articulate, developed searching hypotheticals, and articulated precisely the conflicting policies that shaped the various court opinions. When the class ended, the room was abuzz with students discussing the issues that I had raised. I left the classroom feeling elated, but I was quickly depressed. It was a wonderful class—but what of it? It was so ephemeral. What would it mean to the students a year from now, or even a week? There was no record, no lasting result—nothing but an hour of excitement that I realized would soon fade from everyone's memory. Because I could not sustain such a level of involvement, an individual class on the professional-school level, no matter how good, would make no real educational difference to any of the people who experienced it.

There are many ways in which professors fail as teachers. Higher education is filled with people who were great students but who do not know how to deal with the uncertainties, anxieties and small rejections that are a regular part of teaching. As Christopher Jencks and David Riesman point out, "Most professors become good teachers only if it comes fairly easily and naturally. Those who do not have much natural flair seldom know how to begin remedying their failings even if they have the impulse. They certainly get little help from their colleagues."[14] For such people, teaching can be a bewildering, even a shattering, experience. They go from academic success and universal expressions of esteem to failure and student disdain without understanding what is happening to them. Many respond by getting angry at the students and by telling themselves that their ideas are too sophisticated for those not academically gifted. I know of several intelligent and dedicated academics whose careers have been marred from the beginning by the combination of unexpected student resistance and their own defensive response to it.

Success as a teacher over a long period requires far more than knowledge, sympathy with students, or the ability to articulate. It requires the ability to change, to give up successful roles for more daring ones, to confess confusion, to expose weaknesses, to place student priorities ahead of one's own, to seek out and encourage students who feel inadequate while confronting successful students with the limits of their knowledge.

Such teaching is, of course, rare. Most of us must learn to live with the regular recognition of our failure.

Research and Scholarship

Publication, Scholarship, and Research

Professors are expected to produce scholarly writing. This obligation and the teaching function coexist uneasily. While research often supports teaching by giving professors a deeper understanding of important issues in their fields, the two frequently conflict. Faculty members are often compelled to devote their efforts to one or the other.

Successful research is, by definition, elitist. It functions on the border of accepted knowledge and, by pushing that border forward, it enlarges the distinction between what is known by the academic expert and what is known by the ordinary, educated person. Anyone who has done successful research is for a time the most knowledgeable person in the world about some aspect of the topic and is likely to view the issue from a unique perspective.

The model for great research is Einstein's development of the theory of relativity. His famous articles explaining relativity announced concepts of great subtlety and elegance that were understood by only a handful of people. After their verification, through a complex scholarly process, scientists' concepts of the universe have been forever changed. Einstein himself is probably the patron saint of academic elitists. His very appearance—the face of a dreamer, eyes that radiated subtle comprehension, clothes that showed a complete disinterest in fashion—proclaimed the distance that separated him from others.

Research thus provides the dress suit for academic elitism, clothing with respectability the attitudes that the academic enterprise is more important, demanding, and complex than other endeavors and that first-rate academics are different, smarter, and more creative than other people.

Research also has egalitarian aspects. At its best, it connects the academy with the real world. It often reminds us that reality is more complex than professors sometimes pretend and that thinking and ideas are not our exclusive province. Moreover, true scholars, those whose contributions have an important, illuminating impact on an area of thinking, are rare, the tiny base of a large enterprise. Like cowboys in Texas or seafarers in Maine, their manners of speech, dress, and demeanor are frequently copied by those who would claim membership in their numbers. It is, of course, much more difficult to develop the quality of mind and personality that lead to creative scholarship than it is to affect the manner: it is far easier to look like Einstein than to discover relativity.

As anyone who has read academic journals learns, an enormous amount of pretense is connected with scholarship and publication. The great bulk of writing for which scholarly status is claimed involves no more than the recycling of currently fashionable ideas, using graphs, formulas, and esoteric language to suggest originality. Nevertheless, during periods such as the present when the emphasis shifts away from teaching to research, the production of such writing is important to academic institutions and individual faculty members. For most universities, institutional status and the availability of funds is tied to the scholarly reputation of the faculty. For young professors, productivity means promotions, raises, offers to teach elsewhere, and the crucial awards of tenure. For senior faculty, it can lead to appointments to special, named professorships, the chance to enter administration, opportunities to travel, and national recognition in their fields.

Increasingly, colleges and universities proclaim their primary mission to be "pushing back the frontiers of knowledge." At traditional research institutions, journals filled with inquiry into esoterica, carefully worded footnotes, and stylized academic prose abound. Howard R. Bowen and Jack H. Schuster report:

> At most of the campuses we visited, we were struck by the rapidly changing value system present. Taking advantage of a strong buyer's market, campus after campus has been moving aggressively to upgrade the importance of scholarly productivity as a criterion for academic personnel decisions. Thus, almost every institution of higher education, from leading research institutions to the most modest campuses, has today been able to hire by its standards excellent faculty, and a considerable number of institutions have moved rapidly towards new reward structures. The result is a veritable surge towards research.[15]

Although many people use the terms interchangeably, I distinguish among publication, scholarship, and research. I define "publication" as academic writing that is essentially the restatement of other people's thinking, "scholarship" as writing that introduces or challenges academic concepts. Scholarly writing involves a debate within the academy. Its concern is with the organization, rationality, and persuasiveness of ideas. Its focus is inevitably elitist. I reserve the term "research" for the effort to discover something significant about the way the world works. Its focus is reality. Its impact on the academy need not, indeed should not, be elitist. A policy that promotes publication may actually reduce scholarship and discourage research.

The Appeal of Scholarship

Academics approach the task of scholarly writing from a variety of different perspectives. Some see it as an opportunity to advance understanding, others as an opportunity to make their brilliance more widely known. There are always those who consider the need to publish a meaningless chore—a requirement that will divert them from their first love, teaching. Most young academics are frightened by the prospect and very few truly understand it. For those who do not upon entry in the academy think of themselves as scholars, its appeal is often discovered slowly and with a sense of surprise. I am in some ways typical of this latter group.

I came to Indiana University with the draft of my master's thesis at Harvard Law School in tow. It was a long, rambling discussion of the *Midwest Piping* doctrine, a National Labor Relations Board (NLRB) policy that required an employer faced with conflicting claims for recognition by two different unions to do nothing until the board held an election.[16] I had argued a *Midwest Piping* case when I was with the board, and I was aware that the law was often confused and sometimes contradictory. My paper ran for about seventy pages, most of which was taken up with descriptions of cases. My hope was to publish it and, thereafter, having established my claim to tenure, devote myself exclusively to teaching. I asked Howard Mann, one of my most critical colleagues, to look at my paper. After he read it, he told me it was "all right," a phrase he used to describe things considerably below his own high standards of achievement. But he added quickly, "I kept asking myself, Where's Jack? I don't want to learn about a bunch of old cases. I want to know what you think." I was disappointed, but his comment that I was not present in the work stirred feelings of recognition and hope as well as dismay. My most successful advocacy and teaching has had the quality of personal presence that Howard was urging me to put into my writing. I have since passed along this bit of advice many times. The element of personal commitment is a factor that separates students from scholars and one that makes scholarship enjoyable for many of us.

After pondering Howard's criticism I made my article less pedantic and more personal. The resulting article was much shorter and more direct, forceful, and controversial.[17] Because it was well received, I decided to work on another article addressing the meaning of antiunion discrimination under the National Labor Relations Act. This issue confused my students and puzzled me when I worked at the labor board. I began work on the article in the spring of 1965. Each afternoon after teaching class, I would go to my cubicle in the faculty library and work for two or three hours. To my surprise, I enjoyed the combination of intellectual effort and social isolation that it required. I stopped attending coffee hour, gave up billiards, and cut down on my socializing.

Many evenings I went back to the library after dinner. A colleague, Val Nolan, and I were generally the only two there. We spoke rarely, sometimes working at adjoining cubicles for hours without a word being said. But I was conscious of a mutually understood scholarly link between us. This was my first realization of how individual an enterprise scholarly writing generally is, and how pleasant the loneliness can be, particularly when one simultaneously feels a part of a community of scholars. My interviews suggest that pleasure in working alone and delight in discovery and in working through intellectual problems are common traits of successful scholars. Success as a student is not necessarily predictive. As a student I hated homework and was well known for being gregarious. I was an unlikely bet to enjoy scholarship. But in working on my second article, I once spent almost three hours rewriting a single paragraph. As I tore up my latest effort and gazed at the blank yellow pad with anticipation, I discovered that I was enjoying myself. This sense of pleasure has continued throughout my career. I, who could never force myself to complete writing assignments as a student, suddenly found the hours flying by when I worked on my articles. When I completed a section that pleased me, I had a gratifying sense of achievement and self-definition.

The Organization of Scholarship

Not so long ago, most scholarship was internally motivated and done in whatever time one could carve out from other obligations. No such thing as research leave existed when I first joined the faculty at Indiana University, and, if it had, I would have been at the bottom of the list for it as a young faculty member. I was expected to teach and fully prepare for my classes, take part in all law school activities, and do any writing I wanted in such spare time as I could find. In all but the sciences, we thought of ourselves primarily as teachers, not scholars.

Research and Scholarship

In the 1960s, there were far fewer faculty research seminars in which to try out ideas, far fewer research leaves, and much less thought that the senior faculty had any special responsibility for helping the junior faculty. Generally, only informal exchanges took place among a small group of scholars interested in similar topics. Those who began at that time in any but the most prestigious schools had a great advantage over young scholars today. We could choose topics on the basis of interest and find our own scholarly voice without much pressure from senior faculty.

It is all different today. Expectations are much higher. Young faculty fresh from graduate schools, clerkships, or fellowships are expected to develop sophisticated research agendas before they ever meet with a class. At any school that claims to be a scholarly institution, colloquia, works-in-progress seminars, research leaves, mentors among the senior faculty, and periodic reviews of scholarly progress will all be present. Today's vision of what scholars should attempt is more ambitious. Articles are more theoretical, elegant, interdisciplinary, and ambitious than were those of my early years. In schools seeking to improve their positions in the great hierarchy of higher education (and this includes almost all), publication quotas must be met before a person may be considered for promotion or tenure. Unfortunately, as Jencks and Riesman point out, "Judging . . . by . . . output . . . puts a premium on a particular type of research for which there is relatively little need." [18] New journals spring up regularly—not because they have anything to add but because the supply of writing is so great that it creates a need for a depository. And the creation of new journals is thought to help institutional status. At least six journals were published at Yale Law School when I left. Similar transformations have taken place in almost every academic discipline. Research has become more esoteric, interdisciplinary, mathematical, and professionally oriented so that nonacademics are far less likely to understand or be interested in what is written.

The gap between educated laymen and academic specialists constantly grows. I do not think the gap is attributable to the speed with which the frontiers of knowledge are being pushed back; instead, it reflects the desire by academics to be thought part of a special, elite, intellectually rigorous world and the fear that, if what we wrote was intelligible, the claim would be more easily dismissed.

I approve of little in the current system other than research leaves, and I am even ambivalent about them because they remove young faculty prematurely from the classroom. Teaching is a wonderful source of research ideas because preparing for class often makes faculty aware of their ignorance, and awareness of ignorance is crucial to innovative research.

The pressure to publish hurts both the young professors and their students, and its effect on scholarship is negative. The tension under which many young faculty work is difficult to exaggerate. Not surprisingly, many ignore class preparation and are frequently unavailable to students. They are not likely to experience the scholarly tranquility, the easy communication, or sense of self-discovery that were the best parts of my early experience. As Bowen and Schuster report: "The junior faculty at many of the campuses we visited had become in a sense 'privatized,' that is, the overwhelming pressure to produce and publish had isolated them. According to a number of deans and department chairs whom we interviewed, the junior faculty had ceased to function as fully participating members of their campus communities, even within their own departments, as they 'burrowed toward tenure.' "[19]

In general, this generation's young faculty members write more than young faculty members did only twenty years ago. They are under greater pressure from deans and senior colleagues who will be evaluating them for tenure. Although the current system has produced much writing in almost all disciplines, it has not led to very much useful scholarship. Publication and scholarship are different, a simple truth often ignored today. Useful scholarship requires a willingness to risk failure and to take the time necessary to pursue a scholarly vision, both of which are discouraged by the current system.

THE ROLE OF SCHOLARLY JOURNALS

Innovative scholarship is discouraged by narrow disciplinary journals. This is true in almost every field. Legal scholarship is peculiar in that the academic fate of young professors is placed in the hands of law school students who are editors of the majority of the "professional" journals. I can still recall my elation when I got a letter from the editors of the *University of Chicago Law Review* stating that they would publish my first article. I read the editor's letter over and over, slowly realizing that my status in the world of legal education would be instantly and permanently changed. I would henceforth be a published author, someone likely to get tenure, possibly offers to visit at other schools, and entitled to refer to myself as a scholar—all because a group of third-year students, whose chief claim to distinction was having gotten good grades during their first year as law students, saw fit to publish my article. Because students are generally unfamiliar with basic concepts of research, the only standard they can employ in determining the worth of an article is whether it conforms to the concept of legal analysis that they have just acquired from their professors. Thus the process is confined to a small circle familiar with the same academically fashionable ideas. Because of the great pressure to publish in good journals and the acceptability of multiple submissions, the power of student editors has grown in recent years and the process has become more demeaning and less rational. A great deal of faculty effort has gone into determining when to submit articles, how to attract the attention of editors, and how to play one journal off another to obtain publication in the more prestigious ones.

In most academic disciplines, articles are evaluated by established scholars, but since those who decide upon publication are likely to represent current academic thinking, the problem of publishing only that which conforms to accepted norms is still great.

To read through current scholarly journals with their self-centered displays of learning without daring or originality makes me wonder: What interests are we serving by requiring young professors to devote their best years to this enterprise? The impact on untenured professors, as Jencks and Riesman report, is to push them away, perhaps permanently, from "important problems . . . and substantive issues that actually matter toward a display of professional narcissism . . . a roller coaster ride along a well-worn track." [20] Bowen and Schuster indicate that the new emphasis also has negative consequences for their senior colleagues, whose status was achieved from different—and newly diminished—criteria: "Some were angry, embittered, alienated from a new order. Not infrequently they expressed outrage about market-driven compensation, differential pay policies they consider unjust and even humiliating. From the viewpoint of some of them, such compensation policies tended to favor not only the new breed of self-centered new faculty but also the high-demand academic fields. Many members of the senior arts and sciences professsorate, 'the old guard,' felt that they had been relegated to subordinate status." [21]

The current system turns a process that should be enjoyable and useful into one that causes great pain and produces very little. It is difficult to understand why academic institutions are run in such a self-defeating way. One reason may be that the current system gives too much weight to the skills possessed by excellent students—such as the ability to put one's own gloss on somebody else's ideas and the ability to organize ideas in a linear fashion. Because the system is essentially established by those who were excellent students, this result may not be mere coincidence. Rewarding the skills of students may increase publication, but it is bound to reduce research, the successful completion of which turns on different traits.

The Impact of Scholarship

All young academics secretly expect that publication of their articles will be a momentous event. This is almost never so. When my first article was about to be published, I anticipated its being discussed by the NLRB, cited by the courts, responded to by scholars in the history of labor law scholarship, and referred to in the casebooks. Actually, the article evoked little reaction, as is typical in narrow scholarly writing. Almost all the response came from friends, mentors, and family. I did receive a letter from a professor at the University of Oregon whom I had never met. He described my article as "a real contribution," but when I met him at a law school association meeting a short time later, he did not remember me, my article, or his letter.

The feeling of being inadequately recognized, together with envy of those whose writing is more widely read, is a chronic state for academics. Almost everyone who publishes in law, literature, or social science has to recognize that the writing so important to him or her is unlikely to have an impact on reality or even on scholarship, both of which go on almost precisely as they would have had one not written. Most of us envy physical scientists in this regard. Not only does one scientist's work build on another's contribution, but also the work seems immune from the problems of evaluation that create so much insecurity among social scientists. Science research is testable, cumulative, related to reality, and has practical consequences. Yet discussion with scientists of various ranks suggests that they face the same problems as the rest of us—fierce competition, irrational hierarchy, and feelings of inadequate recognition and constant failure. An internationally recognized experimental physicist told me that he was often treated like a technician by second-rate theorists.

Harvey Greenspan, a friend who is a professor of applied mathematics at the Massachusetts Institute of Technology, commented that the original and seminal contributions in his own field—dealing with such fundamental areas as turbulence, shock waves, and dimensional analysis—were largely ignored by other scientists even as their impact on different areas of science grew. In his words, "Applied mathematicians are the aborigines of science. Nothing is regarded as a major discovery until a white man sees it."

That our writing lacks obvious impact makes many academics defensive and concerned with small indications of importance or recognition. One way that faculty can overcome the feeling of being ignored is by banding together in scholarly movements. This makes one's work fashionable, likely to be published, and certain of favorable response from other members of the movement; however, joining a scholarly movement reduces independence as to subject matter, conclusion, and even language—thereby reducing the likelihood of original research. When rival scholarly movements exist in a single faculty department or school, relations not infrequently deteriorate, mutual respect evaporates, and bitter debates about appointments, promotions, and tenure erupt.

Some faculty respond to the lack of response to their writings by becoming ostentatiously unconcerned with readership. They liken themselves to Einstein or Mendel, whose writings were too advanced, complex, and sophisticated for the vast majority of their colleagues. Those people whose works are actually read are often dismissed as "trendy" or—even worse—"journalistic." A more realistic approach was taken by my colleague at the University of Texas, Michael Sharlot, whose father was a carpenter. Asked if he thought his work was more meaningful than his father's, he responded immediately, "Of course not. Nobody ever took shelter under one of my articles."

Scholarship and Failure

FAILURE AND AMBITION

Scholarly writing involves little risk of obvious failure because it is possible through careful reading, concentration on detail, and critical reasoning to discover analytic errors in current theory, small gaps in what is known, or possible errors in what others have advocated—and that's all most scholarship is about. Professors use such discoveries as the basis of articles that make them known to others in the field. As long as the prose is literate, the writer evidences understanding of the literature and appears erudite, and the issues are currently fashionable, the writer will eventually come to be recognized as a legitimate scholar. Given the fact that scholarship is enjoyable and relatively easy, it is surprising that many academics never attempt it. Some do almost no writing at all. Nonwriters are often articulate and interesting original thinkers and intelligent critics. Attempting to understand their failure to attempt scholarship becomes a parlor game among colleagues and a source of anguish to close friends. Typical was Henry Jonathan, who taught civil procedure at Indiana University.

The first time I saw Henry in action, just after I arrived at Indiana University in 1963, he was arguing with Scott Daily, the constitutional law professor, about then–Chief Justice Earl Warren. Henry was talking excitedly. "It's a wonderful paradox. Eisenhower thought he was appointing a conservative Republican politician and instead he appointed the greatest libertarian activist in the Court's history."

Scott attempted to disagree, but Henry went on excitedly. "Law is the most basic expression of our ideals of justice, and a good Supreme Court justice must understand justice in its most profound sense. He must also understand history, literature, philosophy, poetry, psychology, and above all humanity." He paused and sighed, "It's too much, too profound, obviously too demanding for any one of us, and yet we expect men chosen for political reasons, many with obviously limited intelligence, poorly read, and narrowly educated, to make these basic decisions, and the great paradox is that, somehow, they do. What's worth noticing and writing articles about is not their failures but how often they are right. It's too profound for most of our so-called experts to notice." He smiled, obviously pleased at his own eloquence.

Scott did not respond. His expression suggested that he considered it a waste of time to argue with Henry. A short time later the conversation turned to football. Scott took the position that the university should give up its athletics program and concentrate on academics. Henry would have none of it. "I'm always amused by people who think that nothing at a university counts except scholarship. They consider themselves so high-minded. What they don't realize is that they should be more concerned with what passes for scholarship at most universities. Athletics is what's right about American higher education. It requires teamwork, commitment, and intelligence before it can be done well. It's not accidental that athletic teams were integrated before almost anything else in our society. It shows people what the world should be like and it gives nonacademic people who live in the state a reason to care about the university."

Henry was so eloquent and enjoyed using words so much that I was amazed to learn that he had published almost nothing. Perhaps coffee hour had replaced the law review for him. He used the lounge as the forum in which to express his most original insights and an arena in which to battle his colleagues for intellectual supremacy. He rarely missed coffee hour. He would generally arrive after the discussion had already begun.

Research and Scholarship

His arrival was like shifting a car into a faster gear. He would inevitably change the subject to something that had attracted his notice. The new topic might be a recent movie, a comment by an athlete, a line of poetry, a non sequitur in a Supreme Court opinion, a statement by the president of the university. Sometimes Henry would try to connect his comment to the topic under conversation; sometimes he would wait for a pause in the conversation before speaking. When he was particularly excited, he would simply interrupt.

Henry pretended to be indifferent to academic status, but in fact he was quite ambitious. He hoped to burst upon the world of legal scholarship as he entered a coffee-lounge discussion, giving it new direction and establishing his own central position. He talked of harmonizing law and theoretical physics to show how jurisprudence could be enriched by adding to it the insights and techniques of scientists. After twenty years with no serious scholarly writing, he announced to his friends that he was now "ready to do major work." During this period he regularly read esoteric works of scientific theory. In 1970 he went on leave to Princeton University, sending his books and papers ahead. He told his friends that when he returned his book would be substantially completed. He came back full of stories about life at Princeton but without a manuscript, and he stopped talking about the great work he was planning to write.

I find it difficult to understand why a person capable of coming up with more lively and original ideas during a luncheon than are contained in entire issues of most law reviews was not able to present his ideas in the form of articles or books. Why did something that could have been accomplished fairly easily become such an unconquerable psychological burden? His failure to write was not the result of laziness or unwillingness to put in the hours necessary for successful scholarship. Henry was capable of working around the clock on minor research tasks that he occasionally undertook for lawyers around the state. The questions would invariably get him thinking about issues far deeper than those for which he was hired, and would, as a result, provoke a series of fascinating reflections to enliven lunch and coffee hour for the next week or so.

My conclusions apply not only to Henry but in varying degrees to most of the academic underachievers in all disciplines I have known. First, he was so eloquent and he so easily impressed people with the quickness and ingenuity of his mind through casual contact that he felt he could only disappoint by doing something in which he played the role of advocate rather than that of critic. Second, because he was perceptive enough to regularly spot the flaws in major works by leading scholars, he knew that should he ever put his ideas into print, others would be in a position to do the same to him. I do not, however, believe that such intellectual timidity would have been enough to keep him from publishing and thereby circulating his insights to a wider audience. In other situations, Henry was prepared to take chances and battle for his ideas.

He failed because the level on which he planned to work was so highly intellectual and theoretical that it ruled out the basic insights into human personality that motivated his best conversational ideas. His mind didn't naturally turn to questions of physics and law. He was led to law and science by his ambition. Otherwise, he would have spoken of these areas more and tried out his ideas at coffee or lunch. Truly original scholarship is frightening enough, lonely enough, and difficult enough to make intellectual enjoyment crucial for its successful completion. Much of the enjoyment comes from engaging one's mind with issues one cares about. In Henry's case, had he picked topics equally challenging but less elevated, I think he would have enjoyed scholarship and been a successful scholar. Unfortunately, he did not really believe that what he could do well and enjoyed was worthy of his scholarly focus. And he was too honest, perceptive, and respectful of scholarship to do either traditional or fashionably pretentious work. This doomed him to be the type of academic who scattered his best ideas and deepest visions into the coffee cups of the faculty lounge. I have encountered this personality type at every school at which I have taught. I always like the "Henry Jonathans" and enjoy their company far more than the great majority of the scholarly successes. Nonwriters are sometimes thought to be lazy. Almost always, however, they are like Henry, highly ambitious but fearful that they cannot live up to their own standards.

For those who begin teaching at elite schools, inhibition about scholarship is often exacerbated by the conflicting scholarly theories of their seniors and the chilling vision of their contemporaries assembled in the faculty lounge, eager to point out errors and dismiss other people's work as pedestrian. When I was on the Yale faculty, I realized that I could not have enjoyed writing or done well as a scholar if I had begun there. The assumption that a young scholar should do great work dealing with major legal themes would have inhibited me from doing anything. At one time it was common for young faculty members at elite schools to respond to this pressure by developing writing blocks. Currently they are more likely to write pretentious and meaningless articles. In either case, their ability to do useful scholarly work is diminished by the stature of the school and the expectations it creates. Most current articles that I read are a profound form of failure because they do not change ideas or provide significant information. They are no more scholarship than those novels that lack character, image, and idea are literature.

THE UBIQUITY OF FAILURE

While all academics are capable of success, none can avoid failure. Failure takes many forms. Some fail because their work is too ambitious, some because it is too prosaic. A few fail because they are too daring; many fail because they are too careful. Some attempt innovation that does not work; some lack any shred of originality. Many scholars fail because their work is based on a faulty vision of reality that they neither challenge nor seek to test. Scholarly failure is not limited to the intellectually pretentious. Almost every able academic that I am familiar with has had to wrestle with the problem.

In scholarship more than anywhere else in academic life the line between failure and success is often hidden. Recognizing failure is a matter of perception and acknowledging it a matter of personality. What constitutes failure will vary with the standards being applied and the posture from which work is being evaluated. Almost any completed work can be successfully criticized.

The impact on academic life of living with the constant possibility and frequent occurrence of failure is profound. It makes some academics frantic, some defensive, others driven. It helps to explain the preoccupation of many academics with the indicia of success: how often one's work has been cited and by whom. One of the principal ways that friendship is manifested is through reciprocal citation. A labor law professor with whom I used to be friendly invariably cited my work in his early articles. We had a falling-out and my name no longer appears in his work, even when my writings are directly relevant to his own. Not uncommonly, professors seek job offers they know they will not take. This is only sometimes done to force their home institution to increase their present salary. More often it is a way of obtaining reassurance with respect to the quality and significance of the person's work.

COPING WITH FAILURE: PRETENSE AND GRACE

Pretense. Responses to failure are as varied as its causes. Some acknowledge failure and try again, some become embittered, and many pretend that they have in fact been regularly successful. Scott Daily, the person with whom Henry Jonathan regularly argued, responded to failure as do many academics—with pretentiousness spiced with anger. His concern with his status affected almost all of his relationships and the quality of his professional life. Scott rarely missed coffee, but he always acted as though he were reluctantly taking time out from far more important tasks. He would lean way back in an armchair as though to remove himself from the group, and he would smile to himself, evidently amused by the shallowness and pretense of the discussion. He particularly liked to talk about "legal education," a term he used almost reverentially, and of his days as articles editor of the *Harvard Law Review.* His comments were typically angry, self-praising, and indirectly critical of one or another colleague.

His office was crammed with books, piles of papers, and uncompleted drafts. Yet in fifteen years he had written only one article. He had labored on it for many years. It was overly technical and badly written, which meant that its readership was tiny. Yet hidden in his inflated prose were ideas of subtlety and originality. His article was an example of the way in which failure and success combine in scholarship. It failed to stir response or to influence future writing. It did not demonstrate Scott's brilliance or his mastery over words and ideas. It succeeded, however, by developing new ways of analyzing a significant topic.

Scott assumed the manner of a major academic figure with such insistence that most faculty members outside the law school who knew him were convinced that he was a prolific scholar whose articles and books were frequently cited by the Supreme Court on difficult questions of law and whose original ideas were admired by prominent academics at Harvard, Yale, and Chicago. At the faculty club he would tell stories that he announced were currently making the rounds in the Harvard Faculty Club. He once told a group of political science professors who did not laugh at one of his stories, "Most of my jokes aren't that funny to people who do not really know what's going on among leading jurists."

Scott's way of coping with failure was both ludicrous and tragic. It was ludicrous in his ostentatious efforts to suggest recognition he had not achieved. The tragedy lay in the great wasted talent, the huge, unfilled, palpable need for acceptance in his angry, malevolent response to his sense of inadequacy. The sense of self-contempt about him was made more poignant by the glimpses he showed of the person he might have been but for the feeling of unworthiness that constantly escaped from his self-erected barricades of anger, competitiveness, scorn, and intellectual pretension. Scott was frequently in a state of inner torment. He once told his students that he liked to take long walks at night because that was the only time he was at peace with himself. I believe that part of the battle that raged inside him was between his basically decent farmboy standards and his overpowering desire to demonstrate how far he had come and how greatly superior he was to most of the people he had grown up with.

I used to think of Scott as a special case—a person whose high academic ambitions created a wall that separated him from almost everyone. But now I think of him as typical of the many academics who have great ability and ambition but who end their careers without contributing anything new to the world of ideas.

Today as little scholarship goes on as ever, but far more is written. Pretense similar to Scott's occurs most often in print. One of the common misuses of academic writing is to publish what appears to be a major work without going through the painful process of investigating reality, substituting academic style or the use of mathematical formulas for originality. A variety of techniques may be used to do this, such as creating jargon, formulas, models, and esoteric citations. Certain topics automatically announce their own importance. Articles titled "Toward a New Model of the First Amendment" or "Deconstructing the Hermeneutical Circle" would by their very names suggest the high level on which the authors approach scholarly issues. It is tempting to write these articles because all one needs to do it well enough for publication is to have read the relevant literature and have invented a new vocabularly for expressing familiar ideas. Currently fashionable are articles that contain mathematical formulas, cite European philosophers, develop models, talk in terms of cost-benefit analysis, and use the term "hermeneutic" or the term "story" to describe something without plot or obvious meaning. All of these things may be done without finding out anything new. Such writing is as much an effort to deceive as Scott's self-awarded national reputation. It brings no news despite the trappings of erudition. Its main purpose in any discipline is to win admiration, not to instruct. We are in a period where not publishing is rare but nonscholarship is common.

Grace. The most admirable academics can be identified by the way in which they deal with failure. My late colleague Ralph Fuchs dealt with failure with the same grace that he used in responding to adversity or success. Ralph was a first-rate scholar and teacher, and his life was built around service to the community. His sense of community did not have the narrow institutional focus so common among academics but extended to the profession generally and beyond to the broader national and international society. He had been president of the American Association of University Professors, had been faculty advisor to the Indiana University Chapter of the NAACP when the school desegregated, and had been a founder of the Indiana Civil Liberties Union during the height of the McCarthy period. When I first came to Indiana University in 1963, I learned that Ralph, who had published many excellent articles in a variety of fields, had been working on a treatise for some years. Because our offices were next to one another, I would occasionally hear him dictating case notes or summaries of articles for his secretary to transcribe. Long after Ralph had formally retired, he continued to come in every day to work on his treatise. He told me at lunch one day of a dream in which he learned that Dean Acheson, an old friend of his, had prepared a reception in his honor but Ralph had discovered that he would not have time to attend. Ralph was sure that the dream meant that he would not complete the treatise before he died. Ralph spoke in his normal, reasonable tone, but his anguish and disappointment were apparent.

It turned out that after all these years of work Ralph had not yet begun to write—nor had he figured out precisely what it was he wanted to say. He had begun working on this project when he was a candidate for an advanced degree at Yale. Administrative law was in its infancy then, and Ralph was encouraged to write a treatise that would explain or at least explore all of the cases in which courts passed on the legitimacy of actions by administrative agencies. By the late 1960s, however, the amount of case law was so huge that all of Ralph's energy was devoted to keeping up with the new law and with scholarly writing in the field. Ralph stubbornly and patiently continued to collect cases long after the impractical nature of the plan should have been clear. Only after he developed cataracts did he recognize the impossibility of completing the treatise and reluctantly decide to use some of the material he had collected as the basis for a law review article. The product of the years of careful investigation was a single article, "The Prerequisites to Judicial Review," published in 1976 by the *Indiana Law Journal*. It ran for eighty pages, preceded by a graceful note explaining that the material was a "small portion of a text on Administrative Law which I have long had underway, but which the burgeoning ramifications of that subject have rendered it impracticable to complete as planned." The note thanked the student editors for publishing his article "in a medium that is largely devoted to innovative writing such as I have not attempted here." [22]

It is still difficult for me to understand how Ralph Fuchs, a person of solid achievement and scholarly intelligence, could get caught up in a treatise that from the beginning lacked focus or point of view. It demonstrates to me how vulnerable we all are to failure in pursuing tasks that give the promise of major scholarly significance. Failure is to some extent a natural adjunct of serious scholarship.

In thinking about Ralph's last years, I realize that what distinguished him was the grace with which he responded to failure. Ralph never complained, never turned hostile toward those whose work flourished, and never was unavailable for young colleagues. He did not remove himself from family or friends, and he never refused to contribute his services to causes in which he believed. He did not act in any way like a person who felt his professional success was in jeopardy. He never gave any sign that he regretted his choice of career.

The universality of failure should give academics a sense of being involved in a common risky and frustrating enterprise, but it often drives us apart. No one should be condemned for scholarly failure, but we may all fairly be evaluated for how we deal with it.

Research, Pain, and Serendipity

In interviews with successful scholars I have been struck by the importance of luck and the mysterious ways in which important insights arise. This has also been true in my own work. My first effort at field research started out to be something far different. Professor Steve Goldberg, another former NLRB attorney, and I decided to write a treatise on the law of union representation elections. Such elections play a key role in U.S. labor law. When the project began, we intended to write a standard treatise describing and evaluating the intricate system of legal rules that governs union-organizing campaigns. Along the way, we realized that no one—not the courts, the NLRB, or labor law scholars—knew how the rules work in practice and that the assumptions on which they were based were questionable. Steve suggested that we allocate some of our time to study how employees behave as a result of unlawful campaign behavior by employers. We anticipated that it would take between six months and a year to do the empirical part of our study, but when we met to plan our research design we got an inkling of how complex the task was. We realized that before we could even begin to collect data, we needed to develop questionnaires, learn interviewing skills, hire interviewers, learn how to code answers, and figure out a way to identify illegal behavior and measure its impact.

We realized soon that we were doing something that would take years rather than months, but along with this came the realization that we could thereby contribute something valuable. Steve Goldberg and I worked for

The Basic Academic Processes and the Search for Meaning

almost eight months developing a preliminary design, preparing question-naires, and devising ways in which we could secure cooperation from unions, management, and employees. As the pleasure and potential value of the empirical project we had set for ourselves began to penetrate, we soon dropped the idea of a traditional treatise.

It took us more than a year and a half to complete our pilot studies and work out our research design. The collection of data took another 2½ years. I enjoyed this period more than any other part of the study. I en-joyed the partnership with Steve, the endless conversations about research design, the pleasure of editing each other's writing, and the sense of mu-tual dedication to the study. I enjoyed the junior-partnership relationship that developed with our student interviewers, the rehashing of interviews, and the fun of eating meals together in some motel late in the evening, after all the interviews were completed, while we laughed and swapped stories about what we had learned. I enjoyed the constant flow of ideas about the process of union organizing that stemmed from our interviews and conversations, and I was excited by the variety and basic decency of the working people whom we met. We kept a special file of interesting quotes that did not fit any of our coding categories. Some were humorous, some powerful, and some poetic. I felt certain that if we carried this study through successfully, it would profoundly and permanently change the way people think about the organizing process.

The final stage, during which we analyzed the data, was less exciting and more complex than I had expected. The need to be scientific squeezed out much of the humanity, and some of our most interesting speculations could not be tested through acceptable scientific methods. The worst as-pect of the study by far was the need for funding. Six years passed between our first meeting and the study's completion. The resulting book ran 150 pages.[23] It is not surprising that our study took so long. We were seeking to test the validity of generally accepted assumptions about reality. It is rarely, if ever, easy to discover the error in generally shared assump-tions. Error becomes accepted because truth is hidden. That is why it is far easier to publish articles spelling out the implications of what is gen-erally believed than it is to test the validity of the beliefs, and why pressure to publish is likely to decrease the likelihood of reality-testing research.

Our conclusion had the common ingredient of successful research: we carefully documented that "the emperor has no clothes." The standard vision of reality is wrong. This is not a message that is ever easily acknowl-edged, but it has the advantage of forcing people to respond and some-times to change their thinking.

The Problems of Empirical Research

There are rewards for those who complete major empirical research projects.

Most important is a sense of contribution. The data collected become a part of the body of knowledge. Successful field research can lead to professional advancement. Recently, for example, three colleagues of mine at the University of Texas, law professors Liz Warren and Jay Westbrook and sociologist Teresa Sullivan, completed a major study on bankruptcy. Liz moved to the University of Pennsylvania, where she became head of the appointments committee for the law school. During the 1991–1992 academic year, Jay visited at Harvard, and Terry is now chair of the sociology department at the University of Texas. Their work was the focus of a symposium on bankruptcy and they are all in demand as speakers and presenters of papers. Despite the possible rewards, major empirical studies are rare in the social sciences. The body of accumulated data grows slowly while the amount of theoretical writing derived from secondary sources grows at an exponentially increasing rate. In law it is possible to count on the fingers of one hand the major empirical research of the last decade. Similarly, major research is surprisingly rare in political science, international affairs, philosophy, economics, women's studies, and African studies. In all of these areas, much current controversy and thinking exist that could be resolved or clarified through carefully designed field research. Yet little is actually done. One of the most important questions about the current nature of academic institutions is what in their organization, administration, and culture discourages the development of the sort of research that might actually help us to resolve societal problems. This is not to ignore the fact that a considerable amount of data is developed in certain fields, such as psychology, sociology, and anthropology, but the data developed tend to be discrete, often isolated from social issues, and the research limited in terms of design and possible value. Even in these fields, the current emphasis is increasingly on theory, elegance, and analytic rigor.

Because major field research is costly, it entails the time-consuming processes of obtaining outside money. Also, because it inevitably depends upon the cooperation of others, even well-designed studies can go wrong. For a young, nontenured person, all of these characteristics make field research risky. Unfortunately, academics, particularly young academics, are notoriously risk-averse. The reasons why field research is rare can be illustrated if one considers the matter from the perspective of an untenured faculty member. Imagine a political scientist interested in whether the wealthy have too much political power. He or she could attempt to collect data about the ways in which the wealthy influence the processes of government. Such data might include how much the wealthy contribute to politicians, what form the contributions take, the ways in which they make their desires known at different political levels, how likely politicians are to do their bidding, or what happens to politicians who dare to oppose positions generally held by the wealthy. The political power of the wealthy could be compared to that of groups, such as unions and civil rights organizations, that generally oppose them. Collecting data on any of these issues would be very difficult. To do such a study in the quickest possible way, a researcher would need to obtain cooperation from the wealthy and from politicians. Complete cooperation in admitting their activities would be unlikely, however, and answers to direct questions suspect. Developing alternative techniques would be difficult. Even deciding which people count as wealthy for these purposes could be confusing, controversial, and perhaps arbitrary. To engage in direct data-gathering without informing the subjects would create design problems and perhaps legal complications. It would be impossible to study all of the wealthy on all issues. Inevitably the researcher would have to select a small part of the project for intense scrutiny. If the research is to be done well, considerable time would have to be taken in sharpening the design and technique of data-gathering and analysis by doing a test study. For a significant study, a team including coprincipals and assistants would have to be put together. All of these activities take time and the possibility of mistakes and confusion exists. None of the crucial work adds to the participant's scholarly visibility. If the study were well done and counterintuitive information developed, the methodology, assumptions, and analysis would be bound to be heavily criticized and the conclusions rejected by many. If serious mistakes were made or the results were confusing or obvious, the end product would do little to advance the person's career; the researcher's publication record would appear thin when the person was considered for tenure. Even if the study were good, few would see in it the brilliance that is so important to academic reputation.

With less work over the same period, this same person could have written a series of scholarly papers analyzing the same issue from a group-interest, Marxist, economic, or public-choice approach. He or she could have developed a new vocabulary, suggested a new paradigm, developed a new theory, or deconstructed some of the underlying assumptions in the field. Any of these approaches could have made him or her a "recognized expert" and tenure would be assured.

If one does field research in an area of scholarship where little such work has been done, the intended audience, including other faculty in the field, is likely to have difficulty in evaluating it and may accept or reject it without knowing why. This was true for our study of NLRB elections. The study did not significantly affect the behavior or thinking of people in the field. The academic response has ranged from strong praise to unthinking criticism based on political considerations or academic fashion.[24]

I once had a discussion with a major labor law scholar who has been accorded almost every honor and form of recognition bestowed upon someone in my field. Our discussion occurred during a cocktail party when he came up to me and, after exchanging a few amenities, said, "You made a good try, but your study is a failure. Your conclusions don't hold up. If you understood the situation, especially in the deep South, you would know that the South is really different."

"What data do you have about the voting behavior of Southern employees?" I was annoyed and worried that he had access to a source of information unknown to me.

"You have to realize that I am permanent arbitrator at the Torrington Mills plant in Mississippi. I had a long tour of the factory once, and I had a chance to ask lots of questions."

"Weren't you accompanied by the union steward and members of plant management?"

"Yes."

"Has anything remotely related to organizing ever come up in one of the grievances you have heard?"

"Well, not directly."

"How can you, on the basis of such an experience, say that our conclusions are wrong?"

"It's mainly based on a feeling I have when I am there that the employees are more docile and easily frightened than employees are in the North."

It is difficult to convey the anguish that such assurance from an arrogant academic with no relevant information caused. Both Steve Goldberg and I have had similar conversations with other, generally less distinguished, labor law professors who are unwilling to confront the indications of our study because to do so would involve considering conclusions inconsistent with what they think they know.

Very few scholars can easily trace the impact of their work. Those whose research is descriptive generally seek no specific impact other than use by other scholars. Those whose work supports an existing approach do not know whether they play a role in its continuity. Those whose work is critical of existing institutions are bound to meet resistance. Impact tends to be cumulative where it exists at all. Change may result from the gradual development of a scholarly consensus that previous ways of analyzing or ordering things were misguided. In such cases, it is rare that any one piece makes a critical difference, although an entire body of research of a particular type may be significant in leading to change. Whether an issue will produce a body of work of this type is difficult to predict. It turns upon such things as the availability of funds, the attraction of follow-up work to other professors, and the amount of time that will be needed to do further work.

I consider it a weakness that I have been so concerned with the practical impact of my work. Some of the best scholars I know, mainly anthropologists and filmmakers, are able to enjoy the process and content themselves with writing and filmmaking that tell people about the lives of those they would not otherwise know, demonstrating through their work the common threads that bind different parts of humanity together. Such creative research is wonderful and rare.

The impact on my own thinking of doing field research about law was powerful and irrevocable. Once I began investigating reality, the traditional articles I had earlier worked so hard on seemed to me empty and pretentious, filled with naïve assumptions about aspects of labor relation that I had neither studied nor understood. I realized that my reliance upon untested assumptions was typical of legal scholarship. This was as true of writings in the *Harvard Law Review* as of those in less prestigious journals. The difference between the two was in thoroughness, elegance, logic, and vision, but not in their familiarity with reality. The more contact I had with leading scholars, the less impressive they seemed. I was embarrassed by my early efforts to emulate their work and resentful of my continuing desire for their recognition and approval.

Conducting the union-election study forced me to recall things I had known about working people before I became a lawyer. During many of the interviews, I felt as if I were touching base with my roots. I sat in apartments similar to the one in which I grew up and talked to men with the familiar broad shoulders and round bellies of middle-aged workers, men who wore undershirts like the ones my father used to wear around our house. What they had to say was frequently shrewd and sophisticated, a far cry from the image of the easily cowed and misled employee that informed legal rules. The more I noted their resemblance to my father, the less rational the rules appeared. Before I went to law school, I knew that workers are complex, interesting, and often thoughtful, but when I became acculturated to academic thinking, something in my increased sophistication caused me to forget that knowledge. When I relearned it, I simultaneously became suspicious of the process by which lawyers and academics define reality.

Those who write scholarly articles without leaving the academic environment often act removed from and superior to ordinary people, those who they assume can comprehend neither the complexity of the issues nor the logical symmetry of their solutions. Conversely, those whose work involves observing or sharing part of people's lives often feel empathetic with them and separated from the scholarly community.

When Jerry Mintz, a professor of anthropology at Indiana University, returned in the 1970s from Spain, where for two years he had lived in an Andalusian village, going out to the fields with cork workers and sharing wine and cards with poor Spanish peasants, he for a long time dressed himself in the peaked cap and plain denim jacket common among Andalusian peasants. He dressed this way during the year he worked on films about Spanish expatriots and wrote a fine book, *The Anarchists of Casas Viejas.*[25] At the time I thought his style affected, even silly, but I realize now and respect his desire to express that the kinship he felt with those whose lives he studied and who became his friends was stronger than the ties that bound him to his academic colleagues. The best social science research often has the capacity to remind academics of the dignity and intelligence of those whose lives we study.

Research and the Fine Line between Success and Failure

As already noted, one way in which high-level research differs from other endeavors is that the possibility of failure is not only present but its regular occurrence is almost certain. A good carpenter can succeed in building something worthwhile on each try. A good lawyer can accomplish something for the clients in the great majority of cases. Cab drivers regularly reach the appointed destination. Chefs, stockbrokers, and police all take chances, but able practitioners in each of these fields are far more likely to succeed than to fail. In basic scholarship, however, one or two significant successes in a lifetime are the most that one can hope for.

Steven Weinberg, the 1979 Nobel laureate in theoretical physics, whose name is attached to the most commonly accepted model of the universe, told me that the periods of pain in his research far outweigh the moments of pleasure because, as he said, "most of the time I'm not getting anywhere. I don't even know what to think about." He also told me that the greatest pleasures of research for him are suddenly realizing what he should be working on and recognizing the solution to something he thought was impenetrable.

In *The Hunting of the Quark*, Michael Riordan describes a meeting in 1970 where the solution to a major problem of theoretical physics was discussed by a group of leading physicists, including future Nobel laureates Sheldon Glashow and Steven Weinberg. The answer to the problem they discussed was contained in a 1967 paper written by Weinberg, but none of them recognized it:

> An impromptu seminar soon gathered in [Francis] Low's office, with Weinberg listening intently and asking some probing questions. "We argued a lot," [John] Iliopoulos remembers, "and spent all morning discussing these things"—gauge theories, symmetry breaking, the whole lot—but nobody made a peep about Weinberg's 1967 paper, "not even Steve himself." Glashow himself was "totally unaware" of that particular paper at the time. Here was a marvelous explanation for the apparent lack of neutral currents in kaon decays, the very same currents *required* by Weinberg's theory, and nobody in the room made the connection.
>
> Years later, Iliopoulos quizzed Weinberg about the oversight. "Steve, why didn't you put us on the right track?" To which Weinberg confessed that he'd had a "psychological barrier" against his 1967 paper. He had encountered enormous frustration in trying to purge the theory's infinities, and somehow just did not want to think about it in 1970.[26]

Although most academics would love to have the problem of living up to great scholarly success, early success can sometimes cause severe problems, as it did to the 1988 Nobel laureate in physics, Melvin Schwartz.

Schwartz's early career as a student and young scientist was filled with achievement. He attended PS 75 in the Bronx in the early 1940s. He then entered Bronx High School of Science, a school with the goal of identifying intellectually gifted public school students and preparing them for college. Once again he was a superb student.

Like the students at Bronx Science, the faculty were specially selected. Among them were several practicing mathematicians and scientists. Theodore Benjamin, who taught Mel physics, had worked on the Manhattan

Project, which developed the atomic bomb. His classes had a sense of immediacy, practicality, openness, and conceptual vitality that Mel found inspiring. He determined while in high school that particle physics was the area in which he desired to work. It was challenging, connected to reality, had profound consequences, and placed a high premium on understanding how things work—something that Mel seemed to intuitively grasp.

Mel began to study physics intensely. While his earlier academic performance had been directed toward success and high grades, when he studied physics he became motivated by a desire to understand. He joined the physics club, which during his time at Bronx Science included future Nobel laureates Sheldon Glashow and Steven Weinberg. Even among this gifted group Mel seemed to have a rare ability to recognize issues on the frontiers of science. One of his classmates, a prize-winning scientist himself, later described Mel as a "hero of my youth."

When Mel graduated from high school he received a New York State scholarship and entered Columbia because the university gave him the chance to stay in New York and because of the eminence of its physics department. Among Mel's first teachers at Columbia was Jack Steinberger, whose classes sometimes consisted of students helping him to resolve his research problems. This was a method ideally suited for Mel, who appreciated the respect that Steinberger showed for his ideas. They became friends and then collaborators.

Despite an opportunity to do graduate work at Chicago with the great Enrico Fermi, Mel decided to remain at Columbia to continue his graduate studies with Steinberger. In 1956 he was granted a postdoctoral fellowship at the Brookhaven National Laboratory, even though he did not formally meet the requirement for a Ph.D. While at Brookhaven, Mel worked with bubble chambers to study strange particles. As soon as he received his Ph.D. degree in 1958, he was appointed assistant professor of physics at Columbia.

Columbia at that time, the mid-1950s, had one of the greatest physics departments ever assembled. It included Nobel laureates Polykarp Kusch, T. D. Lee, I. I. Rabi, and Willis Lamb. Mel loved the department and the work that he was involved with. As he later said, "Every day we learned something new and wonderful. There was no chance of our not succeeding."

During faculty discussion, the ideas, not the rank of the presenter, were what counted. Nobel laureates listened when assistant professors spoke. At the center of the exchange of ideas was T. D. Lee, young, intense, and unwilling to accept truths that seemed obvious to almost everyone else. One day at coffee, Lee was talking about the so-called weak interaction that destabilizes the nucleus of atoms. He hoped that experimental data about its functioning would shed light on the similarities and differences among the four basic forces known to physicists.[27] He urged the experimentalists to find a way to use high-energy particles (previously used mainly to study the strong force that binds nuclei) to learn about the weak interaction.

As Lee spoke, Mel became increasingly excited. Lee's suggestion sparked his imagination and his fascination with designing intricate experiments. He spent the rest of the day mulling over ways to achieve what Lee had urged, but without success. His wife, Marilyn, recalls that he came home very disturbed, hardly ate at all, and went immediately to the small bedroom where he had his study. He spent most of the night there thinking about a way to study weak interactions through experiments measuring neutrinos.

Neutrinos, produced when nuclei destabilize, are a product of the weak force and are the least interactive of all subatomic particles. They have no mass and they can pass through almost all objects in the universe without leaving a trace. Mel realized, however, that if they could be isolated through use of a pion beam, their activity might be recorded in a spark chamber and basic information about the weak interaction might be obtained.

The more Mel thought about it, the more elated he became. Unable to control his enthusiasm, he called T. D. Lee that evening before going to sleep and described his plan. Lee was as excited as Mel. He immediately recognized the potential value of the experiment. The next day Lee told people in the faculty lounge that Mel had just come up with a wonderful idea for studying the weak force using neutrinos.

Mel later presented his idea to Leon Lederman and then to his former teacher Jack Steinberger, both of whom joined him in developing the experiment, which was complex, expensive, and time-consuming. It involved use of the newly developed sychrotron at Brookhaven and five thousand tons of cruiser deckplate. The formidable machinery designed for the experiment was known among physicists as the "S.S. Schwartz." When the experiment was concluded two years after it had begun, the scientists had demonstrated the existence of the muon neutrino and its fundamental difference from the electron neutrino. As a result of the experiment, physicists determined for the first time that "leptons are governed by two separate conservation laws: a specific conservation law for the election family and a second conservation law for the 'muon family' behavior."[28] This discovery had profound implications with respect to the fundamental nature of matter.

The contribution that Mel Schwartz, together with Lederman and Steinberger, made to science was quickly recognized by his colleagues at Columbia, by physicists generally, and even by the national media. He was promoted to full professor and had his picture prominently featured in *Life* magazine.[29] He was increasingly treated as a celebrity by his students, more and more of whom sought to do graduate work with him. He heard that he had been nominated for the Nobel Prize. He was sought after by universities great and ambitious. In the mid-1960s, Mel accepted an offer from Stanford for a joint appointment at the physics department and the Stanford Linear Accelerator Center (SLAC). He accepted the offer, not because of any unhappiness with Columbia but because moving to Stanford and California seemed at the time the next step forward in his career.

Stanford was putting together an outstanding physics program. It had built a new linear accelerator that made it possible to do high-energy experiments that could not be done elsewhere. Mel approached the move to Stanford with the enthusiasm that had marked each of his previous academic ventures. No one who knew Mel and no one who was familiar with his work would possibly have predicted that a little more than a decade later he would resign his position at Stanford and give up physics.

His problems at Stanford were anticipated shortly after the neutrino experiment in an unusual conversation he had with Nobel laureate Polykarp Kusch, then a senior member of the Columbia physics department, who told him: "Mel, you've just done a great piece of work, the sort most physicists try for all their lives and never achieve. You should think about changing to another field. The odds are really against your ever doing anything this good again and you are bound to wind up feeling frustrated."

Mel was surprised. The idea of becoming dissatisfied with physics and his place in it seemed far removed from his current feelings of pleasure and success. "I love physics. Besides, what else could I do?"

Kusch suggested that he go to law school. Mel found the idea surprisingly attractive, but he decided that it would be a mistake to give up a career that had been so productive and pleasurable.

Many years later he recalled, "I understood what Kusch was saying intellectually but not emotionally. Now I realize he was trying to spare me from going through what he went through."

What Kusch was able to foresee was that Mel would search in vain for another experience like the neutrino experiment. Mel did good work while at Stanford. He was able to develop a technique for creating, for very brief intervals of time, atoms which had never previously existed. The work was interesting and the techniques ingenious. Rather than feeling pleased, Mel felt frustrated because he knew that it would not have nearly the importance or resonance of his early work.

Important contributions in most academic fields, experimental physics in particular, inevitably involve a large element of good fortune, and the neutrino experiment was no exception. Mel stated years afterward that "the amount of serendipity was just tremendous. I was just looking around for something to work on. I had been doing bubble experiments which involve similar technology. I was lucky to be in the faculty lounge when Lee suggested using high-energy particles to study the weak force. If I had tried to do a similar experiment just a year earlier the technology would not have been available. I wouldn't have the technology for spark chambers of the pion beam. I was lucky that Steinberger and Lederman were available and willing to work with me."

He was not happy at Stanford. He missed the spirited discussions and sense of common enterprise which had marked the Columbia physics department. At Stanford he found the quality of his interaction with many of his colleagues painful. He later described it as a place where "people stayed to themselves and concentrated on protecting their own turf instead of trying to help each other."

He was particularly unhappy with the administrative leadership of SLAC. Wolfgang Panofsky, who headed the program, was described by one physicist as a "very smart man and a very bad scientist." He had control over funds and use of the linear accelerator. Mel found the need to obtain Panofsky's approval both harmful and demeaning. The most unfortunate experience occurred when Mel was not given funds and accelerator time he needed to study the residue remaining in the rear of the accelerator after the occurrence of particle collisions. Panofsky objected that Mel did not adequately articulate what he hoped to find in this way. Mel felt that his intuition that something interesting would be found should have been respected. Had it been, he might have been able to demonstrate the existence of the weak "neutral currents" that were, according to Michael Riordan, a crucial aspect of all unified gauge theories.[30] The idea was never

Research and Scholarship

carried out properly because it needed Panofsky's approval. The incident is described by Michael Riordan in *The Hunting of the Quark:*

> In 1970, Schwartz had shipped his spark chambers to SLAC and installed them in a hole carved into the hillside behind End Station A. It was an imaginative, speculative experiment . . . "that ran a couple of weeks," Schwartz recalled, "and lo and behold, we see these two events that don't have any muons on them. Good energetic, solid events, with *no* muons. And of course lots of events with muons on them—just the neutrino background. And the two events with no muons, God knew what to do with them."
>
> Schwartz went back to the SLAC program committee and implored them for another month on the machine, this time as prime user in a full-fledged experiment. He wanted to dig a deep hole right smack behind the beam dump, where the event rate had to be much higher, and put in a lot of iron shielding to filter out backgrounds. Schwartz figured he needed about a hundred such muonless events to determine what in fact they might be.
>
> But Panofsky granted him just a few more days in the existing hole . . . and the experiment ended abruptly when a vacuum pipe burned out suddenly with an earsplitting bang.
>
> All told, Schwartz had four or five "oddball events," which he showed the next year at Amsterdam, the same meeting where 't Hooft and Veltmann excited field theorists with their news of renormalization. But nobody there drew any connection. "I was puzzled by those events, everybody was puzzled by those events," Schwartz recalled. "In retrospect, they were probably neutral currents."[31]

Mel became even more unhappy when physicists at Brookhaven and the European Center for Nuclear Research began to conduct very useful beam dump experiments using the very approach Mel had suggested.

Mel eventually realized that he was not looking forward to his daily trips to the Stanford campus. He did not enjoy academic small talk or gossip, was not good at or interested in administrative committees, and thought faculty meetings petty and boring. Instead, he found himself looking forward to the small consulting jobs he did occasionally for some of the private scientific research groups in the area. When he was with business people he felt somehow freed from the pressure of the university. In addition, he enjoyed the feeling of inevitable success that seemed at that time, in the mid-1970s, to attach to the computer companies in the San Francisco Bay Area. Scientific entrepreneurs flourished, particularly those connected with the development of computer technology.

The effort to do something imaginative with computer technology seemed a challenge worthy of his ability. He began to think seriously about resigning his professorship. He went through a period of great internal conflict. A part of him thought that doing anything other than high-level physics was shameful and meaningless: a form of surrender to the very forces in academic life that he despised. Another part of him felt that computer technology afforded a great opportunity to succeed once again in an atmosphere of creativity and openness. He finally decided to leave Stanford.

In the early 1970s, Mel had, for tax purposes, created a small company called Digital Pathways. He left Stanford with the idea of making the company a functioning business reality. He set about seeking investors, borrowing money, hiring staff, and determining the direction of the company. He devoted himself for ten years almost entirely to the company. The challenge proved as great as he could have expected, and the company's fortunes have by turns prospered and ebbed. It is now a multi-million-dollar enterprise.

He often enjoyed the sense of adventure involved in business but he also missed physics. He would sometimes wake up early in the morning thinking, "This is all make-believe and crazy. I should be doing physics."

The award of the Nobel Prize in 1988 encouraged him to return to science. He is now associate director of high energy and nuclear physics at Brookhaven. His enthusiasm for research has been rekindled, and although he now rails against government's indifference to science, he hopes to do work of comparable originality to his earlier experiments. He notes wryly, "The best thing about changing jobs is that I am a better physicist than a businessman."

Mel Schwartz's story and those of every successful scholar I know make clear that while the process of discovery is exciting and gratifying, anyone who devotes a life to the narrow confines of scholarship will inevitably have to confront frustration, anger, confusion, and one or another form of self-doubt.

THREE

The Relationship of Faculty to Academic Institutions

In 1914, a group of distinguished professors at major universities, disturbed by the growing number of incidents in which professors had been fired or punished by administrators for expressing controversial views, issued a call for a convocation of faculty. Out of this convocation arose the American Association of University Professors, the stated purpose of which was to "maintain and advance the standards and ideas of the profession."[1] Over the next few years the new organization issued a series of statements about the governance of academic institutions. The statements set forth in elegant academic prose the organization's basic vision—that colleges and universities should be free of outside constraint and governed primarily by the faculty. These ideas had great appeal to faculty at a variety of different institutions and the organization quickly grew in membership and importance.

The AAUP's auspicious beginning was in large part attributable to its leaders. They were almost all intellectually distinguished men of serious expression, conservative dress, and bold ideas—people like John Dewey of Columbia, Arthur O. Lovejoy of Johns Hopkins University, and Roscoe Pound of Harvard—fearless innovators, prominent in their disciplines, and highly respected in the small circle of elite institutions from which they came. I visualize them sitting around elegant oak tables, speaking in measured tones, listening carefully to each other, and slowly working out and making more forceful their statements concerning basic aspects of academic life. The special role of faculty envisioned by the AAUP's founders and enunciated in its later documents has significantly transformed American higher education. Its impact is summed up in three basic concepts: academic freedom, faculty governance, and peer review.

Academic Freedom

The Role of the AAUP

When the AAUP was formed, its first president, John Dewey of Columbia, appointed a committee to consider issues relating to academic freedom and tenure. This led to a committee report mainly composed by Arthur O. Lovejoy, professor of philosophy at Johns Hopkins. The report eloquently stated the case for academic freedom—the right of professors to teach, write, and investigate their concepts of the truth without fear of professional reprisal:

> Great issues in the adjustment of men's social and economic relations are certain to call for settlement in the years that are to come and for the right settlement of them mankind will need all the wisdom, all the goodwill, all the soberness of mind, and all the knowledge drawn from experience that it can command. Toward this settlement the university has potentially its own very great contribution to make. For if the adjustment reached is to be a wise one, it must take due account of economic science and be guided by that breadth of historic vision which should be one of the functions of the university to cultivate. But, if the universities are to render any such service toward the right solution of social problems in the future, it is essential that the scholars who carry on the work of universities shall not be in a position of dependence upon the favor of any social class or group, that the disinterestedness and impartiality of their inquiries and their conclusions shall be so far as is humanly possibly beyond the reach of suspicions.[2]

In its practical recommendations, the committee put great stress on faculty participation in decisions relating to appointments, tenure, and discipline. It concluded with one of the best-articulated claims ever made for special status for faculty in the running of colleges and universities:

> To the degree that professional scholars, in the formation and promulgation of their opinions, are, or by the character of their tenure appear to be, subject to any motive other than their own scientific conscience and a desire for the respect of their fellow-experts, to that degree the university teaching profession is corrupted; its proper influence upon public opinion is diminished and vitiated; and society at large fails to get from its scholars, in an unadulterated form, the peculiar and necessary service which it is the office of the professional scholar to furnish . . . A university is a great and indispensable organ of the higher life of a civi-

Academic Freedom

lized community, in the work of which the trustees hold an essential and highly honorable place, but in which the faculties hold an independent place, with quite equal responsibilities—and in relation to purely scientific and educational questions, the primary responsibility.[3]

Having defined, endorsed, and explained the need for academic freedom, the AAUP undertook the mammoth task of defending it. The technique it developed involved it in the role of investigator, prosecutor, and judge. It worked as follows: "The president of the organization appointed a committee (Committee A) that received complaints of violations of academic freedom and created subcommittees to investigate the facts of alleged violations. Thereafter, the whole committee and the organization itself would decide, based on the investigating report, whether a violation of 'generally understood standards of academic freedom' had taken place. If the organization concluded that an 'academic freedom violation had taken place,' it passed a resolution censuring the offending university administration. The reports concerning the alleged violation were always written in a careful, judicious manner. The debates about censure were never pro forma. The published findings created a common law of academic freedom."[4]

It is remarkable how well the system worked. Neither Committee A nor the organization itself had any formal jurisdiction and the censure list was without any legal significance. Yet, from the first, both administrators and faculty members paid great attention to its finding. When an institution was censured, administrators found it troublesome in a variety of ways. Faculty members at other schools were less likely to be interested in joining or even dealing with censured institutions. This meant fewer prestigious appointments and fewer academic meetings. Faculty members and the local AAUP chapter at the censured school would generally continue to protest the action that gave rise to censure and the administration's failure to take adequate steps to prevent such incidents from arising again. Censured administrations almost always eventually sought to have the vote of censure removed.

It is not clear why this informal system worked as well as it did. Part of the answer had to do with the outstanding academic reputations of the AAUP's early leadership and the members of Committee A. These were difficult people to ignore, and they gave to the enterprise the full weight of their prestige and intellect. Eventually, many college administrators came to seek AAUP advice in structuring their internal processes dealing with promotion, reappointment, and tenure. Even John Silber, the controversial, academically conservative president of Boston University who fought the AAUP on his own campus, has recognized the importance and "high-mindedness of the early AAUP and the righteousness of its approach to academic freedom."[5]

In 1940, the AAUP, together with the American Association of Colleges, promulgated a statement on academic freedom and tenure that has been adopted by almost all disciplinary societies and most major large universities and colleges, either formally or through language in administratively issued faculty handbooks.[6] In accordance with the 1940 statement, most academic institutions have standing committees of faculty to internally adjudicate complaints of violations of academic freedom. When cases arise, the committees regularly look to the 1940 statement and AAUP's formal interpretation of it. Academic freedom covers both controversial statements on public issues and statements critical of university officials. The AAUP agreed in the 1940 statement that the faculty member has a corresponding responsibility to behave with appropriate restraint. The boundaries of academic freedom and the meaning of "appropriate restraint" are regularly addressed by the AAUP and by the courts.

Because it promotes professorial independence and serves to insulate professors from control by students, administrators, and the outside community, academic freedom is often thought to be an offensively elitist concept. The public is sometimes outraged to discover that a professor whose salary it is paying is entitled to both promote ideas that the public rejects and also reject ideas that the public embraces. The offending views may question the rightness of U.S. policy, the wisdom of organized religion, the legitimacy of Zionism, or the concept of racial equality. When that type of sentiment is expressed, politicians, pressure groups, and alumni will often demand that university administrators punish the offending faculty members.

Within the field of higher education, however, academic freedom is an egalitarian concept. It promotes the vision that professors at different institutions are engaged in a common effort to discover the truth and are protected by a common standard. It has been one of the few issues on which professors at elite institutions make common cause with professors elsewhere. It also limits hierarchy within education by protecting younger and less elite faculty from control and supervision by their seniors. Academic freedom is thus egalitarian within the profession and elitist outside of it.

The AAUP harnessed academic elitism on behalf of egalitarian values. This was not done unwittingly. The AAUP's founders and early leaders

Academic Freedom

combined the best of academic elitism (seriousness of purpose, intellectual achievement, and commitment to excellence) with more populist attitudes, many of them derived from the ideology of organized labor. They were progressive, committed both to individual excellence and to making common cause with other educators. Rarely in academic life do elitist and egalitarian attitudes reinforce one another as they did in the furtherance of academic freedom. When this happens, the results are likely to be powerful and enduring.

Over the years, faculty throughout the country came to accept the AAUP as their voice when academic freedom was threatened. Walter Metzger, a noted historian who specializes in the study of academic freedom, summarized its growth:

> Professor Arthur O. Lovejoy, the chief protagonist of self-protection, made use of his secretarial office to involve the Association in [academic freedom] cases, he himself being the chief and sometimes sole investigator; . . . his reports were models of their kind, the monumental products of a truly magisterial intelligence; . . . the publication of these reports immediately publicized the Association as the avenger of academic crimes, and led to further calls for intervention; . . . in time, the Association had to lower its admission standards to enhance its income, . . . [when] it evolved from an elite to a mass society, the Association began to deal with complaints in a routine, rather than ad hoc, fashion.[7]

The organization, in its early years, lived up to the vision of its founders. It was particularly active during World War I and its aftermath. It also played a large role during the turmoil of the 1930s and during World War II. Unfortunately, the AAUP, like many organizations, responded very poorly during the early McCarthy period. Ralph Himstead, its general secretary and chief executive officer, for either ideological or personal reasons held back investigations of academic-freedom violations committed in the name of anticommunism. This made the organization ineffective at a time when it was sorely needed and almost led to its disintegration. However, after much turmoil in 1956, Himstead was replaced. Ralph Fuchs, a person dedicated to academic freedom and prepared to battle for it, was appointed general secretary in his place. Thereafter, the organization became far more active and effective. It regained its former status as the chief defender of academic freedom. It was Fuchs, later my colleague at Indiana University Law School, who, in his tireless, gracious way, played the leading role in the transformation.[8]

The Contribution of Academic Freedom to University Life

The great battles of academic freedom have involved a small number of unorthodox professors espousing controversial ideas, but the victories in the struggle have benefited all professors, enhanced our dignity, and made our professional lives secure. Most young academics today take the existence of academic freedom for granted. They know little or nothing of the early struggle for it and little or nothing of the mechanisms by which academic freedom has been advanced. However, because academic life is concerned primarily with the expression of ideas, the feeling that one is able to express ideas freely is crucial to a feeling of professional and personal security. At times when and in places where this feeling is absent, academic life becomes threatening rather than rewarding.

When I entered academic life in the aftermath of McCarthyism, academic freedom was less secure, the cold war was at its peak, and suspicion of liberal academics was widespread. Fear of being forced to espouse ideas I did not believe caused me to delay accepting an offer from Indiana University. What little I knew about the state and the university in this regard was worrisome: Indiana was represented in the Senate by William Jenner, an ally of Senator McCarthy, who had publicly questioned the patriotism of General George C. Marshall, and by Homer Capehart, a political reactionary with simplistic views. When I was told that part of the process of appointment involved meeting with a subcommittee of the board of trustees, I was warned against saying anything the least bit controversial to them. All of these things combined to make me nervous about beginning a teaching career in such a place. A short time after I accepted the Indiana offer, my nervousness turned to fear when I read a short article in the *New York Times* stating that three Indiana University students had been indicted for conspiring to overthrow the state government. The evidence against them seemed to consist of speeches on campus on behalf of the Young Socialist Alliance. According to the article, university officials refused to comment on the case, a nonresponse into which I read all kinds of sinister meaning.

The reality of Indiana University was far different from my apprehension. The YSA case, as it was known, galvanized the local AAUP chapter to collect funds, make public statements, hire lawyers, and use its influence with the local bar to help get the indictment quashed, as indeed it was by a local conservative judge. The faculty who took part in the AAUP's effort were of every political persuasion.

Because of the AAUP's role in the YSA case, I was pleased to join it when Ralph Fuchs first solicited me. The AAUP chapter at Indiana University was vocal. It issued a strong statement when Allen Ginsberg's erotic poetry reading came under attack, when a new policy limiting the ability of student groups to invite speakers was proposed, when a self-proclaimed Marxist faculty member was criticized by the state's attorney general, and when a new dean was appointed without significant faculty involvement. When the local AAUP chapter issued its statements, the central administration paid close attention. Meetings to resolve issues were common between administrators and AAUP's officials. Indeed, common gossip on campus had it that the quickest way to be appointed as a dean was through leadership in the local chapter of the AAUP.

Meetings of the local chapter on campus issues were well attended, long-winded, and tumultuous. They were punctuated by applause, expressions of general outrage, and questions shouted from the floor. I enjoyed the give-and-take and the seriousness with which people spoke about the issues. I began to speak out, tentatively at first and then more and more easily. Instead of feeling isolated and out of place as I had feared, I began to enjoy Indiana University.

Being active in the AAUP gave me a greater sense of community with colleagues in different disciplines, a more sophisticated understanding of the importance of the academic enterprise, a new knowledge of its historical heroes and standards, and a greater commitment to the cause of academic freedom. I was one of many unwitting beneficiaries of the great work of the AAUP and its early leaders.

Dealing with Violations of Academic Freedom

Minor violations of academic freedom occur regularly. Faculty members are punished in small ways for statements criticizing administration. Teachers are denied leaves and promotions for taking positions contrary to accepted academic thinking; candidates for appointment are rejected in part because they have views different from those in their fields. Although administrative machinery in the form of faculty review boards exists at most universities, small violations are rarely challenged, and for good reason. Generally, establishing improper motive for academic decisions is difficult and the process of review is long, expensive, and emotionally wearing. Because, however, the concept of academic freedom is generally understood and supported by most faculty and most academic administrators, it serves to limit, if not eliminate, their willingness to violate its precepts. Thus it serves as an inhibitor rather than as a bar to improper conduct.

The Relationship of Faculty to Academic Institutions

Periods of academic tension parallel periods of national upheaval. In the 1960s and 1970s, a great deal of abusive, unpopular speech took place on college campuses. Most of it was protected by the allegiance of institutions to academic freedom. The AAUP deserves much of the credit. The extent of its achievement is illustrated by comparing two cases that I handled during the period.

The first case in 1968 involved Terrence Doran, who taught English literature at Granville Wells High School in West Boone County, Indiana.[9] Terry, who had a gift for teaching, could make literary characters and situations connect with the lives of the students, and he encouraged students to articulate their feelings in classroom discussion. His colleagues did not know what to make of Terry. To them, a student like Mike Bradford, who read political books, wore his hair as long as he could, and showed contempt for the pronouncements of school authorities, was a menace to be fought and contained. To Terry, he was a kindred soul. Mike, who sat through most classes with a sneer of contempt, was active and cooperative in Terry's class, and the two struck up a friendship that served to infuriate most of the other teachers.

In his literature course, Terry assigned books and plays that were meaningful to him. Some, like *A Catcher in the Rye* and *A Separate Peace*, dealt with alienation; others, like *MacBeth* and *Lord of the Flies*, dealt with violence, self-destructiveness, and the difficulty involved in maintaining moral standards in a changing, threatening world. He related the literature to current political and social issues. He was one of the speakers in a Parent Teacher Association program on "The Vietnam War: Dress Codes and the Draft." During the discussion, Terry stated his opposition to the Vietnam war and the draft—a dangerous admission in the politically charged atmosphere of the 1960s. Rumors about Terry's political beliefs and social philosophy began to circulate.

According to local gossip, Terry was the leader of a hippie gang that was planning a raid on the community. Rumors abounded that he was a homosexual, had seduced almost all of the female students in his class, had smoked dope, had burned his draft card, and was a card-carrying Communist. Letters protesting his influence and requesting his dismissal were received by the principal and the school board.

One Tuesday evening in December of 1968, Terry, who was the senior class advisor, went to the school with a group of students to trim the Christmas tree. The tree, according to consensus, was too small, and some students were sent to get another one. While they waited for the new tree, Doran had a television set brought into the faculty lounge. He and a few students watched an educational program in the lounge. Some of the students smoked cigarettes. Afterward, they watched part of an Elvis Presley special during breaks. The entire process took about four hours.

The next day Terry was called into the principal's office, where he was accused of being immoral and irresponsible because he permitted students to smoke in the faculty lounge. He tried to defend himself but was summarily ordered out of the office. Shortly thereafter, he was summoned by the school superintendent, who also told Terry that he had violated school policy. Terry was also accused of permitting a female student to sit upon a desk in an unladylike posture. The superintendent claimed he had no choice but to suspend Terry immediately and to recommend his dismissal to the board at its next meeting on the grounds of insubordination. A sit-in followed, which led to the suspension of most of the senior class.[10]

A friend of Terry's was a student of mine and asked me if I would represent him in a hearing before the school board. Meeting with Terry and a group of his students shortly thereafter, I was appalled by his description of the incidents that were the basis of the formal charge against him. I could not believe that anyone would seriously dispute a teacher's right to invite pupils into the faculty lounge in the course of an evening extracurricular activity that was a service to the school.

I questioned Terry closely about his relations with the students, whether he had done anything improper, illegal, or immoral. He gave convincing answers to all of my questions. I decided that Terry was being punished because he was a stimulating teacher who excited his students about ideas and literature and raised challenging issues. His real offense was getting his students to question established truths and recognized authority. This meek, unprepossessing young man timidly asking me to represent him was the spiritual descendant of Socrates and a stirring reaffirmation of the importance of academic freedom.

The hearing was scheduled for the school board's offices, but so many people showed up that we were forced to move to the Thornton Cafeteria. It was clear from the start that the board meant to uphold the discharge. The school board's attorney, who presented the case against Terry, was treated with total deference by the school board president, who presided. The president did not rule in Terry's favor in a single dispute over evidence.

In putting on the case for Terry, I put a great deal of effort into establishing what a good teacher he was, despite perfectly clear indications from the hearing panel that they were not interested in the subject. Indeed, emphasizing his teaching now seems to have been a significant tactical mistake, since Terry's effective teaching was at the root of the discharge. In some hidden, irrational corner of my mind, I hoped for a miraculous change of mood once I was able to show the board how successful Terry had been in conveying the wonders of literature to the students at Granville Wells. I hoped to show that this was not something to fear. How could anyone fail to be moved by the touching regard and affection shown by these burly athletes and wholesome cheerleaders who clamored for the opportunity to take the stand and testify on his behalf? The student witnesses were also important for another, less gratifying, reason. Not a single member of the school's faculty was willing to testify on Terry's behalf—although several admitted privately how appalled they were at the superintendent's actions.

In making my closing argument, I went over the charges, pointing out their lack of substance. I also stressed that the board did not even claim that Terry had violated a written rule concerning teacher behavior. Nor did it claim that he willfully violated school board policy. I stressed Terry's success as a teacher, the loyalty and devotion shown by his students, and the absence of evidence of intent to disobey. I pointed out that under union contracts a worker could not be found guilty of insubordination on such evidence and argued that it was vital that schoolteachers be treated with professional respect, that they should be given the same rights as steelworkers, janitors, and others protected by such contracts.

When the board reconvened, they unanimously found Terry guilty of the charges against him. The dismissal was upheld. After a lawsuit funded by the National Education Association, Terry was able to get the board's determination set aside because of procedural irregularities, such as the fact that opposing counsel was present at the board's deliberations. The court decision merely entitled him to another hearing and the school board indicated that it would not rehire him. Several years after the original charges were brought, the matter was ultimately resolved by an unsatisfactory compromise. In the meantime, Terry attempted to establish an alternative private school but it failed for lack of funds.

Terry's case demonstrated the vulnerability of schoolteachers during that period [11] and the inadequacy of the legal process as a means of protection. He was without funds to hire a full-time lawyer. His fellow teachers were frightened, his principal malevolent, the local community hostile. The school board was indifferent at best to his great ability as a teacher. No contract, legal standard, or professional organization existed to protect him.

The second case involved someone I will call Allen Miller, a self-

Academic Freedom

proclaimed radical who joined Indiana University as a graduate fellow in political science in 1968.[12] Almost immediately after coming to the university, Allen became one of the leaders of the quickly growing radical movement. He had the ability to crystallize sentiment, to express widely shared outrage in catchy phrases, and to suggest actions that caught the students' fancy. He spoke at rallies, organized marches, attended virtually every public meeting, and constantly sought to turn student opinion against the administration.

Allen enjoyed using language as a weapon. Before a meeting between a trustee and students, he came on stage and gave an impromptu speech in which he referred to a trustee, Carl Grey, as a "honky motherfucker." At another meeting the president tried to justify a fee increase. Allen rose from the audience, pointed his finger at the president, and said in a bold, angry voice, "No more bullshit," and sat down. The students rose to their feet cheering, and the phrase "No more bullshit" became their rallying cry at all subsequent student-administration confrontations. After leading a march to protest the university's ROTC (Reserve Officer Training Corps) program, he engaged in a vitriolic attack on Colonel Robert B. Jones, an assistant professor of military science at the university. That confrontation, taped by university officials, began with Allen's lecturing the colonel about Nuremberg laws and then became more personal:

Mr. Miller: I see you've been in Vietnam by your ribbons.

Colonel Jones: Yes, I was in the military there.

Mr. Miller: I can accuse you personally . . . the people in this room think that it's indecent and inhuman and absolutely the most obscene thing we've ever seen that you can be occupying an office rather than a cage in a zoo or a jail cell. As far as people in this room are concerned, you know, you're the scum of the earth . . . and it is unfortunate that we have to deal on a personal level . . . but the establishment for which you work, the organization which you are a part of, makes you guilty and it's unfortunate that you are tricking and conniving young men to engage in what I consider one of the most unholy professions. And the fact that this goes on at the university, the fact that you're a part of this is just an incredible thing. . . . I think you need a lot of forgiveness. I don't think it's forgiveness that we can give you. I think it's forgiveness that [can only come from] the Vietnamese people . . . beating the hell out of the United States Army. The only thing that we have to work for now is a victory of the Viet Cong and hope that they kill, unfortunately, as many of you as possible to end this war, cause that's the way it's going to end.

Colonel Jones: I'm willing to take that chance because I think this country needs it.

Mr. Miller: I hope you don't die taking that chance. I know that I won't, because I'm going to stay over here and fight so we can bring people back home because you're too stupid to realize what's happening so some of us will have to serve your interests and make sure you don't get over there. Maybe you don't think so. You're too stupid, too ignorant, and too pigheaded to realize it. But we're going to work to make sure you don't get blown up over in Vietnam.

Colonel Jones: Thank you, Mr. Miller. I appreciate you for bringing your views in.

This incident was followed by a march on the draft board in which a window was broken. That evening Clark Kerr, former chancellor of the California University System, gave a lecture in the university auditorium during which he was hit in the face with a pie thrown by James Retherford, a former leader of the radical students who was no longer connected with the university. Retherford was arrested and put in jail, and, at a subsequent rally, support for Retherford was encouraged by Jerry Rubin of the Chicago Seven, who was then visiting the campus. Rubin's speech was followed by one by Allen Miller, who urged the students to collect bail to "get our brother, James Retherford, out of jail."

All of this activity, violence, and disruption dismayed most faculty and townspeople, who feared the transformation of the university from a peaceful and respected institution into a revolutionary battleground. There were editorials, faculty resolutions, letters, and statements by politicians urging university administrators to locate and punish the guilty parties.

On October 17, 1969, Byrum Carter, chancellor of the Bloomington campus, publicly announced that he was suspending Allen Miller immediately and without pay from his duties as teaching assistant. Allen was notified by a brief letter: "This action is being taken on grounds of professional misconduct," but the letter did not specify the conduct upon which the conclusion was based.

The suspension of Allen Miller aroused passionate debate within the university almost instantly. The absence of advance warning of specific allegations of misconduct, the failure to provide Allen with an opportunity to be heard either before or after the suspension, and the immediate suspension of pay were all disquieting to many faculty members.

The local AAUP chapter issued a statement calling for a hearing. The statement also charged that "Chancellor Carter's handling of the case thus far reveals grave violations of academic due process." [13] Eighteen members of the zoology department signed a statement expressing their "concern over the apparent departure from fair standards of academic procedure in the suspension" of Allen Miller. The political science department, which was not only Allen's department but also Carter's department, met and voted 21 to 3 to send an open letter to the chancellor in which they stated, "We believe that the action taken in the case of Allen did not follow due process as it is normally understood in an academic community." [14] A left-wing faculty group called the New University Conference issued a vitriolic mimeographed statement entitled "The War Comes Home," which described the suspension as "a clear act of overt political repression." Allen's suspension was also attacked by the Teaching Assistants Association, which threatened to strike over the issue. [15] Eighty-five of the 107 teaching associates in the English department signed a letter condemning the lack of appropriate procedures prior to suspension: "We insist . . . that basic principles of academic freedom apply to everyone who teaches at Indiana University." [16]

On October 21, 1970, Chancellor Carter dealt with Allen Miller's suspension in a meeting of the Faculty Council. In response to widespread criticism, he assured the council that he was prepared to grant Allen a hearing before a faculty committee. I agreed to represent Allen at the hearing.

Evidence in the hearing seemed to favor Allen in every respect. Much of the factual basis of the university's case was stated by two students, whom I will call Rod Smith and Randy Baker, who had acted as wandering informers for the dean of students, following Allen from march to meeting. They were as similar as a pair of dolls, with handsome and square-cut but empty faces; earnest, eager-to-please expressions; and careful good manners that did not completely hide the secret contempt with which they seemed to view the world. They might have been effective witnesses in other settings, but before a committee of academics their clean-cut, nonintellectual style weighed heavily against them.

The university lawyer called both Chancellor Carter and Vice Chancellor Henry Remak as witnesses. Both had been active members of the AAUP—the vice chancellor had been active at the national level—and neither disavowed their basic commitment to the concept of academic freedom. The vice chancellor was particularly uncomfortable on the witness stand, attempting to be loyal both to the chancellor and to the cause of academic freedom. He made clear that he had argued against suspension without a prior hearing.[17] The chancellor, Byrum Carter, was similarly unwilling to challenge accepted notions of academic fairness.

Carter's testimony was carefully reasoned and articulate but clearly unconvincing to the large academic audience and to the members of the committee. He tried to defend his action by claiming that Allen, through his use of inflamed rhetoric and ugly personal confrontation, was a threat to academic freedom,[18] but he conceded on cross-examination that he acted primarily in response to general community pressure:

> *Chancellor Carter:* The nature of the statewide coverage of the events both in the press and in television had tended to concentrate themselves substantially on Mr. Miller and his group and their activities . . . I got phone calls from people whom I cannot identify, you know, about what you are going to do in this kind of way or that kind of way in connection with this or that awful thing they had seen on television. . . .

> *Mr. Getman:* This was an action which you took in response to the feeling of a substantial part of the faculty and the calls and letters and other things you were receiving because of the publicity?

> *Chancellor Carter:* Yes.[19]

When the case for the defense was presented, I tried to explain the perspective from which Allen Miller and his followers were acting and harmonize their radical confrontational approach with the values and beliefs of most members of the university community. This not only helped Allen but also was an attempt to ease tensions and reconcile different parts of the community. I argued that a convincing victory for Allen would be an affirmation of the university's commitment to academic freedom.

Several witnesses testified that Allen's suspension engendered widespread fear among other members of the faculty. The witnesses included the woman who was considered the ablest young professor in the political science department, the head of the Teaching Assistants Association, and the most recent winner of the Young Teacher of the Year award. All three testified to their own increased feelings of vulnerability after Allen was suspended. I also called a well-known English professor who was the chairman of a meeting that Allen was supposed to have disrupted. Both the chairman and the professor then speaking testified that they were "in no way disrupted or bothered by Allen."[20] In my closing argument, I was able to appeal to the shared belief in academic freedom that was common to all members of the committee regardless of political belief. I argued that the basis of the case against Allen was his radical beliefs, and that this was an inappropriate basis for positive action in an academic community. I admitted that his own style was inflammatory and disturbing, but I insisted that it had to be tolerated to support the academic community's commitment to robust debate and free expression of ideas. I could tell from their careful attention and occasional head-nodding that the members of the panel agreed.

A short time later, the committee issued a carefully worded opinion in which it went through the charges against Allen and urged the dismissal of all but one. The board unanimously recommended Allen's reinstatement, although it concluded that Miller "had failed to exercise 'appropriate restraint' in his verbal attack on Colonel Jones," [21] a conclusion with which I agreed. The recommendation for reinstatement was made public, as was Chancellor Carter's prompt acceptance.

The contrast between the two cases is striking. The hearing accorded to Terry was a travesty; that accorded to Allen was a model of fairness. Terry was abandoned by his colleagues. Allen was supported by all elements of the community. The unfairness in Terry's case is a reminder of the fear by outside community members that ideas fresh from the campuses could corrupt their children and disrupt their world. That the entire matter was eventually dealt with through litigation and in an unsatisfactory manner is also one of the legacies of the 1960s.

Despite the excellent work of the committee, Allen was required to leave Indiana University to avoid public prosecution on another matter. This, too, reflects an important fact, that no matter how careful the academic process, universities cannot divorce themselves from the communities in which they are located.

Allen's case demonstrates to me the important commitment made by universities during earlier periods to the concept of academic freedom. The success of the AAUP in providing standards by which such matters are to be handled is amply demonstrated in a number of ways. First, a hearing was held in which the faculty sat to pass judgment on the administration. Second, the administration witnesses, many of them deans, went out of their way to demonstrate their acceptance of the right of free expression and fair procedures. Third, the hearing was conducted in an exemplary way. Both my brief and the administration's brief cited the AAUP's famous 1940 statement on academic freedom, and the committee's final decision relied on it.

Allen's case was far from unique during the Vietnam War period. A great many ugly speeches calculated to inflame opinion were tolerated because of the allegiance of academic institutions to the concept of academic freedom. That basic commitment continues to significantly shape academic freedom. Many years later, as president of the AAUP, I was surprised to discover quiet heroes who put themselves on the line in support of academic freedom. These included a president of a junior college, himself a practicing Catholic, who refused to bar the play *Sister Mary Ignacious Explains It All for You*, and the president of a conservative theology school who advised his young faculty to join the AAUP and made sure that they had tenure to avoid their being purged by new fundamentalist trustees. The commitment of professors of different ranks in colleges and universities all over the country to the concept of academic freedom is well stated by Burton R. Clark: "But whatever the mood of state officials, populous groups, and radical students in the period at hand, the ideologies of the professorate view academic freedom in all its varying means as a necessary condition for acting with integrity in the service of knowledge. That one concern shades into another." [22]

While academic-freedom cases have usually involved conservative forces seeking to silence the expression of radical or liberal ideas, left-wing groups have also attempted censorship regularly of right-wing ideas. This has taken many forms, ranging from shouting down speakers deemed to be associated with repression, racism, and sexual oppression to the denial of tenure. Recently, this movement has gathered strength. The idea that freedom of speech includes the right to engage in personal attacks based on race, religion, or sexual preference, once a recognized tenet of civil libertarians, has come under increasing attack by influential academics. The issue has been raised most directly with respect to proposals to enact antiharassment codes. Such codes have been proposed at many universities and colleges. They have been supported by a variety of feminist and minority groups and are often opposed by civil libertarians and traditional liberals. The issue has divided the liberal-minority coalition, once a standard feature of academic life. [23]

Violations of Academic Freedom Today

The system of faculty committees loosely overseen by the AAUP's Committee A is increasingly inadequate to deal effectively with the great variety of injustice and interference with academic freedom that takes place in academic institutions. Many cases involve relatively minor decisions by administrators within the areas of their discretion: salary raises, leave requests, teaching assignments, and the like. Such cases are difficult to investigate, remedy, or monitor through committees. The effort is rarely worth the aggravation. And the faculty member usually remains subject to the authority of the person who committed the violation. Moreover, violations of academic freedom by administrators are rarely blatant today because administrators have become more sophisticated and almost always have access to expert legal advice. Violations are also made possible by the fact that a far larger percentage of faculty today than ever before do not have the protection of tenure and are therefore not entitled to evaluation before being let go on some vague ground, such as institutional need.

As the discussion of peer review in the next section demonstrates, the system is particularly ill-equipped to deal with violations that arise from the faculty rather than from administrators. In such cases, the complainant rarely has a strong case that the procedures employed were inadequate or unfair, and faculty committees will rarely conclude that other faculty members were improperly motivated.

Because faculty involvement is greatest and standards of evaluation are most stringent and most subjective, the possibility of injustice is built into the very fabric of elite institutions. Almost anyone is vulnerable if the standard is high enough. At Harvard Law School, serious accusations were made in the late 1980s that professors were denied tenure and appointment because of their adherence to the philosophy of the critical legal studies movement. This is the type of issue that a faculty committee would be ill-equipped to determine.

Academic freedom has its costs, and they are usually related to the concept of professorial autonomy. A fine line exists between academic freedom and unfair use of the podium. It is not unknown for professors to take advantage of the students, who constitute a captive audience and are subject to control through the grading process, to indoctrinate them on issues outside the professors' areas of expertise. Faculty also seek on occasion to justify unfair grading or assignment policies as aspects of academic freedom. Furthermore, the tradition of professorial autonomy, a corollary of academic freedom, militates against cohesiveness and common curricular approaches. But I believe, as do most academics, that the costs are minor compared to the contribution that academic freedom has made to the openness of investigation and debate in academic institutions.

Academic Freedom and Public Opinion

During the mid-1980s, I expected that the issue of academic freedom would once again become a great battleground because the political atmosphere in the nation had once more become conservative. Right-wing activists had formed an organization called Accuracy in Academia. Its purpose was to monitor and publicize what it claimed were efforts by radical professors to use the classroom for political indoctrination. Accuracy in Academia urged students to report Marxist and anti-American statements by professors. The organization received a great deal of publicity, and something in the nature of a national debate on the fairness of its tactics took place. Accuracy in Academia was attacked not only by the AAUP but by many academic administrators, the press, and even by William Bennett, Reagan's highly controversial secretary of education. It was lampooned in comic strips and became the butt of routines by comedians. Within a short while, it dropped the tactic of advocating that students report on their professors, and it thereafter gradually became ignored. The episode was frightening in many ways—the first professors the organization went after became the target of vicious attacks from hate groups and anonymous sources. The end result indicates, however, that academic freedom has more popular and political support than most academics realize. This increased public understanding and willingness by administrators and faculty to abide by its precepts, rather than any of the processes discussed, provides academic freedom its greatest protection.

Faculty Governance

When Dwight Eisenhower became president of Columbia University, he met with the faculty, to whom he referred as "employees of Columbia." According to academic legend, a distinguished senior professor corrected him by saying, "General, we are not employees of Columbia University. We *are* Columbia University." This story is dear to the hearts of many faculty because it makes the point that professors, not administrators, determine an institution's nature. Faculty organizations and many faculty conclude as a corollary that faculty should play a major role in developing educational policy for colleges and universities. This idea, when adopted, gives rise to what is known as faculty governance.

Faculty Involvement in Decision Making

Faculty governance requires faculty members to participate in the decisions that affect educational policy. The range of issues with which faculty

Faculty Governance

are involved at most accredited institutions is broad, including such matters as budget, curriculum, promotions, appointments, and admissions.

Faculty governance is simultaneously an elitist and egalitarian concept. It is elitist because part of its rationale is that the academic enterprise is so complex that only professors can properly make its administrative decisions. It is egalitarian as an academic version of the theory that those who do the basic work in any enterprise should take part in formulating policy, a theory currently being put forward by workers and labor unions all over the world. Given the dual nature of its ideological foundation, it should not be surprising that in practice faculty governance is strongest at elite institutions and at those where the faculty bargain collectively. Those are also the institutions where faculty are most powerful. In elite institutions, professors have great bargaining leverage because of their individual distinction; in institutions where faculty bargain collectively, they obtain power from banding together. One of the hallmarks of a top-flight school is meaningful faculty participation in major academic decisions. Participation is achieved through faculty meetings, governing boards, faculty senates, and academic committees.

Faculty Meetings

Faculty meetings are an important instrument of academic governance. But, as almost all academics learn, such meetings are where the least rational aspects of academic life most frequently arise. A variety of the professors whom I interviewed made this point, which also has been borne out by my own experiences.

When I began teaching at Indiana University, our faculty meetings quickly disabused me of the expectation that reason held sway in academic life. The issues were often petty, the arguments irrational, and the exchanges marked by anger or discontent. Prolonged debates but very little productive discussion took place. After a while, I could predict how each person would react to a proposal for change.

The dean, Leon Wallace, would oppose change on the grounds that our existing policies were successful and had important historic justification. Howard Mann would oppose it because it did not direct itself to the "real question." Jerome Hall, the most prolific and best-known person on the faculty, would refer to discussions he had with leading scholars around the world. Harry Pratter would point out that the issue was more complicated than anyone had yet suggested. Ralph Fuchs would address the question of faculty participation. Austin Clifford, who had been in law practice for many years before joining the faculty, would warn that the state bar was upset. Wence Wagner, our comparative law professor, would urge us to emulate the European model of his youth. Doug Bashkoff and I would evaluate the change in terms of current practice at Harvard, and Val Nolan would look impatiently at his watch and grumble that the entire issue was unimportant and the debate an unconscionable waste of his time.

Powerful feelings were evoked by the most technical or trivial of issues. When we considered a minor change in the exam schedule, the debate was barely civil. At the end of the meeting, the faculty would typically split into small groups earnestly analyzing the meeting, grading and reviewing each person's arguments. I was as involved as anyone. When the cause I supported carried or when my comments were well received, I was elated. When the other side won, I was upset, depressed, and often outraged.

Now that I have attended faculty meetings at a variety of institutions in different parts of the world, I have learned that the dynamic at Indiana University was typical and that my own reaction of simultaneously deploring and replicating the conduct of my colleagues was also quite common. On almost all faculties, the most competitive, emotion-laden, acrimonious, lengthy, and pretentious debates are about faculty appointments. Questioning the ability of the candidate is often an indirect way of asserting the speaker's superiority and usually of simultaneously insulting someone currently on the faculty.

Debate at faculty meetings often resembles one-on-one schoolyard basketball more than it does serious academic discussion. The level of competition is high. There are a variety of standard moves by average players and tricky moves by the very good ones. There are sucker moves, "in-your-face" moves, blocking-out moves, and fierce fighting for the ball. When I was on the Yale faculty, I once mentioned to my colleague Geof Hazard that I thought a union caucus that I had witnessed was far more intellectually impressive than a Yale Law School faculty meeting. "So is a sandbox," he said with some feeling.

Committees

Most institutions have an appointments committee, a tenure committee, a curriculum committee, a student relations committee, an academic-policy committee, a budget committee, and myriad others. Faculty help to establish policy and play a significant role in administration primarily

Faculty Governance

through these committees. Faculty members' attitudes toward participating in academic committees vary. Some regularly complain about being appointed to committees that are likely to be time-consuming, while others complain about being bypassed. Many faculty members, myself included, favor the idea of governance but find the actual practice to be burdensome. Governance requires faculty members to undertake administrative tasks that are important to the institution but often boring and time-consuming. Faculty appointments committees try to locate and evaluate teaching prospects. They arrange campus visits, set up lectures, and organize dinner parties so that the person can learn about the institution and be evaluated by the faculty. Generally, budget committees pore over financial reports and tenure committees read great quantities of scholarly writing in fields other than their own. At Yale, as a member of the appointments committee for several years, I met with the committee for at least one afternoon a week and was expected to put in from ten to fifteen hours of work prior to each meeting, reading the collected writings of those we were to consider. I also read admissions files, advised people interested in law teaching, and served on the graduate committee. The chair of the committee did considerably more work.

When I first began teaching, I welcomed the opportunity to become involved in committee work, particularly if the committee was university-wide. Periodically I received a letter signed by the president of the university appointing me to serve on such committees. Their titles were always promising: "The Social Science Advisory Committee," "The Academic Priorities Committee," "The Committee for the Advancement of Teaching," "The Faculty Review Board."

Much ceremony and much administrative effort by secretaries was involved in setting up meetings. Before the meeting, an agenda, reports, and memoranda would be circulated. At first, I read the materials carefully and went to the meetings prepared for interesting and significant academic discussions, but they rarely ensued. Committee work, like faculty meetings, cast an unflattering light upon the entire enterprise. In large committees, discussion was almost always both heated and boring. The members seemed to talk past each other. Inevitably, the meeting would include at least one person who would be intent upon making an issue of principle out of some minor point, several members who welcomed the opportunity to make speeches, and others who had private agendas involving arcane issues of academic politics. Discussions were contaminated by personal ambitions, jealousy, and factionalism. Law school committees were generally smaller and less combative but also involved considerable aimless discussion. We rarely accomplished anything. In my interviews with faculty members, a surprising number listed involvement in committees or academic administration as the worst aspect of academic life.

What comes as an unpleasant surprise to many people is to learn how political academic institutions are. My mother told me that when she first visited us at Indiana University, she was eager to find out "what real professors talked about." She was amazed to discover that discussions among academics were far less intellectually stimulating than the discussions of books, music, and politics that took place in our working-class neighborhood. "At our house the world was at stake. At the university all they talked about was school politics—who the dean appointed to a committee, who got a big raise, things like that."

The Pain and Satisfaction of Administration

Administrative work is demanding. It requires patience, attention to detail, and the ability to make and live with decisions. Administrative tasks that are most interesting and significant are likely also to be the most time-consuming and to have the most potential for conflict. They often present basic issues of justice and raise fundamental questions concerning institutional goals. The tension between elitist and egalitarian values frequently arises in the course of administrative decision making, particularly in the key areas of appointments, curriculum, and admissions.

In appointments, the tension manifests itself in the evaluation of credentials. An English department may have to decide between someone who has written a popular book and someone who has completed a scholarly dissertation on Rilke or Spenser. In law schools the appointments process at any stage may require a choice between a young person with excellent grades from a top law school and a successful practitioner with less impressive academic credentials. During the current elitist period, most schools seek young scholars capable of manipulating theoretical concepts and give low priority to teaching and practical experience. Similarly, today's curriculum reflects the elitist trend in education. The desire for "relevant" courses that marked the 1960s has given way to an emphasis on the profound and theoretical. In law, courses on law and literature, interpretation, deconstruction, dispute resolution, and feminist theory are fashionable. Labor law, debtors' rights, and clinical programs are out of vogue.

At many schools the battle between elitist and egalitarian views of education is fought out most directly over admissions policies. The issue has historically presented itself as a conflict between admissions based on discretion and admissions based on objective criteria. Originally, discretion was an elitist instrument. Admissions officers would give preference to the children of alumni, to the wealthy, or to those who went to elite prep or graduate schools, attended the right churches, or had political influence. During the 1950s, led by the Ivy League, admissions became more objective and therefore more open. I was able to gain admission to the Harvard Law School despite my lack of elite credentials because I did well on an objective test purporting to measure my aptitude for the study of law. Also in the 1950s, grades became more important than the prep or undergraduate school attended.

The system that most schools adopted with varying degrees of rigor involved a numerical prediction of future academic success based on undergraduate or high school grades combined with results on an objective test, like the SAT (Scholastic Aptitude Test) or the LSAT (Law School Aptitude Test).

I learned about the conflicting approaches firsthand early in my career at Indiana University when I was made an admissions officer in the fall of 1967. Applications were way up that year at all law schools. At Indiana University this meant that for the first time a substantial number of those applying would have to be turned down. The school had just begun using an objective formula based on grades and LSAT scores. Our formula treated all undergraduate grades the same, and that raised basic questions of fairness. Should we consider the school that the applicant attended? Should majors in accounting and theoretical physics be treated the same? Should we consider the pattern of an applicant's grades? Suppose someone did poorly for two years and then very well for two years—was that different from doing mediocre work over the entire course of a student's undergraduate career? These questions convinced us that fairness required a significant measure of discretion. Reliance upon the LSAT raised even more powerful questions because use of the test disqualifies a higher proportion of blacks and Hispanics than white students, as well as most of those for whom English is a second language.[24] The widespread use of the LSAT has aided those whose thinking is linear and organized and disadvantaged those whose approach to problems is more intuitive, creative, or insightful.

At Indiana, every admissions committee meeting became the basis for intense discussions about fairness and the importance of following rules or permitting discretion. The greater use of discretion promoted fairer decisions. The new process was elitist in that we paid more attention to undergraduate schools attended and courses taken, but we also used the process to promote diversity and give preference to those both black and white from disadvantaged backgrounds.

Despite our best efforts, great numbers of people who would have been routinely admitted in previous years were either denied admission or had their applications deferred to later in the year. I had no idea of the furor this would cause. It seemed that a large percentage of those rejected were the children of wealthy alumni, related to high university officials, intimate friends of important politicians, or colleagues of people who voted on the law school's budget. In many of these cases, I was told that the family was connected with the university in some worthwhile way, the applicant's life's ambition was to be a lawyer, and he or she knew of at least ten people with poorer records who were admitted in previous years. I was besieged with phone calls from applicants, their families, and prominent politicians. I regularly got letters from university deans who "just called to let you know" that the chancellor or the president were "really hoping we could admit the boy." I also got many calls from relatives: sometimes their pleas were touching, sometimes infuriating.

We tried to take into account letters of recommendation, experience, achievement, handicaps overcome, and personal problems. I spent a great deal of time listening to complaints, explaining the basis for our decisions, and advising people how to make their applications as appealing as possible. The ethical problems with which I had to deal were baffling and often soul-wrenching. The claims of the applicants with strong recommendations had to be balanced against those of the outsiders, the underprivileged, and minorities.

The most controversial decision we made was to establish an affirmative-action program that evaluated credentials of minority students differently from those of white students. This policy, now common in many university departments, appeared to many faculty to contradict the basic academic standard of individual merit. As a result, it was a source of controversy there as it is at almost every academic institution.

During my period as admissions officer at Indiana, we also established a limited part-time program for students "tied to Bloomington for whom full-time study of law was not feasible."[25] Under this program, then very rare among law schools concerned with their status, a variety of people, the majority of them mature women with children, entered the law school. Almost all graduated, and the great majority have had useful, nontraditional practices.

My brief period as an admissions officer gave me a sense of the potential usefulness of active involvement in the administrative process, if one devoted enough time to it. It also made me aware of the great burdens that inevitably accompany successful administration. Part of what makes administration so painful to many academics is that to do it well is both rewarding and challenging, but the commitment of time and emotion required interferes with the values that made one select academic life in the first instance. During that year, I did no writing, and my teaching was less successful, my tension level higher, and my time for family, friendship, contemplation, and fun far more limited. To undertake administration without significant commitment almost guarantees that it will be done badly. Most academics believe that it is important that faculty are involved in administration, but very few of us are willing to put in the time necessary to do it right. As Lewis Cosner writes:

> Precisely because the modern university is no longer a community of scholars but a huge and heterogeneous assemblage of different schools, it requires large-scale efforts of administrative adjustment and regulation. If academicians are unwilling to let themselves be entirely regulated by professional administrators, they are forced to relinquish large parts of their own "free" time for administrative tasks. We face here an interesting paradox: The very effort among academic men to prevent the academy from becoming too highly bureaucratized leads them to engage in activities that necessarily distract them from those scholarly tasks that the academy is supposed to foster and protect.[26]

Faculty and Administrators

The relationship between faculty and high-level administrators—presidents, provosts, deans, and department chairs—is a complex one. At research institutions and small liberal arts colleges, the administrators typically come out of and often return to the faculty. Those faculty who prefer teaching and research to administration often feel superior to deans and other administrators who are required to raise funds, resolve staff problems, and deal with alumni. High-ranking administrators, however, also have the power to affect the lives of faculty. They play a key role in appointments, have primary responsibility for setting salaries, vote on leave requests, assign teaching responsibilities, appoint committees, and represent the institution to the outside world. Many faculty would welcome the chance to be administrators, and the attitude of the rest of the faculty toward high-level administrators is often a complex mix of resentment, respect, fear, and envy.

Administrators, in turn, often feel that faculty appreciate neither the difficulty of the administrative tasks nor the successes. Faculty regularly conclude that administrators play favorites, fail to recognize their achievements, and are either too eager or too reluctant to use their administrative power. Sometimes the faculty perceive that a particular administrator is holding back the development of a school or department. When negative feelings are widespread, a state approaching open warfare may develop, which makes academic life particularly unpleasant.

At one time, at the Indiana law school, a group of faculty members, including myself, agreed to take turns interrupting the dean when he would engage in long-winded irrelevancies at faculty meetings. We felt that the dean, an intelligent man who exploited his intelligence to think of reasons not to take positive steps, was a major impediment to improving the school. He was fearful of controversy, disliked many of the faculty, and was manipulative in his dealings with us. He was also a poor speaker who represented the school inadequately in public appearances. At one of the first meetings I attended, he announced casually that a board of visitors, composed of distinguished lawyers, judges, and academics, had been appointed to investigate the school's functioning and file a report with the university administration. This board was to have its first meeting in two weeks. He listed the membership and quickly read over the schedule of events, trying, it seemed to me, to ignore that no meeting was scheduled between the board members and the faculty. I asked the dean if I was correct in my understanding.

He looked at me gravely. "Yes, Jack. We felt it would be better for them to get to know each other without the burden of interacting with the faculty during this first meeting." He spoke in a slow, whining voice, as though certain that all his vast efforts on our behalf would be misunderstood. The associate dean hastened to agree with him immediately, but Val Nolan, whose generally affable style only partially hid the toughness that had qualified him for the Secret Service during World War II, said angrily, "Surely you don't think you've answered Jack's point, do you?" This provoked a general debate in which the deans stood alone. At the end of the meeting, the dean promised to arrange for the faculty and the board of visitors to meet. I felt very good about the outcome but uneasy about the sharp look of annoyance that I could see on the dean's usually bland face as I left the meeting. Thereafter, I found myself the victim of various sorts of petty harassment. I was sent memos reminding me of various rules I had broken, was questioned about the number of long-distance calls I made, and was even told by the dean's secretary that I had requested too many stamps.

I got a minuscule raise for the next year—so low, in fact, that after a successful year teaching and the completion of a major article, I, who had graduated six years before, was paid less than a newly hired assistant professor fresh out of law school.

When deans or department chairs are incompetent or tyrannical, it is no easy task for faculty to resist their power. These administrators are the ones in contact with the central administration, so their versions of disputes are likely to be believed. Conflict between faculty and administrators is bound to affect major decisions like leave requests and salaries. Faculty united, however, often have the means to resist administrative injustice. Sometimes they can tell their stories to the central administration, as we eventually did at Indiana University. The committee structure sometimes provides a way for faculty to overcome assertions of administrative power. At one time I represented a group of faculty members in the biology department at Indiana State University in Terre Haute that brought a formal complaint to the faculty senate charging their chairman with improper and dictatorial behavior.

The department chairman was a well-known biologist who had come to ISU with visions of turning the department from a mediocre teaching-oriented group into a dynamic research department. The members of the department were at first pleased that someone of his stature was willing to accept the position. Indiana State had an undistinguished faculty and a provincial student body and was located in downtown Terre Haute, which was shabby, with no sense of ever having been fashionable. The new chairman's willingness to leave the Northeast for Terre Haute was considered an expression of confidence that what had once been an undistinguished teachers' college was on its way toward academic respectability. Within six months, however, most of the biology department were totally disillusioned. The chairman's goal, he insisted, was to make the faculty more productive (this meant publishing more), and his style was ruthless. He reduced faculty prerogatives, disbanded committees, ignored advice, gratuitously insulted members of the department, and tried in various ways, both petty and nasty, to encourage experienced people to leave. He publicly ridiculed at least one person in front of his students, and he took reprisals against those who disagreed with him. As far as I could tell, he evaluated faculty members solely in terms of whether their presence would add to the department's reputation. As often happens in such cases, publication was made a surrogate for excellence. Teaching, work with colleagues, and contribution to the community were all ignored.

The biology faculty were so incensed that they contacted the local AAUP chapter and brought a formal charge against the chairman to the faculty senate, which authorized a hearing by a special review committee. The review committee hired its own lawyer and worked out a process very similar to traditional adjudication. I was asked by the AAUP to represent the biology department faculty and ended up cross-examining the vice president for academic affairs, who strongly supported the chairman and accused my clients of continuous improper behavior. Under polite but insistent cross examination, the president could not specify a single instance. The review committee, made up of senior, highly regarded professors, unanimously recommended the chairman's removal on the ground that he violated basic standards of academic decency. A short while later he resigned and a more acceptable person was selected.

The president of the local AAUP chapter, my clients, and the review board all showed courage and integrity. It seemed then, and still now seems, remarkable that a process existed whereby faculty could challenge the behavior of their department chair and, despite the opposition of the central administration, have it tested against traditional academic norms.

Academic Administration and Collective Bargaining

The governance of academic institutions has, in recent years, become more complex, legalistic, and expensive. This has meant less control by faculty and more by full-time administrators and professional staff: assistant deans, lawyers, and business managers. The traditional system, under which administrators are considered an arm of the faculty, has in many institutions given way to a system under which academic administration is a separate career ladder, with administrators more similar to corporate managers than to professors. These two trends, given impetus during the late 1960s, exacerbated tensions between faculty and administrators. At many institutions, professors came to feel alienated, manipulated, and powerless. Many noted that grade and high school teachers had made themselves more formidable through unionization and collective bargaining. This was a concept in keeping with the more radical and egalitarian ideas then sweeping campuses. Many faculty members, particularly younger, more radical ones, argued that collective bargaining would provide better protection for academic freedom, give faculty more say about policy, and raise salaries. During the late 1960s and early 1970s, unionization had strong advocates on almost every campus in the land.

By the end of the 1970s, collective bargaining represented a significant aspect of university governance. About one-fifth of all professors, a figure roughly identical to that of the rest of the work force, had their working conditions covered by negotiated contracts.[27] The ways in which traditional governance and collective bargaining differ is still a matter of conjecture. Several basic aspects of academic life, including the committee structure, tenure, and peer review, remain the same. Certain differences, however, are apparent. Under collective bargaining such things as leave policy, promotional policy, salary scale, and course load, which were once decided unilaterally by administrators, are now worked out over the bargaining table, and their implementation typically involves greater faculty involvement than before. Because collective bargaining results in a contract that establishes working conditions and a grievance system, it tends to make professional relationships and academic procedures more formal and rule-oriented. Collective bargaining in all areas, including academic life, minimizes differences within the group represented. It is almost always egalitarian in impact. Not surprisingly, it flowered during the 1970s and its expansion stopped during the current elitist period.

The rate of unionization of faculty would have been higher had it not been for the Supreme Court's decision in *NLRB v. Yeshiva University*. In that case, the Court held that the faculty at most "mature" academic institutions are managers, not employees, and therefore do not have the right under the National Labor Relations Act to choose union representation and collective bargaining.[28] This decision by the Supreme Court has meant that the structure of faculty involvement through committees will continue to be the dominant mode of faculty governance into the foreseeable future. This complex system can work effectively only when those involved share basic academic values and trust each other's fairness. When that does not obtain, as, for example, when faculty conclude that administrators are not acting in their interest and administrators feel unappreciated, academic governance becomes a source of pain and a constant reinforcer of alienation.

Collective Bargaining and Faculty Organizations

The AAUP, despite its prestigious origins, has always been much like a union in its insistence that governance be shared and in its desire that faculty speak in a unified voice. Many of its early leaders were quite aware of and pleased by the organization's trade-union aspects. On the other hand, from its inception the AAUP has sought to be something more than, or different from, traditional unions. It is dedicated to protecting academic standards and it stresses faculty responsibility as well as faculty rights. By the early 1960s, when I entered academic life, most of the AAUP's members were far more aware of the differences between it and trade unions than of the similarities.

For many years, the AAUP resisted collective bargaining because it seemed inconsistent with the professional status of faculty. As a result, the two giant organizations that have traditionally represented schoolteachers, the American Federation of Teachers (AFT) and the National Education Association (NEA), both became involved in organizing faculty in higher education. During the late 1970s, the AFT, which had a reputation as a militant and progressive union, had great appeal to those whose interest in unionization was strongly ideological. The NEA had special appeal to many because of its political power, its wealth, and its strong organization. The NEA did best at institutions such as junior colleges and schools of education where the AAUP had long seemed irrelevant and where combining with schoolteachers seemed a natural step.

The AAUP responded slowly and with considerable internal disarray to the challenge of collective bargaining. After much argument and more to forestall its rivals than from any conviction of its own, the organization declared in measured tones that, under certain limited circumstances, collective bargaining might be the appropriate way to secure an adequate faculty role in governance. The AAUP announced at the same time that when those limited circumstances existed it would be willing to act as the bargaining representative for the faculty. During the next decades, a series of union-representation elections were held at campuses throughout the country, involving the AAUP, the NEA, and the AFT.

When the AAUP began to engage in collective bargaining it lost some of its professional acceptance. Many faculty members felt that the organization had forfeited its claim to speak as the voice of the profession. A similar claim was made by many administrators. Some seized on the new unionlike status of the organization to ignore its professional pronouncements. John Silber, the president of Boston University, both personified and articulated this point of view. He dismissed the claims of the local AAUP chapter to have a significant voice in the administration of the university and then attributed his response to the AAUP's transformation. In his book *Straight Shooting*, he states: "But more recently the AAUP has shared fully in the intellectual corruption that accompanied the politicization of the university, and its adventure with unionism made matters still worse. A union is required to defend the interests of its members with little or no regard for external standards; the AAUP as a labor union found itself defending the indefensible in a way that the AAUP as a professional organization would have found abhorrent." [29]

It is difficult of course, to tell from this statement what actions of the AAUP Silber found corrupt or indefensible. Moreover, his statement about unions is as inaccurate as it is uninformed. I have dealt professionally with a variety of different unions—police, steelworkers, paperworkers, airline pilots, flight attendants, and hotel and restaurant workers among them. I have never known one that was indifferent to professional standards or one that thought its job was to defend the indefensible. Nor can I think of any action that the AAUP has undertaken as a collective bargaining agent that disregards its traditional commitments to such concepts as academic freedom and shared governance. Nevertheless, the conclusion that the AAUP inevitably sacrificed professional standards when it agreed to engage in collective bargaining was widely accepted by uninformed people in the profession. This belief was costly to the AAUP in many elite institutions at which it was once quite influential.

At the less prestigious institutions at which collective bargaining was adopted, the AAUP had to compete with two organizations, both more knowledgeable and wealthier than itself. The AAUP had the advantage of tradition, the existence of functioning chapters, and the general goodwill of faculty throughout the country. The other organizations had more money, far larger staffs, greater familiarity with collective bargaining, and rhetoric more suitable to the times. After an initial period of AAUP success, the other two organizations began to win more frequently. Both the AFT and the NEA now have more faculty members than the AAUP. Despite the sometimes fierce battles between them, the ideological differences among the faculty groups are minimal. All favor academic freedom, strengthening faculty governance, eliminating discrimination within the academy, and improving salaries. The main difference is that the AAUP is solely a faculty organization, while both of the other organizations are more inclusive. The AFT is a member of the AFL-CIO, and the NEA's membership includes about two million K-12 teachers.

When the AAUP endorsed collective bargaining, it lost members at traditionally nonbargaining campuses. The membership loss was quite severe. Some members quit because they thought the AAUP too liberal and activist, some because they thought the battle for academic freedom had been won, some because the dues were raised; many retreated from any activities other than their own teaching and research, worn-out by the campus turmoil of the 1960s and early 1970s. On the other hand, many faculty left and new faculty declined to join the AAUP on the grounds that it was not militant enough.

The onset of collective bargaining led to my involvement at the national level of AAUP. I became the AAUP's general counsel[30] in 1980, at one of the lowest points in its organizational history. Membership was dropping steadily and the feud between its collective bargaining and traditionalist components was becoming increasingly bitter.

The legal work was interesting. However, as general counsel I inevitably became involved in organizational politics and this, like all academic politics, was painful and cast the entire enterprise in a bad light. The AAUP that had stood for common faculty rights was split into warring factions that treated each other contemptibly. The general secretary, who is head of the staff, was viewed as an elitist by the collective bargaining people and as an intellectual lightweight with no appreciation for the organization's traditions by the Committee A staff and members. The remainder of the staff was allied with one or another faction, and each group within the staff was angry at every other group. Discussion at executive committee meetings was tedious, the issues boring, the arguments repetitive, and personal relations acrimonious. A high percentage of those with whom I dealt seemed to view the AAUP as a vehicle for personal advancement rather than a way of contributing to the profession.

Given the unhappy nature of my experience as general counsel, it surprised many of my friends in the organization that I agreed to run for AAUP president in 1986. I did so for a combination of elitist and egalitarian reasons. I wanted the prestige of the title and the honor of following in the footsteps of the organization's past illustrious leaders—Dewey, Lovejoy, Fuchs. I also saw the presidency as presenting the opportunity to contribute. I wanted to help unify the organization and to help faculty members in trouble. My goals included organizing new faculty (particularly minority-group members and faculty from less prestigious institutions), strengthening the work of Committee A, improving relations with the NEA and the AFT, and increasing our collective bargaining efforts.

My successes were minimal. Much of the blame is attributable to my own administrative weaknesses, but in many situations progress was substantially frustrated by one or another aspect of academic elitism.

Making the AAUP more effective in protecting academic freedom was

Faculty and Administrators

hindered initially by internal organizational politics. I found that appointing someone to Committee A from a collective bargaining chapter who would be acceptable to the committee's staff and chairman was a major undertaking and one that left everyone involved feeling aggrieved. I decided after a few preliminary skirmishes that any effort on my part to change the organization's procedures in dealing with academic-freedom violations would embroil me in a major battle and lead to little progress. I turned my attention to other areas.

My first presidential involvement in collective bargaining, which involved Fairleigh Dickinson University, turned out to be a failure because the newly elected officers of the local chapter refused to take advice from me, the organization's lawyers, or their own counsel in a technical area of labor law related to the Supreme Court's *Yeshiva* decision. They rejected a deal that I had negotiated with the university's president that would have averted a strike and permitted the continuation of collective bargaining. The result was a bitter strike and a hearing before the NLRB on the question of whether the faculty at Fairleigh Dickinson University were employees or managers. It was determined by the labor board that the faculty were managers and not entitled to bargain. The strike was inevitably lost. Today the AAUP's chapter at Fairleigh Dickinson is much smaller, less than one-half its former size. It no longer bargains on behalf of the faculty.

My first experience as president in a union-representation campaign was equally upsetting. It arose at Northern Illinois University. The state of Illinois had passed legislation permitting faculty bargaining in public institutions, and all three faculty organizations were involved in the representation campaign that followed. The AAUP had once been the sole faculty organization on campus and would almost certainly have won the election if its current and former leadership had been united. However, its leaders were badly split, with several prominent former leaders urging the faculty to vote against any union representation.

In November of 1986, I traveled to De Kalb, Illinois, to meet with the leadership of the local chapter and help with the campaign. The meeting convinced me that our chances of winning the election were slim. The discussion of campaign tactics that I witnessed was chaotic, angry, and generally beside the point. The leaders spent almost the entire time composing a single letter. Each word was argued over as though something important turned on the niceties of phraseology, even though they were at a stage of the campaign where no letter could make a real difference.

That evening I gave a talk about collective bargaining to a sparse and generally dispirited audience. I spoke for a few minutes about the AAUP and collective bargaining and then threw the meeting open for questions.

The first questioner wasted little time in getting to the core issue for most of the faculty: "Is there collective bargaining by the faculty at any of the truly great universities?" And almost all of the questions were about the relationship of collective bargaining to academic status, rather than about its relationship to academic values or achievement. I answered in terms of their concerns.

"Collective bargaining has been chosen by the faculty of the New York State system and by that at my alma mater, City University of New York, as well as at such first-rate schools as Oakland University in Michigan and Temple University in Pennsylvania. And many great academics have supported the concept, including Albert Einstein, who was an early AAUP member and a member of the AFT as well."

I did not fool myself into thinking that anything positive would come from my talk. And I was not surprised to learn that the AAUP did very badly in the election. We finished third behind the AFT and "no agent" (or a vote against collective bargaining), which were first and second respectively. A runoff election between AFT and "no agent" was scheduled. Shortly thereafter, the AFT affiliate proposed that the AAUP chapter combine with it in a joint venture. Their proposal was both generous and sensible. I publicly supported the merger. Some of the former AAUP leaders at Northern Illinois were furious with me for this position. I proposed a meeting to explain my position. A former leader of the chapter started a campaign to get the local leadership to refuse to meet with me. For a time, his campaign was successful. The idea of making common cause with the AFT was so troublesome to many of our leaders that it seemed that if I went to Northern Illinois University, the AFT would be eager to meet with me but that the AAUP's leadership would refuse. I was not surprised when the faculty decided against representation in the final vote.

The Northern Illinois experience convinced me that I should make increased cooperation with the AFT and the NEA the chief goal of my presidency. Competition was harmful to all of us and to the cause of greater faculty power in university governance. Acting together, we were quite formidable. The other organizations' combination of resources, trained staff, political power, and collective bargaining experience fit very well with the AAUP's academic experience, tradition, and skillful use of members' technical ability.

My relations with the legal arm of the NEA were particularly close. I

Faculty and Administrators

had, during my time as general counsel, become friendly with Bob Channin, the general counsel of the NEA. Thereafter, the organization used me to help it in various cases. It seemed to me that working out a program which would involve the AAUP and the NEA in greater cooperation on legal matters would be independently valuable and a good way of improving relations between the two organizations. The NEA higher education leadership, after much debate, decided to support the plan, hoping that the development of such a program might be the best way to demonstrate to doubters within the AAUP the values of close cooperation and even of affiliation with them. Thus, after rather friendly negotiations involving the leadership of both organizations, we agreed to set up a joint legal program, to which the NEA would contribute $100,000 for the first year and the AAUP would contribute the volunteer efforts of its membership. The new and as-yet-unnamed entity would provide representation for faculty members in trouble and file briefs in cases of interest to the professoriate. For a time, I thought that the development of such an organization would turn out to be my one significant success as president of the AAUP.

The leaders of the NEA gave the idea strong support and agreed to provide the great majority of the funds while sharing control of the new organization equally with us. Despite the one-sided nature of the arrangement, I did not expect the proposal to be approved by the AAUP without serious debate. I guessed that some of the AAUP members with close ties to the AFT would be troubled by the proposal, but, since I was simultaneously supporting joint programs with the AFT in Illinois and elsewhere, I was sure that the opposition could be overcome. My long-range goal was to have AAUP at the center of a series of cooperative programs, which would eventually lead to all three groups working together, first in higher education and then perhaps on behalf of the cause of education more generally.

Significant opposition to the plan within the AAUP developed sooner than I had expected. Almost as soon as the proposal had been agreed to by the negotiating team, which included the general secretary, the chair of the collective bargaining congress, and the general counsel, the association's senior staff met and unanimously voted to oppose it. I could have taken the position that the staff members were supposed to implement, not make or oppose, policy; instead, I met with them collectively and in smaller groups in an effort to convince them of the plan's wisdom. The position of the Committee A staff was the most intense and at times even irrational. How could we become closely associated with an organization that was dominated by schoolteachers and did not understand or appreci ate and had not contributed to the concept of academic freedom as it had been developed by the AAUP acting through Committee A? Other proponents of the plan and I argued in vain both that the program would be controlled by people in higher education and that academic freedom was as important for K-12 teachers as it was for us. Accustomed as I was to academic snobbery, I still marveled at the contempt that some members of the Committee A staff were able to express toward the NEA through tone of voice, facial expression, and laughter whenever its achievements were mentioned.

Most complicated and difficult to deal with was the opposition of the collective bargaining staff. The staff members were opposed to any structural relationship with either of the other two organizations, in part because they felt it made campaigning against them in representation elections more difficult, in part because past campaigns had left a residue of bitterness, and in part because they feared that the AAUP would ultimately be swallowed up by the other organizations. To be enacted, the proposal required an affirmative vote from the AAUP's council, which met just before our annual meeting in June of 1987. Opposition was intense and widespread. Some members of the council were aggrieved because they had not been adequately notified in advance of the negotiations. Some opposed the plan because of the opposition of the staff. Several people spoke contemptuously of the NEA, criticizing its staff, its lack of political know-how, its lack of commitment to academic freedom, and its lack of knowledge of higher education. Several council members expressed anger at the thought that the NEA was attempting to "buy" us for $100,000. Three things struck me about the opposition members: their anger, the fact that none of them talked about the merits of the proposed program, and the contempt that they expressed for the second largest union in the Western world and the profession of schoolteaching.

Those of us who argued in favor of the plan focused on the value of the program and on the safeguards against NEA domination that were built into the structure. We pointed out that it would be possible to terminate the arrangement at almost any time. In the end, the plan was approved by a three-vote margin by the council.

To everyone's surprise, however, the plan was turned down by a voice vote at the AAUP's annual meeting after some particularly aggressive parliamentary maneuvering by its opponents. The debate was almost totally one-sided. The opponents lined up quickly at the microphones as soon as the proposal was announced and then succeeded in getting a vote "to call the question," which meant an end to debate before other proponents of the program or I could state our arguments. After so much effort, I would have been unhappy with the results even if the procedure had been fair. But I was particularly bitter that the organization most committed to reasoned decision making in academic life was incapable of practicing its own principles.

In part, my limited effectiveness as AAUP president was a tribute to the democratic nature of the organization and to the commitment of many of its members. In part, it reflected my political and administrative weaknesses. In part, it reflected the divisions within any academic group. In part, it reflected the continuing power of snobbery and hierarchy in all aspects of academic life, including the AAUP. Because we were the oldest faculty organization and the one with the most distinguished lineage, many of our members emotionally rejected the idea that we might profit from associating with upstart organizations like the NEA or AFT.

It is often said that academic politics is so bitter because so little turns on the outcome. I did not have that feeling about the AAUP. The issues of policy with which we dealt are fundamental issues about the nature of American society. Higher education, more than any other aspect of our society, has given the children of working-class and immigrant parents, such as myself, the chance to contribute our intelligence and experience to others. I continue to think of the AAUP as an important organization. If it is incapable of living up to its great heritage, that will be a loss for the entire academic world.

Tenure, Peer Review, Excellence, and Injustice

The Basic Concepts

One aspect of faculty governance of particular importance to the running of academic institutions is peer review: the evaluation of faculty for appointments, promotions, and tenure by other faculty. Peer review ensures that basic personnel decisions will be made with the participation of those knowledgeable about the quality of the performance being evaluated and about the academic standards for conducting such faculty evaluations.

The most important decision subject to peer review is whether to grant a junior faculty member tenure. On most faculties, a professor is evaluated for the grant of permanent tenure after a period of full-time membership (usually five or six years). The awarding of tenure means that the person may not be dismissed by the institution unless he or she is guilty of serious misbehavior or unless financial exigency wipes out the position. In practice, charges of misbehavior are rare and financial exigency is a very difficult standard to meet. The grant of tenure thus means job security and a feeling of invulnerability to removal based on academic disagreement, social discord, or political disagreement.

At the great majority of academic institutions, appointment as an assistant professor is understood to be the prelude to a permanent position, as long as the new appointee lives up to some expected level of performance.[31] Most colleges and universities have an elaborate system of evaluation prior to granting or denying tenure. Normally a person is voted on initially by colleagues who are instructed to judge on the basis of three criteria: teaching, scholarship, and institutional service.[32] Information about a person's teaching usually comes from class visits or student evaluations. Conclusions about scholarship are typically arrived at by reading the candidate's published scholarly writing and by sending his or her articles and books to senior professors in the appropriate field for evaluation. Knowledge of service, which refers to committee work and other contributions to the institution, come from the person's annual reports. Service is rarely significant even in marginal cases. Most institutions claim that teaching and scholarship are of comparable importance, but in the past two decades the balance has steadily shifted toward giving greater weight to scholarship. Despite official rhetoric to the contrary, scholarship is almost always given greater weight at the most prestigious schools.[33]

The initial determination of a professor's entitlement to tenure comes from the tenured members of the candidate's school or department. A favorable vote of two-thirds majority is usually required before a positive recommendation is sent on to a campus- or institution-wide committee, where the same evidence is reviewed and sometimes new evidence is gathered.

The review committee makes its own determination, and it, too, generally requires a favorable vote of two-thirds majority before it recommends the grant of tenure to the university administration. In most institutions, the final academic decision is made by the president or provost on the recommendation of one of the deans. The process thus involves review by both faculty and administrators. Administrators have the final say, but strong faculty recommendations are rarely overturned. The tenure decision, being as important as it is both to the individual and the institution, is treated with great seriousness. Faculty members appointed to serve on campus- or institution-wide tenure committees generally put in a great deal of time reading, evaluating, and discussing.

The final stages of faculty consideration do not really constitute peer review because the committees are made up mostly of professors from other disciplines. Pure peer review, in which only those in the same discipline evaluate the candidate, is rare.[34] The concern is that disciplinary colleagues, although the most knowledgeable, are also the most susceptible to the temptations of friendship, disciplinary fads, and personal animosity.

If a person is denied tenure by this process of evaluation, an appeal may usually be taken to a faculty review board. Review boards, however, do not reconsider the case on its merits. Their role is to determine that the evaluation process was fair and that the decision was based on acceptable academic criteria. Review boards typically do not have the power to grant tenure but may recommend to the administration that the person be reevaluated.

The tenure system as it currently works has been significantly influenced by the AAUP, which has fought for tenure and the system of peer review as protections for academic freedom. The justification is that peer review ensures that the tenure decision will be made fairly and knowledgeably, and that the protection provided by tenure, in turn, facilitates willingness to explore and to take positions on controversial issues. The system of colleagues and administrators reviewing professors for promotion and tenure generally works well. Decisions are made on the merits. Those whose teaching and research are considered by others in their field to be good are granted tenure. Those who fail at both are denied tenure. Those whose teaching and scholarship are uneven are given careful consideration and are generally treated with at least a measure of generosity.

Political affiliations, the expression of unpopular opinions, race, gender, and appearance are almost never referred to in the review process. Nevertheless, because faculty members are human, unfair or extraneous factors sometimes affect tenure decisions. Sometimes this works to benefit a professor who has in one way or another won the goodwill of his or her senior colleagues. Sometimes such factors work to the detriment of someone who has, for one or another reason, incurred the enmity of senior colleagues. The process is thus on occasion subject to unfair manipulation. One factor which makes this possible is that the standards by which the untenured person's performance will be judged are rarely spelled out with any precision. It is thus possible for these standards to be applied differently to different candidates. Departments or institutions can therefore change the standards that they apply without acknowledging that they are doing so. Sometimes a person will be denied tenure, despite being more productive and a better teacher than the great majority of the tenured faculty members engaging in the review process.

In some schools, departments, and universities, the prospect of peer review is used to keep younger faculty in line. Untenured faculty learn that it is dangerous to criticize or even disagree with senior colleagues. Past slights may be revenged and new intellectual movements thwarted or hindered through adverse votes on tenure. Those who take part in the review process, generally senior professors, are almost always able to cast opposition in terms of academic deficiencies, arguing that an untenured professor's published articles are too simplistic or too confusing, that they address the wrong issue, that the secondary literature is not well dealt with, or that the best ideas are not really worked through. It may be impossible for anyone, including the person making the criticism, to know whether the criticism reflects legitimate evaluation or the exacting of revenge.

When a meritorious person is denied tenure, the result is a double tragedy. The person's life is blighted for a long period, often permanently, and other junior faculty become obsessed with making sure that being denied tenure does not happen to them. Some become unduly deferential to their senior colleagues. Some change their research agendas to emphasize quantity of publication. Others become completely immersed in their work.

Over the years, a significant proportion of the unremedied cases of academic injustice that I have witnessed have involved the denial of tenure. The injustice is generally committed in the name of excellence, typically when the school or department considers itself great or on the verge of greatness and the credentials of the person being evaluated are suspect according to currently fashionable elitist criteria.

When an untenured academic has worked hard and believes that he or she has performed in accordance with the standards of the institution, the denial of tenure is almost always a monumental and traumatic experience. On a practical level it means moving after a particularly unpleasant final year, leaving friends, students, and home. It may require separation from one's spouse or children. It generally means trying to find a new academic position with one's credentials severely weakened. The internal and symbolic significance of the denial of tenure—the blow to one's ego and to one's sense of the rationality of the academic enterprise—is likely to be even more severe. Professors typically have been accustomed to academic success from early childhood on. They have believed in the benignity of academic institutions and have measured their own worth by academic standards. When they perceive that the process of academic evaluation to which they have previously been committed has worked unfairly, they often expect that they will be able to correct the perceived injustice. They are also likely to be angry and eager for vindication. Thus they frequently take action, usually in the form of an academic appeal, attempting to get the decision reversed. Nevertheless, once the peer review process produces an unfair result, it is unlikely that the injustice will ever be adequately remedied, regardless of steps the aggrieved party takes.

I report here on two cases involving women whose lives were blighted for prolonged periods by the tenure process. The first case is that of Janet Lever, a sociologist who was denied tenure at Northwestern University. Janet chose to battle the denial of tenure in a series of academic forums, before the Equal Employment Opportunity Commission and in court. The result has been a personal and academic tragedy. The second case is that of Adrienne Birecree, an economist at Bucknell University who worked out a settlement of her case despite a favorable ruling from the appropriate faculty committee. She has fared somewhat better, although in her case, too, the result is unfair, unjust, and unhappy.

The Case of Janet Lever

Janet Lever is a scholar. She has a knack for showing how important features of a society are revealed through seemingly minor cultural patterns. Her natural affinity for scholarship was first manifested while she was still in college. She was in England in 1966 during the summer after her sophomore year, while the World Cup in soccer was going on. Although she was not a sports fan and knew nothing of soccer, she recognized its great cultural impact, particularly to Latin Americans. She noted that when the favored Brazilian team was eliminated, "men and women in Rio de Janeiro openly wept; one fan attempted suicide by throwing herself off a boat; Brazilian flags were lowered to half-mast and buildings were draped in black crepe; angry mobs burned players and coaches in effigy."

The following summer, after her junior year in college, she traveled to Brazil to write an undergraduate term paper about the role of soccer in Brazilian society. She translated popular magazine articles, talked about sports with everyone she met, and conducted interviews with players.

The reaction of her professors to her paper was so favorable that she decided, over the strenuous objection of her parents, to drop out of school for a semester to live in Brazil and continue her research. She became part of the Brazilian soccer world. She was introduced to players and coaches; she began a friendship with the great Brazilian soccer player and idol,

Pelé; and she was asked to inaugurate a new soccer field at a local country club, where she was presented with a silver plaque inscribed "to the imperialist Yankee sent to spy on Brazilian soccer."

She returned to school and used the material she gathered to write her honors thesis. A shortened version of the thesis was published in *Transactions*, a social science magazine, a rare achievement for an undergraduate student. The article's reception was even more remarkable; it has since been translated into many languages and has been frequently cited over the years.

In the late 1960s, Janet began graduate studies in sociology at Yale. She made two more trips to Brazil while studying for her doctorate, and another afterward, when she returned for a thirteen-month stay. The final result of her efforts was *Soccer Madness*, a book written in clear, unadorned prose and published by the University of Chicago Press.[35] A writer for *Sports Illustrated* praised it as a "brilliantly analyzed . . . study of people, culture and politics."[36] The then-president of the American Sociological Association said that "it elevates sociology of sport to a subdiscipline of the highest importance,"[37] and another critic commented that "Janet Lever's interest in Brazilian soccer and her friendship with Pelé should become one of the folktales of sociology of sport."[38]

While at Yale, she published a book on the introduction of female students to Yale College as undergraduates and began doing work on the role of play in gender differentiation. She went from Yale to Northwestern, where she was an enormously popular teacher, known for her clarity and enthusiasm. Her teaching ratings were enthusiastic, and hundreds of students signed up for her courses. She continued her research, writing several articles on gender differentiation based on her thesis, and her work on *Soccer Madness*.

By today's standards, which emphasize the quantity and speed of publication, Janet would not be considered very prolific, but she published more than was typical at the time, and the quality of her work was high. Her articles on sexual differentiation were widely reprinted and cited, and her work on the role of sport in society was hailed by experts in the field. Given that her publication record exceeded those of several of the senior members of the faculty, Janet fully expected to receive tenure. In October of 1979, her departmental colleagues voted for her unanimously. An ad hoc college-wide committee of social scientists, which was then appointed, also voted for her unanimously, but some members expressed doubt about the trendy nature of her work and her journalistic style, both severe criticisms among serious academics. Under the system employed at Northwestern, the ad hoc committee's recommendation is then considered by the standing Promotions and Tenure Committee (known as PATC), chaired by the dean of the College of Arts and Sciences. PATC conducts its own vote; a two-thirds majority is necessary before an affirmative recommendation is made to the dean of the college. The dean, in turn, makes a recommendation to the provost, who makes the final decision.[39]

On April 28, 1980, the PATC committee voted on the recommendation by the department and the ad hoc committee that Janet be awarded tenure. She received eleven "yes" votes and six "no" votes, one short of the necessary two-thirds. It would not have been unusual for the dean of the college to have recommended that tenure be granted to Janet, despite her having fallen one vote short of the necessary two-thirds for a favorable recommendation from the committee. The dean, Rudolph Weingartner, however, declined to do so. In May of 1980, he wrote to Janet that he would not recommend to the provost, Raymond Mack, that she be given tenure. In accordance with Northwestern's policy, the dean offered her a final year of employment, to terminate on August 31, 1981.

Although the deliberation of the PATC remains shrouded in mystery, there is reason to believe that Janet's choice of nonesoteric topics as well as her generally unpretentious style counted against her. Janet believes that her informal dress contributed to the decision. "I think that one reason why I didn't get tenure at Northwestern where things are unspoken is that I didn't dress for success. I dressed no worse than my male colleagues, but they could get by with it. I couldn't. And yet it was very much one of the reasons why I was such a rave success as a teacher—because I was communicating to the kids that 'I am one of you. I understand where you are at.' "

Some members of the sociology department suggested to Janet that Dean Weingartner was opposed to granting her tenure because he wanted to shake up the department, making it more productive and more quantitative.

Her students and most of her departmental colleagues responded with outrage when they heard that she was denied tenure. The chairman of the department wrote to the dean protesting the decision. According to U.S. Magistrate Bernard Weisberg, who investigated the procedural aspects of the process, the chairman contended that the dean and the PATC had been unfairly "influenced by the popular and accessible style of Lever's writing and for that reason had judged it insufficiently scholarly, disregarding the judgment of outside experts in sociology who acknowledged her genuine contributions." In addition, a "delegation for the Sociology department called on Weingartner to express disagreement with his decision . . . In response Weingartner took the unusual step of undertaking to reconsider his recommendation."[40]

A reexamination was undertaken and two additional letters were obtained from well-known sociologists at other universities. Both letters were favorable, although each was qualified and written in careful academic prose.[41] The less favorable of the two stated: "The manuscript you sent me is a very interesting and informative discussion of soccer in Brazil. The question one must ask, of course, is whether it is also a contribution of special value to sociology, and I am of two minds on that subject—although the mind inclined to say yes can summon stronger arguments than the mind inclined to say no."

As the letter suggests, in the evaluation of scholarship at major academic institutions, greater emphasis is placed on the issue of disciplinary contribution than on whether the work being evaluated is interesting, informative, and original in its own terms. The other letter stresses the newness of the material and its interest:

> I have finished Janet Lever's *Soccer in Brazil* ahead of schedule, largely because it held my interest but also because it is a remarkable, sustained work; one chapter leads to the next . . .
>
> First there is a thoughtful description of Brazilian society, limited in many respects, available to some extent in other publications but bringing into focus the voluntaristic elements of the society. Then there is an ethnography of Brazilian soccer, its organization, its relationship to national political systems, and its enactment in the stadium itself. All this is fundamental to developing an empirical base on which . . . analysis can begin. . . .
>
> What is needed is really a genuinely comparative study showing that where sports languish, important elements of the population remain provincial, unimportant, . . .
>
> Also there are lots of questions that this study cannot answer. . . .
>
> These are interesting questions and they can be addressed by future researchers. Ms. Lever has helped set the data base for such questions. It is badly needed in the sociology of sports. I think that it is a splendid accomplishment.

After receiving these letters and talking with Provost Mack, "Weingartner decided not to reverse his decision not to recommend Lever for tenure. . . . Lever then went to Mack and asked him to overrule Weingartner's decision . . . he declined to do so . . . ," according to U.S. Magistrate Weisberg in his decision.

During the pendency of the second review, Lever, at the suggestion of the provost, refrained from taking any formal steps to appeal the original decision not to grant her tenure. When that review was complete, she filed an appeal with the University Faculty Reappointment, Promotions, and Tenure Appeals Panel, or UFRPTAP. An ad hoc hearing panel of five faculty members was chosen to investigate her complaint. The panel, by a vote of 3 to 2, decided against recommending any further reconsideration. The majority of the panel stressed that its jurisdiction was limited to reviewing tenure decisions for violations of academic freedom or inadequacy of consideration. It found that neither had been shown to have taken place in Janet's case. However, the entire panel expressed its uneasiness with the tenure decision and its lack of confidence in its correctness:

> Many details that surfaced during our investigation aroused considerable uneasiness in members of our *ad hoc* committee. We discovered weaknesses not only in the handling of Professor Lever's case but in the system as a whole. . . . Our committee, as well as many we interviewed, agree that a different group of faculty with the same evidence and acting on their best judgment might well have reached a more favorable conclusion. . . . Is it reasonable that the work of a sociologist be judged by those outside the field? Did the clarity and liveliness of her writing prejudice scholars who might expect a heavier, murkier prose in scholarly writing? Do subtle biases result in the conclusion that a writer who appeals to a larger audience must necessarily be "superficial" or "theoretical?" And how much attention ought to be paid to teaching and service in the final decision? UFRPTAP is not the appropriate body to address such issues unless they point to an improper motive for an otherwise proper decision. We cannot make a compelling case that improper biases were operative in the decisions in the Lever case, but we want to draw attention to the highly subjective nature of some of the judgments which in the Lever case may have carried too much weight. . . .
>
> Finally we are not convinced that the Promotions and Tenure Committee paid sufficient attention to evidence about teaching and service. Such neglect may be all too common but that does not excuse it; a system that tells its junior faculty one thing and judges it by quite another standard can only lead to cynicism not only about the tenure process but the University as a whole.[42]

This language is rather remarkable in that the committee, while upholding the decision, is rather forcefully, if indirectly, criticizing the process, the result, and the standards used in Janet's evaluation. Two members of the panel would have gone further and recommended, on the basis of procedural irregularities, that Janet was entitled to a rehearing. In their minority report, they stated that "some of the language and labels used by members of the P/T Committee [PATC] seem inappropriate to a serious discussion of scholarship and could reflect intellectual and/or sexual discrimination."[43]

When her internal appeals were rejected, Janet decided to challenge the denial of tenure in court. She discovered that under the law, she could not get the denial reversed on the grounds that the decision was wrong, or even outrageous. Courts will not review the correctness of tenure decisions made by academic institutions in accordance with traditional procedures. To get the decision denying her tenure set aside, she would have to demonstrate that the decision was discriminatory—that a male candidate with her record would have been awarded tenure.

Janet spent considerable time seeking a lawyer to represent her in a lawsuit against the university. She was turned down by a series of civil rights lawyers, all of whom told her that such cases are extraordinarily difficult to win. Courts are very reluctant to second-guess academic decision makers about issues of scholarly achievement. They are also reluctant to ascribe evil motives to high-level administrators or to committees composed of distinguished academics. Academic defendants are typically able to explain even discriminatory decisions in objective academic terms. In addition, academic officials, for a combination of institutional and personal reasons, often bitterly resent and strongly battle the claim that they were guilty of sex discrimination.

In June of 1981, within six months of the decisions on rereview, Janet filed a complaint alleging sex discrimination with the EEOC. The EEOC declined to bring a complaint for the same reasons that many lawyers rejected the case: it thought it would be very difficult, if not impossible, to win. Nevertheless, the EEOC was sufficiently impressed with the merits of her case to hold on to it for almost two years. Janet was finally able to get legal help from Len Cavise, now an associate professor at De Paul University Law School, then associated with the clinical program at Chicago Kent College of Law. Cavise warned her repeatedly of the tough legal, emotional, and financial aspects of bringing such a suit. Janet, however, was determined. In 1984, four years after the original denial of tenure, Cavise filed a lawsuit on her behalf alleging that the denial of tenure was a violation of federal antidiscrimination law.

For almost a decade afterward, Janet's life was filled with legal battles over discovery, motions, arguments, briefs, and transcripts. Northwestern

Tenure, Peer Review, Excellence, and Injustice

University was represented in this matter by the large, prestigious law firm of Sidley and Austin. They assigned a senior partner, a junior partner, and several associates to the case. They battled Janet and Cavise on almost every issue. Many of the battles were over Cavise's attempts to obtain information concerning the decisional process in Janet's case and about the evaluation of comparable male candidates granted tenure at about the same time. University counsel argued that the process of tenure review must be kept essentially confidential.

University counsel also argued that Janet's suit should be dismissed because she did not file her original charge with the EEOC within six months of Dean Weingartner's original letter denying her tenure. Under the law, a charge must be filed with the EEOC within 180 days of the action complained of, and the original letter was dated May 5, 1980. Janet and Cavise argued that the final decision was not made in her case until the reconsideration was completed and that she didn't file earlier because she did not want to prejudice Weingartner's reconsideration of her candidacy. The federal magistrate agreed that "a person in Lever's position faces a difficult dilemma," but he felt that under an earlier Supreme Court decision in a tenure case, he had no choice but to hold that her original charge was untimely. This decision was issued in June of 1991, eleven years after Janet filed her complaint and twelve years after her colleagues unanimously voted in favor of granting her tenure. The magistrate's decision was affirmed by Judge Ann Williams on October 4, 1991.[44]

Janet has decided to appeal this ruling, which is legally questionable. If she loses the appeal, she will never get a hearing on the merits of her legal claim. If she is successful on appeal and continues with the case, the process will take at least another year and cost thousands of dollars. And there is no assurance that she will prevail.

While the case has been languishing, Janet has fought tenaciously to maintain a position in academic life. She sought a tenure-track position and applied whenever a vacancy arose at any respectable school. She estimates that she filed more than one hundred applications, and for almost a decade she was turned down each time. Some schools rejected her because she was denied tenure at Northwestern; some because they thought her overqualified and unlikely to stay for long. During this period, she accepted a number of temporary non-tenure-track appointments. She has served as a consultant to the Rand Corporation, and she has been a commentator on women and sex for the Playboy Channel. In 1990 she finally received a tenure-track appointment at California State University, Los

Angeles. Her teaching load at Cal State is roughly twice as heavy as that at Northwestern—nine courses a year compared to four. She teaches both day and evening classes. Her students are no longer the academic elite. Many have full-time jobs, and nearly one quarter are immigrants who have difficulty with basic English.

Janet has found adjusting her teaching to conform to the altered needs and expectations of her students to be a difficult task. Fewer students seem to be inspired by the intellectual excitement of sociology, and more are simply trying to get by in order to prepare themselves for a better job in some other field. She has little time for research. Nevertheless, she has continued to enjoy teaching, meeting with students, and taking part in academic discourse. She has taken particular pride in encouraging several shy Asian-American students to participate actively in class.

Janet is a splendid scholar, a devoted academic, a genuine intellectual chance-taker, and a person capable of opening the world of ideas to students. She has the ability to get along with people of all types. She investigates powerful, important issues. Yet she has faced ten years of rejection, strife, and denigration, all in the name of academic excellence. Denial of tenure was a personal tragedy for her, a loss to the students she might otherwise have taught, and a loss to the world of scholarship. Hers is the type of story that, when repeated, corrupts the soul of the academy, pushing untenured scholars toward more esoteric and limited topics and limiting teaching to conventional modes.

The Case of Adrienne Birecree

Adrienne Birecree is a labor economist. She originally planned on a career in international relations, and to gain experience she joined the Peace Corps. While serving in Africa, she was assigned teaching responsibilities. The experience changed her and altered her career goals. As Adrienne explained, "I really liked being up in front of the class, I liked teaching, I liked working with the kids over there, and I guess . . . I had a natural affinity for teaching because I ended up being hired to train new people coming in . . . I felt really good. This was something I did well."

She decided to teach at college rather than high school or grade school because of "the intellectual challenge" and because she thought that social change would most likely come from "discussion and ideas generated in the college classroom."

She was admitted to the Ph.D. program in international economic development at Notre Dame University in Indiana, where she shifted her focus from international development to labor. She decided that labor "is at the heart of the system, and I should be focusing on what is going on domestically in this country first."

The senior professor she worked with was Charles Craypo, who is an old-fashioned, thoughtful institutional labor economist. He is interested in the impact of economic change on working people and labor unions. He encourages his students to do field research rather than focus on complex mathematical analysis and modeling.

Adrienne studied a strike that took place in Clinton, Iowa, during the course of which the company permanently replaced the striking workers. The result of the company's action was the destruction of a community and the decertification of a militant local union. Studying the development of company strategy and its impact on the employees in a case such as this is a difficult and time-consuming process. It is far harder to do and in today's academic climate carries far less prestige than a more mathematically sophisticated study developed from more easily available data. Adrienne was aware of this:

> I knew that case work was not popular but also felt that it was one of the most valuable things I could do and it was becoming a lost art . . . I made the decision knowing that it probably was going to cause trouble, but I really felt that to be true to myself as an intellectual and an academic, I wanted to choose the method I thought best and try to make a valuable contribution . . . I didn't want to just crank out a traditional Ph.D. thesis. I wasn't worried about publishing my thesis because I intended to concentrate on teaching—I wasn't planning on going to a big research institution; that wasn't my orientation.

Before her thesis was completed, she was hired as an assistant professor in economics at Bucknell University. She chose Bucknell over schools such as Skidmore College and Hobart College because "it was part of the tradition of that department" that tenure could be earned by effective teaching and community service.[45]

Initially her experiences at Bucknell lived up to her expectations.[46] Adrienne concentrated on her teaching, did a great deal of community service, and continued to work on her Ph.D. thesis. Her thesis was completed in 1983 and her Ph.D. was awarded in 1984. She worked on scholarly papers deriving from her thesis but gave little thought that either publication of these papers or their presentation in scholarly forums would be necessary for the grant of tenure because many different types of activities were included under "scholarship," according to departmental criteria and past practice.

Her academic evaluations, conducted in 1983 and in 1985, were quite positive. The 1983 review, signed by Robert H. Chambers, then dean of the College of Arts and Sciences, stated, "During your relatively brief time as a member of the Bucknell faculty, you have impressed your colleagues with your energetic teaching, your promising scholarship, and your willingness to serve both your Department and the University beyond the classroom." [47]

The second evaluative report, written in December of 1985, was by a new dean, Larry D. Shinn, who had recently replaced Chambers as dean of the College of Arts. The letter notes that her teaching was highly evaluated both by students and colleagues: "[Y]ou show a 'profound commitment and genuine gift for teaching' which produces a powerful classroom presence in the eyes of the student." The letter was less complimentary about her publication record, but it was far from negative, stating, "We are pleased to know of your future plans to develop aspects of your dissertation research for publication." [48]

The letter was favorable enough that, when Adrienne's husband Dan read it, he said, "They have almost guaranteed you tenure." To Adrienne, the only disturbing note in the second review was a request to demonstrate how "your fine professional contributions to public agencies" (consulting with the Interfaith Council on Crisis in Appalachia) "relate to creative contributions in the field of economics." She attributed this request to the new dean, Larry Shinn, who she said "was clearly coming in and going to up the ante for publications at the university."

It was soon clear to her that Dean Shinn meant to change the focus of the university from teaching and community service to research: "I sat in a meeting with him at which he was constantly talking about deadwood. At one point in this meeting I turned to him and said: 'You know, some of the deadwood you are talking about includes people that were the most outstanding teachers I have ever had. It really bothers me that you are describing them this way.'"

During the time Adrienne was at Bucknell, there were two strikes in the region by locals of the United Paperworkers International Union (UPIU) against International Paper Company. In each case, the company sought to replace the striking workers by hiring permanent replacements ("scabs," in labor union slang). The strikes involved issues similar to those of the strike that she studied for her Ph.D. thesis. The second strike by the Lock Haven local was part of a major four-unit strike that has since been studied by various academic scholars.[49] Adrienne became involved first as a scholar and then as a supporter of the union. She was instrumental in forming Friends of Labor, a group of faculty and students that supported the union through money, advice, and speeches at union rallies. In 1987 she presented a paper on the strike she had studied to the faculty. After her presentation, she was criticized by the president of Bucknell, who felt that she was much too supportive of the union.

Before Adrienne was considered for tenure in 1987, the university-wide review committee, which passed on tenure recommendations by the departments, was changed. According to Adrienne, the committee was made more conservative by faculty vote and it was instructed by the dean to be more critical of scholarship in making its tenure decisions. As Adrienne said:

> When you get new administrators, they've got to put their mark on the damn place. It's never good enough. One of the things I felt the dean was trying to do was centralize his control over the departments that were under his jurisdiction. We vigorously fought that in our department.
>
> One afternoon after one of our meetings, when we had gotten an irritating memo from the dean asking us to explain something that we thought was none of his business, a member of the department marched over to the dean's office at 5:00 P.M., walked right past the secretary, looked the dean right in the eye, and screamed, "Get the fuck off our backs!"

By the time she came up for tenure, Adrienne, who had served on the university's Committee on Academic Freedom and Tenure (CAFT) that was examining the operations of the University Review Committee (URC), was nervous that she would be turned down as a way of disciplining the economics department, which, as she expected, had voted unanimously to grant her tenure. The two papers she had been advised to move forward with had been completed. They were sent out by her departmental review committee to labor scholars at major research institutions. According to Adrienne: "The reviews were fine" in terms of the quality of her research, but they were sent to professors at institutions that had traditionally required more scholarly output than Bucknell, so when the reviewers were asked if her work would qualify for tenure at their institutions, some commented that she would have to do more work unrelated to her thesis.

A short time later Adrienne received a short letter from the chairman of the URC informing her that her scholarship had been found inadequate: "Your work to date does not provide evidence of the mature scholarship commonly achieved by Bucknell faculty at their sixth year tenure review."[50] The letter was filled with generalities about the importance of scholarship but contained little to explain how Adrienne fell short, other than in her failure to go beyond the articles growing out of her Ph.D. thesis and her failure to present scholarly papers at professional meetings.

Shortly thereafter, the dean wrote and informed her that, because of the committee's decision, she was denied tenure and would not be renewed. Her own explanation parallels the discussion earlier in this chapter about the failures of peer review: "I think that what happened was that the new administration planned to change the whole way that Bucknell dealt with tenure. I was vulnerable because they changed the standards for tenure six months before my tenure decision . . . I had many people tell me two and three years before that, based on my teaching, I wouldn't even have to publish a word to be tenured."

Adrienne's students and colleagues were outraged. A petition protesting the denial was signed by fifteen hundred students. The signatures were collected "in 10 hours over three days."[51] Many of her colleagues urged her to battle the decision, and she and Janet Seiz, a woman denied contract renewal by the same committee, filed complaints with CAFT. Adrienne's complaint alleged sex discrimination, violations of academic freedom (for prejudice against the field of labor economics and her prounion positions), the application of arbitrary and unfair standards, prejudice as well as improper involvement by Dean Shinn, and lack of adequate notice, in that in her fourth-year review "I had been told to do one thing and then [was] evaluated with totally different criteria." The committee proceeded to investigate the complaint. It rejected the charges of sex discrimination and concluded that Adrienne's academic freedom had not been violated and that Dean Shinn had not behaved inappropriately. Nevertheless, it came to the conclusion that, because of the disparity between the standards conveyed to Adrienne and those actually applied, she had been denied academic due process: "It is clear from the evidence that some members of the URC required scholarship beyond the two publications arising from the dissertation as a condition for tenure. This position is contrary to the contents of the 4th year review letter." The committee also found other procedural irregularities. It came to the same conclusion with regard to her friend and colleague, Janet Seiz. As a remedy, the committee "unanimously and respectfully" recommended that "the URC reconsider Prof. Birecree's tenure review."[52] The URC agreed to reconsider. Adrienne was asked to submit and then submitted new material. Four months after the resubmission, the URC issued its second opinion, essentially resting its conclusion on the same grounds. They also reaffirmed their decision with respect to Janet Seiz. Both decisions were appealed once more to CAFT, and once more that committee concluded that the applicants were denied fair procedure in the review process. According to Adrienne: "CAFT called for a new committee to be formed. So it became a battle between the Committee on Academic Freedom and Tenure and the University Review Committee, two of the most powerful committees in the university. People were now putting their careers on the line . . . CAFT was not very popular with the administration and some people on the URC, and some elements in the university community said that CAFT was now stepping beyond its bounds."

Inevitably the issue, which was widely reported, split the faculty. Rumors and information leaks were all over the campus. Those who supported Adrienne, Janet, and CAFT saw the issue in terms of fair procedures, the importance of teaching, and the need to combat unconscious sexist attitudes. Those who supported the review committee and the administration saw it in terms of the university's commitment to scholarly excellence and the need to hold women scholars to the same exacting standards as men. There is little doubt that the turmoil affected the junior faculty. According to Adrienne:

That's when teaching became less important and everybody started concentrating on scholarship . . . It changed the whole tenor of the place. [The administration] then introduced junior leave before tenure. Junior faculty now get a whole semester off to work on scholarship.

The students started complaining that you couldn't find any of the junior people. This decision changed the whole tenor of Bucknell, that is what it was supposed to do. Just to give you an example, I taught in a program that was called Freshman Humanities Semester. It was for first semester freshmen who were very gifted. . . . We team taught and discussed various critical thinking issues. The students talked a lot, read a lot, and wrote a lot. . . . I had taught two years in this program and had received complimentary letters from the people who had founded this program. It had been in existence somewhere from thirteen to fifteen years. Well, after our case they couldn't recruit any junior people to teach in it and it went under within a year. It's gone now permanently from the curriculum. What these guys were up to was changing the focus of the university from liberal arts education to cranking out publications, all in the name of academic excellence.

The Relationship of Faculty to Academic Institutions

The atmosphere became so charged that Adrienne determined to leave. She joined the faculty at Radford University, near Roanoke, Virginia, and a year later negotiated a settlement of her academic-freedom claim with the university. Despite carrying a much heavier teaching load, Adrienne is now more committed to scholarship and somewhat less to teaching. She has done excellent scholarly work, continuing her studies, begun at Bucknell, of the strike by the United Paperworkers International Union against International Paper Company. She said:

> I get almost obsessed about writing now. Part of it is because a lot of people assumed at Bucknell that I did so much service work, curriculum work, and teaching because I couldn't do research. That really pissed me off because I thought we had to make some very difficult decisions. You make decisions about how to use your time and the things you choose to do. When I first started, I had a commitment to Bucknell. It was the institution that trained me and I was committed to education. I used my time in certain ways and stood for certain values, but it wasn't because I was incompetent and couldn't write. What has stuck with me is this urge to disprove the critics, to show that if I put the same amount of energy into writing that I put into other things, I'm a better scholar than most of them.[53]

Adrienne's current excellent scholarship will undoubtedly bring her opportunities to move to more prestigious institutions and do more sophisticated research. But she will never have the academic life she first sought, and she will never again have the same attitudes toward academic institutions:

> I'm not as naïve as I was before and I no longer believe academic institutions are bastions for pursuing truth. They are very nasty political cauldrons and a lot of bullshit passes for scholarship. No matter how hard you work, if there is someone out there who doesn't like you, is threatened, or offended by you, they use excellence to get to you.
>
> I don't really trust anybody in academia. I'm much more cautious than I was because I have seen what can happen. Academic institutions are among the nastiest places you can work.
>
> Sometimes when people are bright, that makes them even nastier. They attempt to destroy people's lives—and that's the side of academia that I didn't see as a student—people meddling in other people's lives and trying to hurt them. . . . There were some older faculty who said, "What could these women have possibly done to have deserved this treatment?"

I must have been threatening to people since they went to that much trouble to get me out of there. There had to be an agenda. I think they wanted to get our department under control. The department was the real target, but Janet and I represented it. We were the type of people that they didn't want on that campus. They wanted people who don't cause trouble, who defer to authority, and who work within the bounds that they define—people who defer to authority. I don't think either one of us was good at that; I wasn't.

Academic Injustice and Elitism

Taken together, these two cases tell us much about academic injustice and also about its relationship to elitism.

To a considerable extent, the victims of academic injustice are selected accidentally. Janet Lever and Adrienne Birecree had the bad fortune to be candidates for tenure at times when academic standards were changing and at places where the administration sought to give a message to the faculty that publication (particularly esoteric academic publication) would count more and teaching less. Had they come up for tenure earlier, each would almost certainly have received it. Each had a record far more impressive in terms of the standards that had traditionally been applied than most of their tenured colleagues. In each case, they were a small part of a larger battle within the university of department against central administration. In each case, their real contributions were undervalued because they were directed to the wrong people. Janet's writing was directed to the general literate public and not primarily to sociologists. Adrienne was interested in helping and working on issues of interest to working people.

Yet they were not simply randomly selected victims. The fact that they are women was not irrelevant. Both came up for tenure at a time when many faculty were determined to show that the recruitment of women would not lead to a diminution of traditional standards. Thus, they, like many women denied tenure at that time, were victims of unconscious but powerful sexism. More significantly, each posed a challenge to elitist values. Janet's choice of topic, her prose style, her dress, and her speech were and remain nonelitist. Even the fact that her scholarship concerning soccer was begun long before she acquired the professional tools of sociology undoubtedly hurt her. Much about the formation and carrying out of her research suggested that a person did not have to be specially trained to do effective scholarship.

Adrienne overtly eschewed the fashionable elitist aspects of labor economics. She was less interested in demonstrating the relevance of sophisticated econometric analysis than in probing the current state of labor-management relations from the perspective of someone sympathetic to labor. Even more significantly, she deliberately rejected the life-style associated with professional success for both liberal and conservative academics. She chose to teach union members rather than present papers. She was more interested in working on real economic problems than in publishing articles about them.

Most ominously, each was deemed a threat to institutional advancement in the great hierarchy of American higher education at a time when the administrations of their schools were determined to make a push for such advancement. Each case demonstrates that the processes for remedying academic injustice are inadequate even when the procedures utilized and available are entirely consistent with AAUP standards. In each case, the committee—although bothered by the possibility of sex discrimination—lacked the resources and the technical expertise to investigate the issue fully. In each case, the faculty review committee was notably reluctant to conclude that senior colleagues and administrators were guilty of bad faith or prejudice. Each case also is a reminder of how often injustice in academic institutions is perpetrated in the name of excellence.

Almost all cases of academic injustice involve instigators and supporters. Instigators, those who lead in making the case against the person being evaluated, tend to be motivated by the same base and ignoble impulses that exist everywhere in the world. However, like other academics, instigators pride themselves on being fair, rational, and humanistic. Commitment to excellence offers a way for them to rationalize their hostility and clothe it in the colors of nobility. Because standards for performance are so difficult to define and because great schools always can recruit able people, the temptations and opportunities to act on the basis of such feelings are unusually great. Claiming to act on the basis of academic standards provides a way of dealing with people harshly—without recognizing that one's baser motives are at work.

Those who support, as opposed to those who instigate, academic injustice frequently do so with great personal reluctance. They generally become convinced that they are acting on behalf of supervening academic virtues, such as rigor, scholarship, or artistic achievement. One of the saddest features of academic life is that commitment to excellence frequently causes professors to reject their own best values, such as intellectual understanding, modesty, and appreciation of variety.

The term *excellence* is so often used to support injustice that I have come to have an almost visceral negative reaction to its use. Yet I am foolish to disclaim excellence: academic excellence is once again fashionable. There is great national desire to achieve it. All polls show that the public strongly supports academic excellence, and, to achieve it, many would even be willing to pay higher taxes. Anyone interested in improving higher education would be foolish to reject or deny the concept. Unfortunately, many cases of academic injustice are aspects of a continuing struggle between competing visions of excellence. The important task is to define academic excellence in such a way as to focus on substance and learning rather than style, pretense, and the imposition of unrealistically high standards.

FOUR

The Struggle
for Change

The Legacy of the 1960s

Colleges and universities are at all times subject to pressure, either to change or to resist change. Such pressure comes from students, legislators, voters, minority groups, foundations, alumni, faculty organizations, employee unions, and scholarly movements. The conflicting vectors of all these forces and the complex decision-making processes that govern universities mean that permanent change comes rarely, and profound change even more rarely. During my time in academic life, significant pressure for change has come from radical students in the 1960s, faculty in the 1980s and 1990s, civil rights groups, and feminists. Workers and unions have the potential to influence higher education, but they have not done so to any significant extent. Conservative groups—political, religious, and academic—often take part in struggles over the nature of academic institutions, but they are rarely the ones seeking fundamental change. They are, rather, typically in the position of resisting change or of seeking to remove those who advocate it.

Change is generally sought in the name of egalitarian values, such as opening up the academy to those who have traditionally been excluded, and resisted in the name of elitist values, excellence, tradition, and cultural literacy. Nevertheless, groups seeking change are likely to contain elitist values and messages, while those opposing change often rest their claims on consistency with general nonelitist societal values.

The Rise of the Student Movement

At times, university campuses are strangely insulated from the important issues and momentous events of the outside world. The mid-1950s to the mid-1960s, when I first entered teaching, was such a period; the great civil rights struggles in the South and the start of the feminist ferment were barely echoed on most campuses. Students were involved in their personal careers, and faculty and administrators devoted themselves to issues of academic, rather than societal, significance. The metaphor of the ivory tower seemed apt.

In the late 1960s, this calm situation changed very quickly under the pressure of the Vietnam War, the assassinations of Robert Kennedy and Martin Luther King, and the riots in the cities. Indiana University was typical. Before 1967, when I left for India, the campus was serene and nonpolitical, students strolled down the tree-shaded walks and tossed frisbees in the large, open fields. When I returned, all this was changed. The students at I.U. altered their dress, manner, and outlook, becoming more intense, increasingly political, and sometimes violent. Left-wing and anti-war groups were active, leafleting, protesting, and organizing. Political banners hung from many of the dorms and rooming houses near campus: "End the Draft" and "One, two, three, four—we don't want your fucking war." There were teach-ins, sit-ins, rallies, marches in which the Viet Cong flag was carried, and frequent confrontations between students and university officials. Bloomington came to increasingly resemble the Greenwich Village of my youth in mood, dress, and morals. Marijuana was smoked openly. Outdoor bulletin boards advertised "Acid Available," and bearded student speakers talked of armed revolution. The male students wore their hair long and the female students let theirs hang loose. Many female students went braless. The language of the campus more and more self-consciously echoed the slang of the inner city.

The sudden eruption of political activism was accompanied by student demands for academic reform. This movement had three major goals: relevance, which meant that courses should address, in a committed fashion, the great social issues that the society was facing; student power, which meant a major role for students, comparable to that of faculty in the process of academic governance; and an amorphous antielitist tenant vaguely built around the slogan "Power to the People." This meant adopting a less elegant style in discourse, writing, and appearance, in each case making these aspects of life-style less esoteric, formal, and genteel, and more direct, open, and egalitarian.

The Desire for Relevance

As students became more political in the 1960s and early 1970s, they simultaneously began to express discontent with the academic curriculum and traditional teaching methods. They argued that the method of instruction was too hierarchical and that the curriculum was too technical, limited, and removed. The times presented great issues: the war, the draft, the civil rights movement, feminism, and the various inequities with which American society was filled. Very few courses dealt with these issues directly, and those that were relevant in terms of subject matter, such as political science or moral philosophy, were removed in content and tone. Through petition, demonstration, discussion, and resolution, the students manifested their desire for courses addressed to the issues of their times. And they asked that they be taught not with academic distance but with political commitment.

The student demands for relevance coincided with changes in the thinking of many younger academics, myself included. In the late 1960s, we began to be dissatisfied with the narrow professional focus of academic life. I had devoted much effort and emotion to scholarship concerned with technical legal questions: "What was the responsibility of an employer faced with competing recognition claims from two unions?" or "How did Sections 8(a)(1) and (3) of the National Labor Relations Act differ, and what was the reach of protected activity under Section 7?" Implied in these issues were questions of policy and fairness, but they were so remote from the passion-provoking causes of the day that I felt professionally removed and useless at a time when social commitment was called for. My teaching was similarly directed to developing legal competence but not social or political awareness. Many professors felt as I did. As a result, courses in street poetry, poverty law, and protest and social change were instituted on many campuses. Whole new fields—black studies, women's studies, and clinical legal education—were organized; new materials dealing with current issues were added to many traditional courses. The period was one of great agitation, experimentation, and exploitation of the desire for change.

This period of change was followed by one of retreat, but the basic issues of curriculum and pedagogy have continued to arise and have led to an important debate about the nature of academic institutions. In the past few years in particular, as a significant number of young academics who were once part of the student movement in the 1960s and 1970s have gotten tenure, similar curricular issues have arisen.

Two polar positions may be described. Those whom I call "traditionalists" believe that the function of teaching is to make students aware of conclusions reached and approaches taken by academic specialists—they seek to convey generally agreed-to disciplinary conclusions. Those whom

I call "activists" believe that the main function of teaching is to arouse the students' interests in important social, political, and moral issues and to give them a new perspective for addressing these issues. The traditionalists argue that it is improper for the professor to intrude his or her own political values into the classroom. They believe that we are given the podium and the ability to grade students not because we are politically astute but because we are knowledgeable about scholarly issues. Accordingly, they argue, we should discipline ourselves and limit our pedagogy to those matters about which we have recognized academic expertise. Traditionalists who teach courses about the political system will often take pride in the fact that students cannot tell whether they are Democrats or Republicans. Activists believe that this position is itself political because it makes academics apologists for the status quo, either directly or indirectly. They also argue that political indoctrination is inevitable and more insidious and difficult to deal with when the professor is not up-front about his or her ideas.

The debate between these contending positions has arisen on almost every campus. And, although no one believes solely in either position, the debate between the rival camps has recently become quite heated.

The Current Debate: Pressures for and Resistance to Change

From the mid-1970s to the mid-1980s, many of the changes and many of the new courses developed in the name of relevance disappeared. This was inevitable. The forces resisting change and the difficulties involved in developing new courses were both far greater than the proponents of academic reform recognized during the heyday of the initial student movement. One problem that made curricular reform difficult to achieve was the lack of materials for the new courses. Preparing texts to adequately explain such phenomena as the war in Vietnam and the impact of the civil rights movement was no easy matter. Instructors competent to teach such courses had to be located. In general, the more innovative a course, the more difficult it is to teach. By definition, no pedagogic models exist for teaching conceptually new courses, and new generalized themes will not yet be recognized or referred to in the literature on the subject. Pedagogic competence cannot be achieved solely by commitment. Except in the most unusual cases, developing a new course around a current theme requires study and time. As a result, by the time the course is intellectually coherent, interesting teaching materials are developed, themes are identified, and faculty are recruited or trained, the issues may no longer be vital.

The Struggle for Change

In addition to the logistical problems involved in developing new courses, powerful resistance to the idea that academic institutions should adopt a socially conscious or politically oriented agenda has always existed. Those who favored the overt politicizing of the academy have been at all times a minority among faculty and a smaller minority among administrators. In addition, the movement for relevance led by the students in the 1960s had the effect of involving many conservative nonstudent groups in academic issues. Parents, alumni, and politicians suddenly began to inundate administrators with questions, suggestions, and criticisms. Trustees and regents who had previously been content to remain removed from the day-to-day operations of the university began to play a more active role. Mainly composed of lawyers, politicians and business executives, these boards typically have legal authority to make important decisions. Once they undertook to exercise this power to any extent, and they did so in the early 1970s, they asserted a largely conservative voice echoing the concerns of parents and the general public. Thus, the struggle for relevance had the curious aspect that those who marched under the egalitarian banner of social commitment were the academically privileged, while those who argued for maintaining the traditional elitist nature of the academy did so in the name of ordinary citizens whose support they generally had.

The large body of conservative faculty who bitterly opposed many of the more radical ideas then fashionable also became increasingly active in the 1960s. And the idea of pushing universities toward social relevance made many liberals uneasy. Academic-freedom traditionalists, civil libertarians, and non-movement-oriented liberals all feared that a new academic orthodoxy might be developed, that faculty who taught relevant courses would be expected to be committed to politically acceptable points of view. Those who remembered the McCarthy period and the struggle to insulate universities from political scrutiny became alarmed that their hard-won victories would be lost by the political naïveté and academic intolerance of the students and their allies.

Thus during the 1970s and 1980s the forces seeking relevance were resisted and limited by fear of politicalization and the administrative and academic problems that make institutionalized change difficult to achieve. But the movement for relevance was itself a response to powerful forces and ideas. For example, the position that academic institutions should oppose the war and take greater steps to promote racial justice was bolstered by the widespread desire of faculty not to emulate the distinguished German academics who continued to pursue their elite academic agendas before and after Hitler came to power. The activist impulse was also bolstered by the desire of some to curry favor or ally themselves with the activist students who seemed to give power to intellectuality, even as they proclaimed that it "came from the barrel of a gun." Most significantly, the desire for change was abetted by the hope of many that, by pursuing more vital topics, the passion and intellectual abilities of the nonengaged students might be diverted from parties, sex, and athletics to learning and thinking.

Considerable ebb and flow has taken place with respect to curricular change during a relatively brief time span. The early 1970s were a period of change, the late 1970s and early 1980s a period of retrenchment. Nevertheless, during the past two decades many courses dealing with contemporary issues and nontraditional cultures have been added to the curriculum of most schools. Courses on civil rights, feminism, and gay and lesbian concerns have been added; they have helped to spark scholarship in all of these areas. They have been added partly in response to student pressure but primarily to meet the interests of younger faculty, in accordance with the custom of permitting faculty a degree of choice about their teaching responsibilities. In the main, these courses have been added as seminars and upper-year electives and have remained peripheral. The core curriculum has continued to be more traditional, less political, and less concerned with change than with carrying on the Anglo-European culture.

In recent years, many schools have been pressured to change the core curriculum. The claim for reform, although similar to that of the student movement, is no longer made in the name of relevance. The current claim is that the curriculum should better reflect the contributions of the varied groups that make up American society; the concept underlying this claim is known as multiculturalism.

Multiculturalism is not easily defined. It means teaching students to appreciate differences, but it also means "enlarging the canon" by adding to the literature in any field the contributions, concerns, and voices of historically excluded groups. For these purposes, it is not clear whose works and whose voices suffice. A writer like Jane Austen might not be thought sufficiently feminist or alienated or unappreciated to count, because her subject matter is traditional, her attitudes arguably conventional, her style classic, and her abilities long recognized. It should be noted that no single multicultural position exists and views differ among its adherents about what is required for a course to be a multicultural offering. In the 1960s and 1970s, similar disagreements took place about relevance.

No correlation necessarily exists between the professors' own political views and their views on the question of curricular change and classroom activism. Indeed, as already noted, the traditionalists cover a broad spectrum on almost any campus and are likely to include many of the older academic-freedom activists. Nevertheless, those arguing for engagement and particularly those who claim to be multiculturalists tend to be on the political left. Often, but not always, they are younger professors who were activists in the 1960s in the civil rights, antiwar, or feminist movements. They find political engagement stimulating and they miss the sense of intellectual excitement and change that marked the period. Their current emphasis, both academic and political, puts them at odds with traditional liberal academics because it focuses on the rights of groups rather than the rights of individuals. Current political activists on the left are particularly concerned that academic discourse be opened up so that the voices of groups once excluded—women, minorities, gays, and third-world scholars and writers—be heard. They argue that those once silenced or ignored have something special to offer to the understanding of current issues—an approach and a point of view unlikely to come from the white males who have dominated both the society and academia since the beginning. They also argue that hearing their voices will instill pride in women and minority students and reduce prejudice and arrogance among white males. Not coincidentally, the rise of multiculturalism has coincided with the increasing political importance of the formerly excluded groups. Thus, in a state like Texas, multiculturalism has to be taken seriously because it reflects the new political reality. In general, the multiculturalists have a more limited view of the concept of free speech than do traditional civil libertarians. Many of the multiculturalists argue that words can be used to assault, and that personal attacks based on race, religion, gender, and sexual orientations should be outlawed. On many campuses, movements to develop antiharassment codes have sprung up. And carefully worded efforts to limit harassment while protecting free speech have been put into effect at a number of well-known universities.

The current struggle between committed activists and traditionalists has been exemplified by the controversy that erupted at the University of Texas about the teaching of composition.

English 306 is the one required course in composition at the University of Texas. Roughly 60 percent of the students in any class (about three thousand students in all) end up taking it. It is taught almost entirely by graduate-student teaching assistants in sections of twenty-five to thirty students. The graduate students are under the general direction of a faculty committee known as the Lower Division English Policy Committee, or the LDEPC, whose chair is the director of the program and the chief administrator of the course.

The course had provoked unhappiness for some time. The faculty involved felt that the students were not learning enough. The students complained about the variation in approach from section to section.

In 1988, Professor Linda Brodkey was hired from the University of Pennsylvania and subsequently appointed as director of the program in the spring of 1989. It was understood that she, working together with the LDEPC, would change the course in an effort to make it more uniform and effective.

Brodkey is both a distinguished academic and a child of the 1960s, during which period many of her social and political attitudes were formed. She is proud of the fact that she was brought up in a working-class home in western Illinois, and also that through her early experiences in school she was able to overcome the racial prejudice that was accepted as a matter of course by her family and early friends. Partly because she had to deal with them while growing up, questions of race, prejudice, and group differences are very important to her. She thinks of them as the type of issues that "each generation must confront for itself without accepting the answers that came from previous generations." By this, she means that the concept of color-blindness, which was important to her and her generation, is not adequate to resolve current issues. She is also serious about teaching composition and rhetoric. She has been academically successful since childhood. School has always been the place where she has felt most comfortable and successful. She is a multiculturist but is also convinced of the importance of academic excellence and the value of theoretical understanding.

When she first came to the University of Texas, Brodkey spent much time talking with former course instructors about English 306. She learned that writing about gender differences and racial issues was not uncommon and that student attitudes varied widely. This was not surprising to her. The student body at the University of Texas reflects the growing diversity of the state. It contains substantial numbers of affluent students, mostly (but not entirely) white; it also contains poor whites, Chicanos, blacks, and women of all groups—poor and wealthy, white and of color. Brodkey was also told by the former instructors that much of the writing about race and gender was badly uninformed. Many of the instructors felt uncomfortable with and unqualified to deal with such issues on the merits. Several highly publicized racist issues on campus also brought questions of race and ethnicity to the fore. Brodkey saw in all of this an opportunity

The Struggle for Change

both to revitalize the course and to make a contribution to mutual understanding among the varied groups that make up the University of Texas student body.

In the fall semester of 1989, she proposed that the English 306 course focus on issues of difference and that it employ judicial opinions as examples of legitimate arguments about race and racial preference. Brodkey had become fascinated by the style and force of legal debate on controversial issues while she was at the University of Pennsylvania, where she took part in a seminar on race and the law organized by the writer Houston Baker and Regina Austin (see Chapter 2 on teaching). The course Brodkey proposed was much broader than the Penn seminar because it dealt with various forms of difference, including gender, sexual orientation, national origin, and class as well as race. No existing text or set of materials was available for such an approach to teaching rhetoric and composition. When she arrived at the University of Texas, Brodkey undertook, with assistance from Patricia Cain, a professor at the University of Texas Law School, Ralph Smith, at the University of Pennsylvania Law School, and some knowledgeable lawyers, to organize materials for the course. The materials that she developed included a traditional writing handbook co-authored by two department members who would become public opponents of the course,[1] a packet of court opinions, and a text by Paula S. Rothenberg containing materials about the economic, social, and political effects of racism and other forms of prejudice.[2] Brodkey also proposed and offered to conduct a special training session for the instructors who would be teaching the material. Both the basic concept and the materials chosen were approved initially by the LDEPC by a vote of 4 to 0 with one abstention. A member of the committee, Professor John Ruszkiewicz, failed to attend the meeting but informed Brodkey that he was opposed to the new course, and a second meeting was held to permit him to voice his objections. The committee then voted 4 to 2 in favor of the proposal. Brodkey did not vote. The committee reported its decision to the English faculty in May of 1990. In her memo to the faculty explaining the new course, Brodkey concentrated on its suitability for teaching about writing and argumentation—not about its value in improving race relations:

> The revised E 306 curriculum makes it possible to generate the kinds of discussions, research, and critical activities that support young writers who are learning how to construct academically responsible arguments on controversial topics that profoundly affect us all. My own experience with undergraduates here and elsewhere, as well as with the graduate students who teach E 306, has convinced me that:

The Legacy of the 1960s

1) many students introduce issues associated with "difference" into their discussions and essays even though it has not been the official topic, and

2) many instructors would like the topic institutionalized, thereby authorizing the discussion of the topic and specifying the rights and responsibilities of students and teachers.

The rights and responsibilities of teachers and students are serious matters in all classrooms. These and other related issues concerning pedagogy will be addressed in our summer-long deliberations and work on the syllabus for E 306 and they will play a large part in the summer orientation for the AIs [assistant instructors] who will be teaching E 306 in Fall 1990.

We are anticipating difficulties, but because we see them in the light of writing curriculum and pedagogy our concerns are not whether to teach the topic of difference, but how best to teach a college-level writing course.[3]

The departmental meeting was held on May 8, 1990. Members of the department who were present report that although there was vocal opposition, it was largely confined to a few members and that there was general enthusiasm for the proposed course. According to an article in *Texas Academe* by Professor Alan Friedman, a member of the English department and former president of the University of Texas Faculty Senate:

The Committee stressed several points: that the current version was not working well; that the revision in no way altered the curricular goals of E.306; that a support system would be available to assist the teachers of the course; that faculty teaching the course would remain, as they had always been, free to create their own versions; and that graduate students, after they had taught the course once, would be encouraged to create their own variations on the standard syllabus. After extensive and open discussion, it was clear that a large majority of the faculty present felt that the LDEPC was acting within its provenance and according to its charge. As at all such meetings in the past, no motion was offered, no vote was taken, and tacit endorsement of the Committee's action resulted.[4]

The decision to go forward with the course received a great deal of publicity. Standish Meacham, Jr., the dean of the College of Liberal Arts, was particularly enthusiastic, describing the course as a positive response from the university to the problem of racism on campus, a problem that had received considerable publicity because of a few ugly racist incidents.

Neither the dean's enthusiasm nor the department's "tacit endorsement," however, was sufficient to insulate the course from the furor that developed almost immediately thereafter.

Friedman described that "shortly after that meeting, four or five English department opponents of the course revisions, having lost the argument within the academic forum, launched a media and letter-writing campaign (aimed at students, parents, and influential alumnae, among others) attacking the large majority of the Department in highly charged language. In a series of articles, advertisements, and media appearances, proponents were accused of being radical, ideological, biased, propagandistic, intolerant of alternative viewpoints, antithetical to academic freedom and free inquiry . . ."[5]

Friedman's description of the attack on the proposed changes was, if anything, understated. Almost as soon as the course was announced, it became a lightning rod for criticism from a variety of sources who saw in it an example of the dangers of multiculturalism. A conservative group, the National Association of Scholars, and its Texas affiliate placed an ad in the *Daily Texan*, the University of Texas' student newspaper, attacking the concept of multiculturalism and urging the rejection of "proposals being so rapidly brought . . . to change the curriculum in the name of pluralism."[6] A member of the philosophy department stated publicly that the course should more properly be called "Marxism 306."[7] Alan Gribben, a leading opponent of the course, urged, in a letter to a member of the University of Texas Liberal Arts Foundation Council that was published in the *Daily Texan*, that "our problems are so profound and likely to be longlasting that the English department should be placed in receivership indefinitely with someone like Donald Foss (chairman of the Psychology Department) as its director for several years . . ."[8] The proposed course was attacked by William Murchison in the *Dallas Morning News* in a series of columns. George Will wrote a nationally syndicated article specifically attacking the proposed version of E 306 as "political indoctrination." He described the controversy as typical of "skirmishes in the curriculum wars" that "occur because campuses have become refuges for radicals who want universities to be as thoroughly politicized as they are." He referred to the arguments of those favoring the proposed changes as "broken records stashed in the nation's attic in 1968." He went on to attack the concept of multiculturalism and the rise of antiharassment codes associated with it: "These moral tutors have a professional interest in the exacerbation of group tension, to which university administrators contribute by allowing, even encouraging, the Balkanization of campus life. This is done by encouraging group identities—black dorms, women's centers, gay studies, etc." [9]

More moderate attacks on the course were made by those who felt that the instructors would not be able to teach writing adequately while focusing on such complex and highly charged issues. A moderate opponent of the course, Maxine Hairston, herself a well-regarded writing teacher in the University of Texas English department, wrote an article for the *Chronicle of Higher Education* in which she stated:

> We do not believe required writing courses built around politically charged social issues can achieve the goals I've outlined for students learning to write. One reason is that we know students develop best as writers when they are allowed to write on something they care about. Having them write about other people's ideas doesn't work well.
>
> Another reason these courses will fail is that most freshmen enter composition courses with great apprehension about grades. Convinced that they are in a high-risk situation, they are reluctant to take risks. They will be especially reluctant to express their opinions on controversial issues, particularly if their radars are picking up clear signals about what their instructors' views are. Under such circumstances, they will not think critically or write honestly. [10]

The *Daily Texan* ran several articles on the controversy that gave wide circulation to angry attacks on the course by its most passionate opponent, Professor Alan Gribben. [11] Proponents of the course responded with articles accusing its opponents of censorship and political repression. [12]

Even the favorable publicity that the course received had a negative aspect. Many faculty members and others believed that it had been developed primarily to cope with campus racism. It thus appeared to be essentially an effort to indoctrinate. Several of us concluded, based on the public announcements, that the English department intended to use the judicial opinions not to instruct in writing but to preach about diversity. On the other hand, I was told that faculty members in the sociology department resented the publicity that the new course received. They thought it undeserved, since the sociology department had never received similar publicity for any of the many courses dealing with race that it offered.

Much of the early criticism focused on the use of the book *Racism and Sexism*, by Paula S. Rothenberg, as a required text. [13] The book is a collection of materials from different disciplines. It contains short stories, newspaper accounts, autobiographical accounts, scholarly writing, and a fair amount of legal material, including descriptions of leading cases and excerpts from statutes. Because the course was prepared by whites and would mainly be taught by whites, Brodkey said that she wanted a book that contained the viewpoints and the voices of people of color, and the Rothenberg book did that, albeit to a limited extent.

The materials contained in the book are uneven in quality. Many of the stories are moving and much of the social science material is provocative, but the materials seem chosen to present a single point of view: women and people of color as innocent victims, white males as oppressors. Much, but not all, of what is wrong with the book is illustrated by the definition of "racism" that the author claimed to derive from a series of statements contained elsewhere in the book: "1. Racism involves the subordination of people of color by white people. While an individual person of color may discriminate against white people or even hate them, his or her behavior or attitude cannot be called 'racist' . . . racism . . . requires prejudice plus power. The history of the world provides us with a long record of white people holding power and using it to maintain that power and privilege over people of color, not the reverse." [14]

This definition is elitist in that it rejects the commonly understood definition of the term, factually in error in ignoring situations in which people of color have used their power over whites, and patronizing or racist in eliminating from the definition of racism all situations involving the subordination of some people of color by other people of color.

Brodkey did not dispute the book's one-sided aspect, but she argued that it had definite advantages in scope and voice and that she thought it would be useful for the students to learn that an official text could be subject to legitimate criticism. In late June, as criticism mounted, the Rothenberg book was dropped and replaced by a packet of materials that consisted mainly of articles by well-recognized legal scholars. The change did little to silence the critics of the course. The controversy continued, exacerbated by a story published in *Texas Monthly* that was critical of the English department on a variety of grounds and that described a department party at which the guests were invited to "bring something Texan that you wanted to burn." The article by Gregory Curtis quotes "a conservative professor" as calling the party "a kind of victory celebration" for radical professors, "most often specifically Marxist" faculty, in the battle over multiculturalism. [15]

There is little doubt that such a party took place and that it was sponsored quite openly by some members of the English department faculty. Brodkey did not attend the party. She described it to me as "a rich kid's game." In July of 1990, the dean of the College of Liberal Arts announced that the new course that he had previously supported so enthusiastically would be postponed. Dean Meacham simultaneously stated, "I will continue to support strongly, as I have during the past months, the concept of English 306 as a writing and rhetoric course with a unified curriculum centered on the themes of diversity and difference—an idea which I believe to be imaginative and exciting . . ." Meacham added that he had discussed the matter with University of Texas executive vice president and provost Gerhard Fonken and University of Texas president William Cunningham and that he "[has] the assurance of the administration that they support the revised course as well."[16] It is not disputed that Meacham made his announcement shortly after meeting with University of Texas President William Cunningham and Provost Gerhard Fonken. President Cunningham stated that Meacham "made the decision." However, he declined to discuss the content of his meeting with Meacham, and he acknowledged writing a letter to a Dallas woman on July 11, 1990, almost two weeks before Meacham's announcement in which he stated that "after careful consideration the department has decided that the course will not be modified this fall." President Cunningham later claimed that the letter was intended to refer only to the decision not to use the Rothenberg text. Under all of these circumstances, however, it is difficult to dispute the assertion by Professor Kurt Heinzelman of the English department that "it is inconceivable that Meacham arrived at his decision to suspend E 306 without considerable encouragement from Fonken and Cunningham."[17]

In the fall of 1990, the English department voted 46 to 11 to support the LDEPC; the Association of Graduate Students in English (AGSE), composed largely of those who were to teach the course, voted to support it by a vote of 52 to 2. Despite these votes, William Cunningham, the president of the university, who has had a reputation as a strong backer of affirmative action and who has supported efforts to develop understanding among different groups, refused to meet with the LDEPC and refused the English department the authorization to field-test the course. As a result, the entire LDEPC committee resigned in protest. President Cunningham did not deny his refusal to meet with the committee, stating, "I met on several occasions with Dean Meacham and Chairman [Joseph] Kruppa and I felt that was appropriate . . . I have not seen a syllabus."[18]

The decision by the administration is not at all admirable. Instead of protecting faculty decision making, it seems clear that the administration played a key role in overriding it, whether because of internal protest or external pressure is not clear. Since the president and the provost did not meet with the faculty members involved, it cannot be persuasively argued that their actions were based on appropriate academic considerations. The administration's action is, however, understandable. The proposed changes were controversial within the department and unpopular outside of it. They were associated by some with the radicalism of the department and the "burn something Texan" party. The early publicity suggested that the purpose of the course was to indoctrinate about difference rather than teach composition. The proposal did not seem to have been adequately thought through as evidenced first by the selection of the Rothenberg book and then by its quick abandonment. And the proposal involved teaching a basic traditional course in a highly untraditional manner, something likely to arouse administrative suspicion under the best of circumstances.

Although much that was done by the proponents of the course (particularly any involvement in the "burn something Texan" party) was foolish, the proponents followed appropriate academic procedures at every step of the way. According to traditional, generally accepted notions of faculty governance, the decision about the course should have been made by the department in accordance with its own procedures. Since the proponents did this, they expected the general support of the faculty in getting started, but this was in fact not the case. And this lack of support permitted the administration to overrule the department without causing the sort of campus turmoil that might otherwise have arisen.

The absence of stronger general faculty support for the English department was probably based on several factors. First, the course was seen by many as part of the multicultural movement, and multiculturalism is highly controversial. Many faculty moderates and concerned nonacademics think of multiculturalism as a code word for a new form of intolerance. This belief is not without cause. As the many books and articles attacking multiculturalism point out, deplorable attacks on legitimate scholars and texts have been carried out in the name of multiculturalism.[19]

Much of the writing about the proposed English 306 course has assumed that the course is an example of multiculturalism. Brodkey herself disagrees with this assumption. Although she describes herself as a multiculturalist, she points out that the proposed course would have been taught primarily from the writings of white, male, presumably heterosexual judges, and that accordingly it could not claim to be either multicultural or politically correct.

Another foe of basic innovation that was made obvious during the English 306 debate is the fact that much of the basic teaching at large universities is done by graduate assistants. Developing adequate materials and innovative approaches is more difficult when the instruction comes from those who have not yet learned to teach the traditional courses in the traditional fashion. Also, people evaluating proposals for change are less willing to take chances in such situations. For example, some of those who criticized the proposed course did so on the grounds that the Rothenberg book was particularly unsuited for instructors who were not in a position to take issue with its approach.

Many faculty who would have supported the right of an individual professor to teach a multicultural course using whatever materials he or she chose were less bothered by administrative involvement in this case because the course was required and was to be taught almost entirely by graduate students whose competence in matters of law or groups' difference seemed questionable.

An exchange of letters between Professor Douglas Laycock, one of my University of Texas Law School colleagues, and Professor Kurt Heinzelman, a member of the University of Texas English department, illustrates the reaction of many traditional academic-freedom advocates outside the department and the resentment that this engendered in English professors. The correspondence was in response to a preliminary investigation of the case by the American Association of University Professors, which received a complaint. The current president of the AAUP, Barbara Bergmann (herself a strong feminist), wrote to Laycock (a person whom she knew and trusted from his work on the AAUP committee dealing with the status of women in academic life), asking whether postponement of the course constituted a violation of academic freedom. He responded with a long letter indicating considerable familiarity with the issue and very little sympathy for the English department:

> Opposition to or serious doubts about the proposed changes in English 306 are not confined to the political right or to persons whose motives are suspect. Opposition extends across the range of faculty opinion, from conservative . . . to mild leftists. . . .
>
> The proposed changes were to be imposed on individual instructors by the departmental committee. At least some, perhaps many, of the instructors would not adopt these changes if given a choice. The opponents of the changes have never proposed any comparable imposition on individual instructors. Academic freedom is a right of individuals; . . .
>
> The proposed changes demonstrably require the English instructors to teach well outside their competence. . . . The English faculty . . . did not ask for help with the court opinions. . . .

The Struggle for Change

Some proponents of the course have responded to the competence issue by claiming that they can teach techniques of argument in the abstract . . . This is a pedagogical claim that raises honest intellectual dispute from other disciplines. They can teach argument with examples from any subject matter, but only if they understand the examples. . . . the proponents do not really intend to ignore substance, because they also say that a goal of the course is to change the students' attitudes about race and gender issues.

English instructors could organize the course around race and gender problems, without getting into technical material beyond their competence, by using literature and rhetoric on these issues. I am told that the proponents have resisted this suggestion. Dr. King's Letter from a Birmingham Jail has been expressly suggested and rejected.

Opponents of the course charge that the proponents want to use it as a vehicle to attempt to indoctrinate students into a single view of race and gender issues. Proponents deny the charge. . . . Probably the truth is that some instructors will try to indoctrinate and some will not, and that those who try will have a few successes and mostly failures. Some will try to be fair and balanced but fail, because forced to talk about law or social science, they will lack sufficient depth or breadth to test their own predispositions or imagine what a countervailing argument would be. . . .

On both the competence and the indoctrination issues, the proponents forfeited much of their credibility when they adopted the Rothenberg textbook. . . . It was a truly dreadful book. . . .

When the faculty teach outside their competence there is much less basis to defer to their judgement. . . . Much of the faculty believes that the proposed changes would structure the course in a way that inherently tends to bad teaching because it would force faculty to deal with difficult and controversial material well outside their competence, and without even a balanced source of readings for either students or faculty.[20]

Doug Laycock's letter was responded to by an equally passionate and powerful letter from Kurt Heinzelman, who took particular umbrage at the idea that English faculty were not competent to deal with the rhetoric of legal argument. He stated first that the proposal was based not on the desire to indoctrinate but upon the realization that the course needed to be changed:

The new syllabus evolves out of Linda Brodkey's own independent and generally applauded research. . . . She is, in our department's opinion, one of the most eminent American scholars in the field of discourse theory . . .

Whether or not your opinion of the Rothenberg text is just, it did

The Legacy of the 1960s

contain mostly belletristic writing (fiction, personal essays, poems—just the sort of writings you also think an English course should draw upon), and it was soon abandoned.

A balanced view of how texts are actually decided upon by committees might plead for greater tolerance and patience. . . .

No one who objected to the Rothenberg text at the time, and no one who has bad-mouthed that text since it was discarded, has ever proposed an alternative that addresses the same range of issues with the same scope and that is readily available in a published textbook form that can be ordered by the thousands. Some have said that the choice of this particular textbook signals the fraudulence and political bias of the Committee members who considered using it. Such an assertion conveniently forgets, for the sake of polemical skewing, that this book was never adopted and that it has been dropped from 306 for far longer than it was ever considered to be a text. Moreover, such an assertion about personal motives desperately trivializes the difficult business of making textbook selections.

From the start the LDEPC determined that it wanted a uniform syllabus and a regulated set of texts in the first year of the new 306's operation in order to standardize freshman composition instruction sufficiently to evaluate effectiveness.

I can only conclude that your opinions . . . presume a strangely parochial sense of what English departments do; and they promulgate an even stranger notion of what departments like mine ought to do. . . . I do want to focus on one misapprehension of my discipline that you reiterate so often it becomes a professional affront . . .

All of your concerns about the new 306—your indoctrination concerns, reading-level concerns, required-course concerns . . . come down to one overriding objection: that the English Department is not professionally competent to accomplish what it has proposed to perform. The new 306, you say, presumes to teach materials . . . that "demonstrably require the English instructors to teach well outside their competence" . . . Supreme Court opinions exist in the public domain. They have disciplinary applicability in the field of law, of course, but they are also literary documents with rhetorical missions and civic ends. They are texts. They are published in the New York Times. They are studied in many different academic fields, such as political science, history, education—indeed, pharmacy and engineering. . . . In a Biology class an oyster is a bivalve mollusk and in Home Economics it may be principally a kind of nutrition and in Geography it may represent commercial practices and in Anthropology it may be an aphrodisiac or form of money and in a Shakespeare course it may be the bottom of the great chain of being, the exact antithesis of God. I do not understand why it is demonstrably beyond the competence of my discipline to read legal texts in contexts that are not specific to your discipline. Even in the law school you have courses in which literary texts, sociological essays, and films are read. . . . In short, Supreme Court opinions do not have a single audience—law school professors. . . . Surely one does not have to argue that justices on the Supreme Court (or on other courts) write specifically for students who must take English 306 in order to say that there is ample reason why 306 students might find careful attention to the rhetoric of these opinions generally instructive, intellectually rich, rhetorically informative, and compositionally pertinent.[21]

Two more letters of comparable quality followed on each side. While the letters are courteous, they leave little doubt of the strong personal feeling that the debate evoked.

After these letters were written, it became apparent that the course proposed by Linda Brodkey will not be taught at the University of Texas in the near future, if ever. When the members of the LDEPC committee resigned, an ad hoc committee of five professors and two graduate students was appointed. The new committee was chaired by James Kinneavy, a nationally known scholar in the field of rhetoric and a supporter of Brodkey's original proposal. The committee drew up a new compromise syllabus that was approved by a 36 to 0 vote in the department.[22] Despite the unanimous result, many in the English department faculty clearly felt besieged by conservative attacks and abandoned or betrayed by liberals from other departments, especially the law school. Meanwhile, the controversy continues to be analyzed by the press as an example of the drive for, and resistance to, multiculturalism. Some see the case as an example of the power of the political right, as exemplified by the National Association of Scholars, and some see it as an example of the newly tenured left's drive to indoctrinate. Each side sees the other as engaged in an effort to undermine traditional notions of academic freedom.

After reading much of the material and interviewing both proponents and opponents of the proposed course, I am convinced that the decision to teach such a course stemmed from a legitimate desire to catch hold of an important issue and use it in a pedagogically sound way to teach students how to think, write, and argue about difference. The fact that Brodkey is a believer in some type of multiculturalism is beside the point. Everyone recognizes that scholars are apt to have views, some of them politically generated, favoring or disfavoring positions within their fields. The fact that my colleague Lino Graglia, a member of the National Association of Scholars, believes in original intent does not make him incapable of teaching constitutional law, nor does the fact that I support unions make me incapable of teaching a course in labor law. The only serious question is whether the professor treats opposing views by other scholars and by students with respect. Nothing in the way English 306 was developed or structured suggests that Brodkey was intent on indoctrination.[23] The choice of the Rothenberg book was unfortunate, but it contains some valuable material suitable for such a course, and a good course can be taught using a slanted text so long as the slanting is recognized and compensated for by the instructor.

Given the importance of writing and the difficulty of teaching composition and rhetoric to undergraduates, the course offered opportunities to break out of traditional categories and to do something interdisciplinary and exciting. It also posed risks, but surely that cannot be a reason for denying a department the right to alter a course or to experiment with a new form of pedagogy.[24]

In several important ways, the course was done in by elitism, both from its backers and from its opponents. The arrogance and hypocrisy of those in the department who took part in the "burn something Texan" party is both obvious and stunning. The party was both an obvious affront to the concept of multiculturalism to which many of the participants are committed and an insult to the ordinary people whose taxes help to pay their salaries. Also, a more subtle form of elitism was at work. The proponents did not, for a time, take the attacks from within the department seriously enough because they were contemptuous of the academic achievements of those who opposed the course. One of the course supporters described them to me as "academic losers."

The arrogance of the department was certainly matched by that of its opponents. Several presumed to judge the course without studying it and to impute motives to Brodkey without listening to her. The failure of other faculty, particularly those in the law school, to support the English department was based on the elitist view that the department could not deal competently with legal materials in teaching rhetoric. This position, though well refuted in Kurt Heinzelman's letter to the AAUP, was, nevertheless, quite pervasive. It was my own initial reaction to the course.

I believe that if Linda Brodkey had been correctly perceived, there might have been much less concern about the course. Like most people of her generation whom I have met in academic life, she is a very serious and theoretically motivated academic. Her primary purpose was to develop a sophisticated, intellectually respectable, and challenging course. She also intended the course to help students to think more clearly about race and

The Struggle for Change

difference, but that was not an unrelated purpose. For Brodkey, as for many of her fellow 1960s-students-turned-1990s professors, political effectiveness requires academic soundness. Brodkey's academic standards and her concern with the theory of rhetoric were clearly revealed in an interview with Lillian S. Robinson, also an English professor. In discussing Jane Marcus and Ramon Saldivar, two of the course's proponents, Brodkey described them in this manner:

"They are also two distinguished theorists. You know, theorists have created a new climate of enthusiasm in the English Department. . . . about the importance of writing and the teaching of writing. It's the shift of focus that theory entails, the shift to the entire cycle of writing from production through reception that has made writing as well as reading interesting to those in literary studies as well as in composition." [25]

The struggle over multiculturalism has roused considerable angry debate within the academy. The concept has been attacked in a series of bestselling books by those concerned about the impact of multiculturalism on academic standards and traditional notions of academic freedom.[26] These books, while differing in a variety of ways, have several features in common. They stress the excesses of adherents of multiculturalism and the dangers of political correctness. Political correctness is itself a vague, general term. As used by the opponents of multiculturalism, it stands for intolerance of those who do not share multicultural values and the effort to censor or remove them from positions of academic authority. By equating multiculturalism and political correctness, its message is shifted from one of opening the academy to new perspectives to one of narrowing what may be said, written, or thought. Its opponents deny multiculturalism any academic, artistic, or cultural validity. They reflect a remarkable assurance that the best way to educate is to focus on the cultural classics. They appear fearful that their ability to define what is worth knowing will be taken away. Its opponents equate multiculturalism and political correctness but ignore its legitimate pedagogical and cultural insights. They thus distort its message. A typically misleading caricature of the multiculturalist position is contained in Roger Kimball's *Tenured Radicals:*

> The very idea that the works of Shakespeare might be indisputably greater than the collected cartoons of Bugs Bunny is often rejected as antidemocratic and an imposition on the freedom and political interests of various groups. . . . At many colleges and universities students are now treated to courses in which the products of popular culture— Hollywood movies, rock and roll, comic strips, and the like—are granted parity with (or even precedence over) the most important cultural

achievements of our civilization. Typical is the philosopher Stanley Cavell's seminar at Harvard University on Spencer Tracy or a recent graduate course at Columbia University on Victorian and modern British literature that repeatedly took time to ponder the relevance of pop singer Bruce Springsteen and the television series *Star Trek* to the issue at hand.[27]

The passage is misleading, snobbish, and self-righteous and unfortunately is typical of the campaign being conducted in the name of traditional cultural values. To teach about Bugs Bunny and Shakespeare in the same curriculum is not to say that they are comparable artistic achievements, a point remarkably ignored by Kimball. The passage also seems to confuse or, at least, blend multiculturalism and teaching about popular culture. To dismiss the potential educational value of Hollywood films, popular music, and television is educationally foolish. The popular materials that Kimball ridicules are all culturally rich and interesting in their own right and can be used to trace the intellectual and historical links between the classical material and material familiar to students. I was a teaching assistant in Professor David Riesman's famous Soc Sci 136, American Character and Social Structure. One of the course's most notable achievements was in getting students to realize and deal with connections between classical and contemporary culture.

This, of course, is not to deny the value of courses limited to classics but to point out the anti-intellectualization inherent in the idea that popular culture and third-world culture are necessarily unimportant and that the function of education is to show why this is so.[28]

Opponents often ignore the fact that one can be a multiculturalist without being intolerant of traditional values or opposing ideas. The amount of writing that multiculturalism has generated suggests that universities are about to enter another period in which curriculum is the focus of controversy both inside and outside of the academy over what is to be taught and by whom. The controversy is likely to be fueled by the misunderstanding of multiculturalism and its adherents, by its opponents, and by intolerance and elitism from its supporters. Multiculturalism has been important in reminding us that different experiences and different types of expression have contributed to American culture. It also has an intolerant, censorious edge to it. Some of its adherents argue that only certain people are eligible to teach or write about the experiences of people of color or members of the underclass. They deny legitimate scholars the right to speak out because of their race, sex, or class.

Acceptance of such concepts as academic freedom and racial equality by all sides will do little to improve matters. Each camp in this dispute has its own definitions of equality, freedom, and racism, and each can point to examples of ugly, censorial and insensitive behavior by the other. A strange feature of this controversy is that each side, with some justice, sees itself as defending and the other as threatening academic freedom; each side sees itself as committed to and the other as threatening racial and sexual equality.

Despite the dangers, something hopeful is suggested by the effort and even by the controversy. The positive aspect is illustrated by the letters submitted to the AAUP defending and criticizing the course. They constitute an impressive attempt at defining the nature of the academic enterprise and of giving meaning to such concepts as faculty governance and academic freedom in terms of their applicability to current issues.

There is no doubt that change of some sort is on the way. Perhaps it will mainly be about what is taught; perhaps it will reflect a more basic effort to deal with societal problems through academic investigation, in which case the current agitation may be seen as part of the inevitable pain of transformation and improvement.

Student Power

The relation between faculty and students at large academic institutions is almost always a source of dissatisfaction to students. Many students feel depersonalized, ignored, and infantilized by the system. This sense is particularly galling to older students and to those who identify with or admire the faculty and would like to have a more personal and equal relationship with it. The role of student almost always has its demeaning aspects. Typically, faculty determine what is to be read and who may speak in class, set the tone of the discussion, point out error in answers, and evaluate student learning and ability. Students who seek a more equal relationship by going to the professor's office after class increasingly find the professor too busy doing research or engaging in some extracurricular activity to have any time for them. Not surprisingly, students periodically seek to change their role to have more say in what is taught and in who their teachers are. Surges of student activism arise when students are particularly unhappy or tense. This happened during the Vietnam War period; for a time the structure of higher education in the United States and other countries was shaken by the demands of students for academic power. This movement was just beginning when I left for India in 1967. My initial reaction, like that of most faculty, was strongly negative. This reaction was strengthened by the aspects of student power and activism that I observed while in India which were chilling—violent, intolerant, and educationally mindless.

Student power looked very different in France. On our way home from India in 1968, my family stopped off in France to visit with Brigitte, a French graduate student with whom we had become friends. Brigitte was associated with a group of radical students that had led a takeover of the medical school. She got us admitted to a huge rally at the auditorium, where I witnessed firsthand the phenomena of student activism in a context far different from the United States or India. The auditorium was packed with singing and cheering medical students who quieted down with dramatic suddenness when the meeting began. After some preliminary announcements, a panel of speakers representing different factions began to debate what reforms of medical education the students should seek. The debate lasted for almost three hours. Questions of pedagogy, professional responsibility, standards, and academic equity were its focus. The audience listened intently to the passionate statements of the speakers, periodically breaking into applause, laughter, or cheers. I realized that I had never before witnessed a discussion of education in which so many people were so deeply involved or a class in which ideas were taken so seriously. If student activism could provoke such an intellectually stimulating experience, I needed to rethink my initial negative response.

When I resumed teaching at Indiana University Law School, a variety of factors pushed me further in the direction of supporting student claims for greater participation. First, I became friendly with many of the black students, almost all of whom were critical of one or another aspect of our program and many of whom had interesting ideas about needed changes. The older students whom we had admitted through the part-time program included several faculty wives who were my friends. They, too, were full of suggestions for improvement of the school. And they changed my image of students whom I had previously referred to as "kids." Finally, the teach-ins and student programs that I witnessed or took part in over the next several years were always intellectually stimulating, often displaying the sense of intellectual excitement that had so impressed me in France. The vice-chancellor at Indiana University, a severe critic of the student movement, showed up at a teach-in and was so impressed that he volunteered to conduct a class at the next one. The students took him up on the offer. He later declared that the session he chaired on the need for civility in debate was one of the best experiences of his academic career.

The teach-ins and similar student-developed programs got students more involved with ideas than regular courses, even though the programs

The Struggle for Change

lacked intellectual precision and adequate structure. I became convinced that students could provide a positive supplement to the regular courses and useful suggestions about curriculum and pedagogy. I supported their efforts to become members of academic committees and to take part in the governance of academic institutions. This transformation in outlook put me in direct conflict with most of my colleagues.

Most faculty remained strongly opposed to sharing power. Some of the most successful and popular teachers were the most defensive. The matter was eventually settled at most schools by what appeared to be either a victory for the students or a compromise. Students were added to committees and given roles in the formal administration of academic institutions. What happened then was an initial flurry of interest by the students, their discovery that committee work was less interesting than they had supposed, the separation of the students on the committee from the general student body, and the shift of decisional power from committees to the general faculty or to a few committees from which students were barred. At Yale Law School, for example, after a stormy confrontation, students won the right to attend and vote at faculty meetings. Decisional power was thereupon shifted from faculty meetings to a newly organized entity called the Expanded Governing Board, which was limited to full-time faculty. Formal faculty meetings that included students became largely ceremonial. But students do now serve on important committees at many schools and frequently add considerations that would otherwise be lacking.

A lasting innovation developed by the student movement in the 1960s was the regular evaluation of faculty by students. This practice, which became common during the 1960s, is now routine at the great majority of academic institutions. Typically, the evaluation is conducted by having students fill out forms that grade the instructor on a scale of 1 to 5 on a variety of criteria ranging from preparation to innovation. Students also typically provide an overall evaluation on a 5-point scale and give specific comments.

I do not think that this practice has either improved teaching or in any way contributed to the improvement of academic institutions. I am fairly typical in the way I have responded. Although I read the completed student evaluations carefully, I have rarely profited from them. On occasion, my student evaluations have been enthusiastic. When this has occurred, I have found the process gratifying to my ego but not particularly helpful. There is little that a teacher can learn from laudatory evaluations, and thus they provide little motive to experiment. Indeed, it can be a mistake to think of oneself as a master teacher. When I have thought this way, I have frequently been less successful the following year. On occasion, the student evaluations and my own do not coincide. I have taught classes that I considered to be highly successful which received mixed reviews and courses that I felt were not very creative which the students rated very highly. I believe this difference is typically based on the fact that the students and I have different objectives and, therefore, different criteria for evaluation. They are seeking to learn the subject matter so they feel competent to deal with an area of law. I am hoping to stimulate interest, make students aware of confusion and ambiguity, and to help them to understand the underlying policy considerations that shape legal doctrine. To the extent that I try to improve evaluations by giving greater weight to the students' criteria, I am betraying my own vision of what the educational process is about.

For those who are unsuccessful as teachers, the student evaluations are a painful reminder of failure and alienation. Professors who regularly receive such evaluations usually develop elaborate explanations that permit them to continue teaching and help to ease the pain. Sometimes small errors can be corrected, but the major flaws of teaching—inability to communicate, unwillingness to consider opposing ideas, pedantic focus on minutia—are typically aspects of personality and therefore are not subject to amendment by being pointed out.

The Student Movement and Egalitarian Rhetoric

The aspect of the student movement that most upset people was the occasional use of violence as a political tactic. This was accompanied and supplemented by an almost equally disturbing effort to change the nature of academic discourse, substituting fervor, directness, and the language of the streets for civility and articulateness. This self-conscious attack on academic elitism was widespread and effective. The students' new style of rhetoric was an important aspect of the Allen Miller case. The rhetoric was described by one of my witnesses as an effort "to desanctify the person that you are talking to." Radical students claimed that their style of rhetoric was merely a reflection of the violent events that they had to confront. The emotions that gave rise to it were described at the Allen Miller hearing by a student activist from an old, politically active, conservative Kentucky family:

Q: You were on Senator [Robert F.] Kennedy's staff in California?

The Struggle for Change

A: Right. I was in the room at the time the Senator was shot and at that point, I had absolute confidence in all the rules of fair play that had been set up within the system. That was the means to accomplish the ends that I sought to accomplish. But the shooting and several other things at that time and my political dealings here and then Chicago was sort of a capper to it all when I saw the rules of rhetoric violated with tear gas and clubs . . . What happened to me then was that suddenly a rational argument wasn't honest any longer.

There was a good deal of anger within me, and that had to be expressed too, in order to have an honest expression of my political beliefs. It seems to me that the style that I've adopted, that people that I know have adopted, has been a really total political style. You can see it on our heads quite often and on our faces—we wear it, we speak it, our tone of voice, the words we choose.[29]

Part of the linguistic style of the students was an effort to deny or escape from their elitist backgrounds to make common cause with the oppressed, particularly with inner-city blacks. I tried to explain this in Allen Miller's hearing to soften the impact of his calling one of the trustees a "honky motherfucker." The term had not yet lost its enormous emotional impact on respectable citizens, and my strategy was to deflate its impact by scholarly explanation and constant repetition.

My key witness in this regard was Robert Johnson, a research assistant in the black studies department at Indiana University. He was an excellent witness: calm, measured in tone, and scholarly:

Q: Have you ever heard students use the term "motherfucker" in discussion about members of the faculty or members of the trustees or members of the administration?

A: Yes.

Q: Is it a fairly frequently used term?

A: I would say very frequently used.

Q: Can you give us a little background as to how it became so widely used?

A: Specifically, I think the term "motherfucker" is one that has been borrowed from blacks. Its usage is very common. The confounding factor is that the word does not have the Anglo-Saxon connotation that most people ascribe to it and as such is not a sexually related word. I think that's part of the confusion, but I would say that it's one of many [words] that have been borrowed especially by political activists. It's a word that really can't be defined. [Its meaning] depends upon the circumstance under which it's used. It can be anything from a derogatory statement to a statement of endearment.

Q: You've heard it used as a statement of endearment?

A: I've used it as a statement of endearment. I've heard it used as such.[30]

For a period after the Allen Miller hearing, discussion of the term "motherfucker" became something of a campus fad, from the faculty club to the student newspaper. This seemingly minor aspect of the case reflects one of the themes that made the 1960s so interesting. It was a time when people examined assumptions about language and considered why some ways of stating things were legitimate and others were not, why black ghetto language was appealing to some and frightening to others, and what messages people gave when they adopted such language. All of these questions involved an important, rarely examined issue of the relationship between the rhetoric of the street and the language of the academy. It forms the basis of today's adult response to rap music.[31] Concern with language is a valuable aid to education. Indeed, the longer I teach the more significant the role of "voice" becomes in my thinking. The struggle to develop a style of discourse at once rich and capable of nuance but not pompous, wordy, or confusing is at the heart of the educational process and is a significant aspect of social science scholarship. The desire of students in the 1960s and early 1970s to avoid pompous and class-oriented language was a praiseworthy goal, even if the initial effort was to replace it with a prose style as pretentious as the one being abandoned.

An absurd and patronizing quality was present, of course, in the use of ghetto language by people who sought instant identification with a struggle they did not share and people they did not understand. In addition, however, many people felt understandably liberated from the restraints of class propriety and ambition. For me, as for many, there was much that was positive in this reexamination. My father, like many working-class immigrants, almost never cursed and never used language he thought impolite in the presence of company. On the streets, the schoolyard, at work, or in the army, I spoke a different, far more earthy, slangy prose that I never used in front of my parents or in school. At Harvard Law School, I learned to speak in the professional language of law, to mimic the phrases of English judges long since dead. During my early years as an academic, I felt that the language of the streets reflected an aspect of my personality that needed to be hidden and repressed. During the 1960s, I realized that it was possible for this aspect to be acknowledged, transformed, and utilized.

Ultimately, however, healthy aspects of reexamining language in the 1960s were more than offset by its use as a weapon to express anger, hatred, and cruelty. This was apparent in the Allen Miller case, most notably in his vicious confrontation with Colonel Jones, whom he called an "animal" and a "war criminal." Allen's anger was also evident in his regular references to members of the faculty and administration as Nazis and Fascists. Casual references to police as "pigs" were also common features of the period. When I asked Allen what political purpose he hoped to accomplish in this way, he merely shrugged his shoulders.

In many cases, the self-consciously egalitarian style meant to connect the students with the oppressed was a supremely arrogant form of behavior by privileged students used to shock the sensibilities of and express contempt for ordinary people.

One of the reactions to the 1960s that became most noticeable in the 1980s was a return to the most esoteric, theoretical, and complex language in academic discourse. This served in a different way to separate academics from the general society. This reaction seems to be weakening in the 1990s. The recent development of feminist scholarship, with its focus on narrative, seems likely to make speaking and writing in a human voice once more academically respectable.

The Aftermath

THE REACTION TO THE 1960S

It took academic institutions a long time to get over the anger generated during the 1960s. Many people were hurt during the period. Some, like the chancellor at Indiana University who suspended Allen Miller, were placed in a hopeless no-win position trying to mediate between the ideals of the campus with its commitment to robust debate and the general community that demanded the restoration of order and civility. The academy became, for a time, a cauldron in which demands for change, violence, threatening life-styles, and angry protest came to engulf the ordered patterns, traditional issues, and institutional values that had previously marked our lives. Many academics during this period felt that the values on which they based their professional lives were rejected. The dominant attitude that arose in response on almost all campuses was that such turmoil must not be permitted to happen again.

It is easy to understand why. The radical-student subculture threatened to destroy the basic precondition of academic life, rendering scholarly inquiry and intellectual exchange far more difficult than they are normally. Any serious academic must be pleased that these aspects of the 1960s were eliminated and express concern when they threaten to reappear, as they sometimes do in the name of multiculturalism or another activist movement. The reaction against the mood and approach of the 1960s on all campuses has been profound. The life-style that marked the 1960s is in general disrepute. Drugs are condemned and love beads are sneered at. The sexual revolution has taken place, but the great concern on campus now is not to make things more open but to prevent sexual harassment. This generation must also cope with the fear of AIDS.

The reaction of most faculty who went through the period is "good riddance." Allan Bloom personifies the general mood, even as he castigates the academic establishment for its behavior during the period. His reaction is doubtlessly affected by his experience at Cornell University, just as my own feeling about the 1960s reflects my special experiences. It was for me a liberating period, one in which I felt active and put my background and professional skills together. Thus, I feel pleased to have taken part in this momentous upheaval and regretful that the legitimate messages and passion of the 1960s have been rejected, along with the excesses. I see the end of student activism as much as an opportunity lost as a peril overcome.

THE 1960S STUDENTS AS 1990S PROFESSORS

As the response to the English 306 course shows, many people believe that the "children of the 1960s" are a threat to traditional academic standards. The fear may be stated as this: as students their chief concern was not learning; as faculty their chief concern is not teaching or scholarship but indoctrination. This point, clearly spelled out in the George Will article on multiculturalism and several of the other attacks on the course, vastly underestimates the academic commitment of the current generation of professors, particularly those who once saw themselves as part of the student movement.

The impact of the children of the 1960s on academic life is as yet unclear, but several trends are discernable, trends that reveal both continuity with and change from the 1960s and 1970s. Continuity may be seen in their interest in social and political issues from a generally left-wing perspective and in their special concern with particular issues—racism, peace, and poverty. The most notable change is that a generation once dedicated to overthrowing academic hierarchy, distrustful of theorizing, and contemptuous of scholarship has been extraordinarily prolific, deeply concerned with theory, and able both to fit into existing hierarchical structures and to create its own. Perhaps this is not so much of a change. A scholarly and theoretical side was frequently apparent in the student movement. Many of its leaders had been outstanding students earlier in their careers who always focused much direct attention on the academy.

The most notable quality about many of these new professors is their naïve belief that an adequate academic understanding of an issue is the equivalent of dealing with it in the real world. They fill the journals with academic analysis of current issues. They seem to confuse academic writing with the resolution of problems. If sexism is a problem, a scholarly journal on sexual equality must be the solution.

The external struggle that the 1960s activists have provoked has been matched by a profound internal struggle. When many of the children of the 1960s entered academic life, they did so determined not to sell out to the academic establishment. They were in a difficult position—needing the approval of the older faculty to obtain tenure while trying to remain true to their convictions. The only solution was to academize protest, writing articles attacking the establishment in a scholarly mode so that such attacks might be thought of as worthy of tenure by senior professors. They thereby translated their radicalism into academic theory.

Former student radicals who went through the tenure process rarely, if ever, emerged from the process unchanged. As they wrote their articles and developed and shared their theories, many came to see discourse, rather than confrontation, as the path to social change. In addition, those who have achieved academic success (and the number has been significant), have had to either deny or rationalize their pleasure in achieving status in the very establishment that they once castigated so roundly. It is in the minds of the academically successful radicals that the conflict between egalitarian values and elitist satisfactions has waged most fiercely during the past decade. Many have resolved the conflict by more and more savage attacks on the system, even as they have prospered in it; a few have eschewed success, a few have changed their views, and many have become academic tightrope-walkers, carefully walking the thin line between hypocrisy and academic radicalism.

Yet the tenured radicals have performed a valuable service for academia. They have reminded us that scholars have an obligation to address the issues of their times, to be concerned with injustice, to be active on its behalf, and to provide a vision of progress.

The student movement of the 1960s failed because of its basic elitist quality. The radical students focused their energy on the campus, and they behaved in a way calculated to arouse the fear and loathing of the greater community. They seemed to have contempt for the people in whose name they sought power. It is too early to tell whether the academic movements that have arisen to replace the student movement of the 1960s will be able to overcome these flaws. The early evidence is mixed. One unfavorable sign is the failure of current academic radicals to make common cause with labor unions and other nonelitist groups working for social change. A positive sign is the number of people within the multicultural movement who are urging it to expand beyond the campus. There seems to be growing awareness that an elitist student or radical movement cannot bring social change, but an effort to achieve social progress through an alliance between intellectuals and other groups might.[32]

The Impact of Feminism

The Advent of Female Faculty

The academic world was once almost entirely male. When I left Harvard Law School in 1963 to begin teaching at Indiana University, no women were on the Harvard Law School faculty, and only one, librarian Betty Lebus, was on the Indiana University faculty. Betty was not expected to take part in serious academic discussions. She was thought of as an auxiliary, a helper who cleaned up the faculty library, prepared coffee, and washed out the cups. I often thought that she went out of her way to hide the keenness of her mind and her perceptiveness.

A law school administrator, shortly thereafter president of a major university, told me in 1961 that women faculty were "as unnatural as male nurses." And as late as 1969, Jencks and Riesman, in their study of academic life, used the terms "men" and "faculty" interchangeably.[33]

Women today comprise a high percentage of graduate students and a steadily growing percentage of university faculty and administrators.[34] Schools that once disdained women faculty now avidly seek them. The University of Texas Law School added four women faculty in the 1990–1991 academic year. And comparable additions were made on many other faculties. This significant change did not come about easily. The first female faculty were often subjected to ridicule and embarrassment and injustice. It was not that most male faculty thought themselves prejudiced or that they openly discriminated; it was more that they thought female faculty were a challenge to existing standards of excellence. For a long time, many male professors were convinced that the great majority of female faculty were hired because of affirmative action programs and not because of their merits. Women, especially those with children, were often assumed not to be serious scholars. In the 1970s and early 1980s, female faculty were told, either directly or indirectly, that they could not have it both ways: performing the traditional roles of women and being accepted as serious academics. If women were to achieve tenure, they would have to write more and better than the men who preceded them. Standards for tenure, for example, became much more difficult to meet after large numbers of women entered academic life. In addition, young female faculty had greater administrative demands on them than did males. The first women on faculties, like the first minority-group members, were used to integrate the major committees. They served on time-consuming committees. They were also expected to put in considerable time counseling female students. The first female faculty met with unreasoned hostility and unfair criticism from male students, particularly when their teaching styles differed from those of male colleagues. The heaviness of the burden was frequently ignored when women were considered for promotion or tenure. Indeed, the evaluation of women for appointment and tenure in the early 1980s was often marked by barely suppressed feelings of resentment. In my experience, almost every time a woman was evaluated for promotion or tenure during that period, some hostility was manifest. Even when a female faculty member received tenure or was voted an appointment, a male faculty member was bound to comment that, had the woman receiving the vote been a man, the male faculty member would have voted "no."

Women responded in a variety of ways. Some got angry, some were depressed, some left academic life, some became neurotic about their performance, and many worked incessantly. A few lived apart from their mates, and quite a few became more insistent that their husbands share the chores of child rearing. To a remarkable extent, however, the women succeeded in becoming accepted, demonstrating their academic commitment and ability under very difficult conditions.

As a result, the resentment toward women faculty has become less pervasive and more particular. In recent years, not all women but those who have most directly posed a challenge to traditional elitist standards have become the objects of resentment. As already noted in the discussion of peer review in Chapter 3, many of the worst cases of academic injustice have involved such women.

An interesting, and in many ways archetypal, example of the impact of the fear that women threatened standards was the effort of the new dean of the School of Music at Indiana University to terminate in 1973 the services of Ethel Merker, an assistant professor of French horn. Ethel had been hired by Wilford Baine, then the dean at the university, as an assistant professor for an academic year when one of the two French horn teachers resigned unexpectedly. She was at that time a free-lance French horn player of both jazz and classical music. She played regularly with Peggy Lee and occasionally did recordings with Quincy Jones, Pearl Bailey, Ramsey Lewis, and the Chicago Symphony Orchestra. She had taught successfully at Northwestern. Her background, which would have been considered outstanding at most other music schools in America, was weak for Indiana University, then generally considered the finest music school in the country.

During the 1960s and 1970s, the School of Music had recruited many of the country's leading classical musicians for its faculty, among them such people as Janos Starker in cello, Menahem Pressler in piano, Josef Gingold in violin, Harvey G. Phillips in tuba, and Eileen Farrell in voice. The primary French horn professor was Philip F. Farkas, who had once been soloist with the Chicago Symphony. It is doubtful that Ethel would have been asked to teach at Indiana had there not been a sudden need for a competent teacher, but this fact was not mentioned to her when she was recruited by Dean Baine. He selected her rather than others who might have been available because he had heard great things about her teaching at Northwestern. She was, as the dean noted in a memo, "reluctant to accept a year's appointment since she will absent herself from the free-lance field in Chicago." She was persuaded by his descriptions of the "advantages of academic life and the pleasures of living in Bloomington."[35] The entire discussion was based on their mutual assumption that the position was to be permanent if she performed adequately.

Her first few weeks at Indiana University were hectic and unpleasant. The students who returned from the summer expecting to find her distinguished predecessor were angered to find this unprepossessing woman, of whom only a few had heard, taking his place. They treated her disdainfully and openly talked of their displeasure at her appointment to other faculty members. She was, however, an unusual teacher who was available to her students at any time. She played duets with them, advised them about personal crises, invited them to her house, went to concerts with them, and gave them extra lessons. Gradually, she won them over, and, by her second semester when she added students of her own, she had developed a large following.

The Struggle for Change

At the end of her first year, Dean Wilford Baine resigned and was replaced by a fiercely ambitious young faculty member eager to recruit his own faculty. Ethel was notified shortly thereafter that she would not be retained. The memo referred to her lack of national reputation and her failure to perform publicly.

Despite the obvious injustice of being dismissed after teaching excellently under the most adverse academic conditions, Ethel would probably have accepted the decision, but when her students learned of it, they responded with outrage. A petition was quickly circulated and signed by all of them. Three of her students, led by a young woman who, under Ethel's tutelage, had gone from mediocre to outstanding performance, spoke to various university administrators, including the new dean, in an effort to get the decision reversed. Eventually the students came to me, and I agreed to handle the case. I filed a petition with the Faculty Review Board alleging that her dismissal was unfair and that it was based on sex discrimination. My argument was that reputation in an almost all-male field was bound to incorporate elements of such discrimination. I also undertook to investigate whether other forms of discrimination existed as well.

When I talked with people at the School of Music, I was astonished at the overriding concern of the faculty with the school's status. One professor told me that an unnamed musician with one of the great symphonies had told him that "I.U. could do better." He hoped that someone could be appointed whose addition would reinforce the school's reputation for excellence. He assured me that Ethel's claim of sex discrimination was absurd. I asked if any women had the necessary credentials. He thought for a long time and said, "Not really."

I asked how he explained the lack of qualified women. He paused, "You know we have an expression: it takes balls to play brass." When I asked whether he thought the expression might itself be an illustration of sexism, he insisted that it was a reflection of reality.

The review board scheduled a series of hearings to determine whether Ethel's academic freedom had been violated by sex discrimination or in any other way. The first witness was this dean. He spoke calmly, but with a patronizing air: "I know some of her students consider her an excellent teacher and I do not quarrel with that. But I was troubled at her lack of public performance and her failure to earn a reputation for excellence . . . The decision was difficult, but the School of Music is where it is today because such decisions were made regardless of their popularity."

He smiled constantly at the hearing panel. His image of calm leadership was marred only because he occasionally licked his lips when he got nervous.

On cross-examination, I brought out that, prior to Ethel's notice of dismissal, she had never been warned that her performance was deficient. When I asked whether giving concerts was a requirement, the dean spoke evasively for about five minutes, trying, it seemed, to say both "yes" and "no." It was a delicate point for him because several others, whom he considered important to the faculty, had not given any concerts during their years at I.U. He also admitted that he had made no systematic investigation of her reputation, but had relied on negative comments reported by other members of the faculty. He denied that people such as Peggy Lee, Quincy Jones, Pearl Bailey, or Ramsey Lewis might have anything significant to contribute about her reputation.

I asked the dean whether he was actively seeking women faculty. He said with a look of profound sincerity that the recruitment of women faculty was one of the highest priorities of his administration. I asked whether reliance on reputation might itself incorporate the impact of sex discrimination.

"In what way?" he asked.

"Do you think it has been more difficult for women to obtain the positions that would establish their reputations?"

"Perhaps in some instances, but I'm not responsible for that."

"Do you think the people who commented negatively about her to members of the faculty might have been motivated by sexist feelings?"

"I have no reason to think so."

"Have you ever heard the expression 'It takes balls to play brass?'"

"Oh, yes."

"Is that a commonly used expression among brass players?"

"Fairly common."

"Would you say it reflects feelings of masculine superiority?"

"No, it's just an expression referring to the aggressive style necessary for good brass playing, a kind of pulsing virility which most brass instruments require."

"You don't think that's sexist?"

"No, not at all, because a woman might be said to play with balls."

"Can you describe the last time you heard that expression applied to compliment a woman brass player?"

"Not offhand." [36]

I could see a look of astonishment on a female panelist's face and the look of confusion on the dean's.

The Struggle for Change

The case for Ethel was made by her students, who testified about her commitment and success in getting them to play far better than they had ever played. Several testified that she had changed their entire approach to the French horn, making them feel like musicians for the first time.

When the dean was recalled toward the end of the hearing, his testimony was marked by his constant reference to the school's outstanding reputation. At one point he reminded me that, in a 1972 poll of academic standing published by the *New York Times*, the School of Music placed first, while the law school was not even listed among the top twenty schools.

The committee promptly and unanimously recommended that the notice of nonreappointment "be considered invalid." It found lack of adequate notice and discrimination in the use of reputation as a criterion:

> Our finding that the use of reputation in this case was sufficient to render the procedures improper is based on the following reasoning. First, it was so clear that women were disadvantaged in developing a reputation in the horn field that denials of this fact by the Dean and other witnesses indicated an insensitivity which could very well have insinuated itself unconsciously into the reappointment decision. Second, the total inability to grasp the difference between traditional sex discrimination and affirmative action, though completely understandable, was so prevalent in the testimony of many administrators that the risk of improper use of the criterion of reputation was enhanced. Three, reliance on only word-of-mouth and in-house faculty appraisals has a high level of risk of unconscious abuse against women.[37]

The report was a complete vindication of our position, and for a brief period I felt exultant and Ethel felt vindicated. The problem was that all the committee could do was restore her to her temporary status and call for a new evaluation by those who had already found her wanting. It could not in such circumstances award or even recommend the award of tenure. As long as she was at I.U., the dean would have control of such things as salary, leaves, and teaching assignments.

I was able to negotiate a three-year evaluation period, but I suspected that, given the hostility aroused by the hearing, she had little chance of permanent tenure. She tried to win her critics over at the start of the new period, but rumors and slights, real and imagined, quickly became a part of her life. Faced with continuing hostility from the dean and many colleagues, the life-style that had motivated her to enter academic life was rendered impossible. She returned to free-lancing with a great deal of relief, happy to leave Bloomington.

Another example of the confluence of sex, age, and elitist bias involves a friend of mine, a law professor who seems to attract academic injustice like a magnet. She is a splendid teacher, has done first-rate scholarship, and is an unusually stimulating colleague. Yet several law schools of varying ranks have turned her down for tenure. In each case, she had very strong supporters and equally determined opponents. One significant reason for the opposition is style. She neither criticizes nor praises in the professional language of academia. Her speech is generally colloquial, always direct, and often bawdy. Her voice is loud and her laughter booming. By her open method of teaching and her way of relating to students and colleagues, she conveys the messages that neither the practice nor teaching of law requires extraordinary brilliance and that professors are a species of people with intellectual strengths and weaknesses like everyone else. It is difficult to convey to outsiders how contrary this message is to the general ethos of legal education. To make matters worse, she was not an outstanding student and for many years she devoted herself to raising her children. Thus, although I can't imagine a law school which she would not improve, it is difficult to think of many in which she would have been easily granted tenure. She stands in opposition to too many academic prejudices.

Issues of sex discrimination have arisen in almost every field and in almost all universities. While I was at Yale and head of the AAUP's local grievance committee, some of the most shocking cases came from Yale's famous English department. The cases ranged from old-fashioned sexual harassment to the appropriation of scholarly ideas.

Almost every case of injustice involving academic women has involved "sex plus" (i.e., gender bias combined with some other likely source of academic injustice). In Ethel Merker's case, the additional elements were the absence of an appropriate reputation as a classical soloist and her connection to jazz. In Janet Lever's case, the additional element was her refusal to adopt an appropriate academic style in writing, teaching, or conversation. This was also true of Adrienne Biracree, who made it clear that teaching union members was more important to her than presenting papers at academic colloquia.

The women I mentioned have been penalized because of qualities such as openness and lack of pretension in style that are sadly lacking in the academic world. This is not accidental. As already noted, a major cause of sex discrimination has been the fear that the presence of female faculty could change academic institutions so that the qualities that have caused male faculty members to be successful would no longer be valued.

The importance of the struggle for equality affects all women academics, but in a variety of ways. Some find in it a cause that stimulates their teaching, shapes relations with colleagues, and affects their choices of research topics. Some rebel against the easy assumption that all women are feminists, and many struggle with the uneasy relationship between their own interests and ambitions and the needs, expectations, and perceptions of other women.

Despite pain, anguish, and ruined lives, the struggle for gender equality in academic life is slowly being won. The tradition and commitment to openness in American higher education, together with the growing interest of women in academic careers, means that women cannot be permanently kept out or even relegated for long to the bottom of the hierarchy. Women are now a powerful, permanent part of the academic system. The "old-boy network" still exists, but with an increasing number of women members; there is also a "new-girl network," which has less power but greater dedication. For example, in 1991 every high office in the American Association of University Professors was held by a woman. In each case, the female candidate was elected over a well-regarded male candidate.

The movement of women into all echelons of academic life has become inexorable. The desire of academic institutions to acquire those thought likely to make a scholarly mark inevitably makes certain women in demand, even as immigrant scientists were once sought. What is not clear is whether the acceptance of women will mark a significant change in traditional hierarchical and elitist aspects of academic life. This is a battle that is still being fought both by the institutions and internally by many female faculty.

Academic Women: The Internal Struggle

Contemporary feminist theory, much of it extrapolating from Carol Gilligan's important book *In a Different Voice*,[38] increasingly focuses on gender differences. In particular, many female academics today claim for themselves (as contrasted with men) a more nurturing style, a more human voice, and less concern with rules, hegemonic structures, and status.[39]

Yet my own experience suggests that female academics are as ambitious and status-conscious as their male counterparts and have to deal with the same internal conflicts of elitist and egalitarian values. When I acted as advisor to the Yale law students seeking careers in teaching, the female students no less than the men were eager to attain positions at the most prestigious schools. My female colleagues at Yale were as ambitious and as committed to traditional concepts of academic excellence as the male faculty. They were as tough at legal-theory workshops and as choosy about appointments to the faculty. The same dynamic can be observed in the leadership of the AAUP. The women are as competitive and status-oriented as the men. The meaningful distinction tends to be the nature of the institution from which people come—not their gender.

Many female scholars are similar to myself in recognizing the harmful effects of hierarchy but not thereby becoming immune from the lure of status. I know from frequent discussions that many women feel uncomfortable about their ambition and think the feeling unworthy of their deeper aspirations.

The combination of feminist theory and the increasingly important role of women in academic life makes it possible for women to resolve this internal conflict by achieving status through institutions established to pursue feminist, ostensibly egalitarian, goals. Many newly established journals, conferences, anthologies, and research centers devoted to women's issues now exist. They continue to deplore the hegemony of the white male academics and to focus on the negative experiences of women in the system, without much attention to the internal struggles of women and their ambitions. I find an increasingly unreal aspect to such enterprises. I have begun to marvel at the number of articles purporting to express an outsider's perspective on academic issues that are written by prominent women academics and appear in journals sponsored by elite academic institutions.

That women do, and will continue to, contribute to academic hypocrisy and self-delusion is not surprising; that they use egalitarian rhetoric in pursuit of status is far from novel. These developments make it difficult for women scholars to confront their own confusion and do their best research and teaching. It also means that, in feminist circles, competitiveness is often expressed indirectly and sometimes in the guise of nurture.

Another area in which the struggle between personal ambition and feminist values takes place is in dealings between women professors and the regularly exploited members of the academic community—adjuncts of many types, secretaries, and instructors, most of whom are and have historically been women. For example, when newly unionized Yale secretaries went on strike in 1983, special problems were posed for Professor Deborah Rhode. She was both a professor of law at Stanford whose work championed the concept of comparable worth that underlay the union's claim and a member of the Yale Corporation that helped to determine the administration's response. At one point, Professor Rhode was in the difficult position of presenting a paper to a Yale legal-theory workshop supporting comparable worth while she was on record in support of the Yale administration's rejection of the concept in dealing with its own employees. Similar conflicts were experienced by some of the female faculty, the publication of whose articles were delayed by the strike. Several supported the union and several opposed it.

The Changing Nature of Marriage

In the early 1960s, when I entered teaching, almost all of the law faculty were married, and all of the marriages centered on the husbands' careers. The great majority of wives did not have careers. They stayed home with the children, took classes at the university, were involved in charitable or political activities, taught school occasionally but not as careers, and worked at nonprofessional jobs. None of them acted as though their work was of comparable significance to that of their husbands. Each woman took her husband's last name.

Not a single one of the men did a significant amount of housework and, although all with children were proud parents, not one shared equally with his wife in the children's upbringing. Faculty wives seemed to lead pleasant, nonstructured lives. The women were interesting, fun to talk with, intelligent, and congenial, but rarely were they as overtly intellectual or as ambitious as the men. The women invariably got along well with each other even when their spouses were involved in professional disputes and academic rivalry.

Acceptance of the status quo changed rather dramatically in the late 1960s. Many of the younger wives became more openly dissatisfied with their secondary roles. Several, including my former wife Bobby, went back to school. Bobby finished college at Indiana University in the late 1960s and then entered law school. She devoted herself to the student role with great intensity. As Bobby became more involved with school, she began to question the legitimacy of the sex-defined roles with which we began our marriage. I responded defensively, and for a time we had a continuous running argument about the validity of these roles. I rarely won because I could never find an adequate answer to her question: "How would you like to change places with me?"

That we were far from unique was vividly revealed to me at a dinner party given in 1969 by June and George Ewing, who were among my earliest friends at I.U. They were an intelligent, attractive young couple who lived in a lovely home. George was an associate professor in the chemistry department, where June worked as an electrospectroscopy technician. Each had done graduate work in chemistry at the University of California at Berkeley. June was considered by many of the Berkeley faculty the better student, but she was not seriously considered for a faculty appointment. Most of the guests at the party were chemists. We had a long cocktail hour and ate a fine Mexican meal.

During dessert, one of the chemists remarked, "The women's movement is going to destroy scholarship in America. We're a perfect example. I am on the verge of a major conceptual breakthrough that I could achieve soon if only Ginny wouldn't keep insisting that I look after the children all the time." Another chemist joined in. "My wife cannot believe that I have anything more important to do than to help her with the dishes." An English professor added, "Carol has really taken the new civil rights act to heart. She thinks women ought to be hired for everything from lumberjacks to professional football. I think she wants me to stop working on my novel so that she can get her B.A."

The men appeared to be in high spirits, taunting the women in seeming good-nature, but the women responded fiercely. As the conversation continued, the men became more raucous, the women angrier and angrier. The men did not seem to notice the raw nerve they had touched. I was struck by the uniformly passionate feeling of the women and the total scorn of the men. My first reaction was that the behavior of the men showed an astonishing lack of sensitivity. Despite the strong feelings of the women, the men seemed to act as though nothing important was happening. But, in retrospect, they might have been far more aware than I realized at the time. Behind the sarcasm and contempt was the unhappy realization that the comfortable, male-dominated world in which we dwelt was soon to become a thing of the past, as indeed it has.

Within a short time, all of the couples present that evening were separated, divorced, or struggling to restructure their marriages. In no case was this accomplished easily or without resentment. The men had to accept far less pleasant life-styles. The constant cycle of wife-prepared dinner parties, around which professional social life had centered, ended. The women either returned to school or took jobs. Very few of the wives easily found a satisfying professional niche. They were an in-between generation, more dissatisfied than their predecessors but less ambitious or successful than the next generation.

The Struggle for Change

In the years that have gone by since that dinner party, the nature of family life and marriage in academic communities has changed profoundly. There is no longer a common pattern to relationships. Some couples live together without being, or claiming to be, married. Out-of-the-closet gay and lesbian couples have become far more numerous and accepted. The traditional husband-centered marriage of the 1960s is still to be found, but mostly among older couples. Among young academics it has become rare. The two-academic-career marriage is far more common. And, even if both spouses are not academics, it is likely that the nonacademic spouses will have serious careers. It is unlikely that a wife will use the husband's last name.

The marriage in which both husband and wife are academics might seem from the outside an ideal arrangement: the spouses sharing ideas, helping each other's research, profiting from the flexibility of time demands to be available to children. In practice, such marriages seem to me to be generally stressful and frequently unhappy even if the couples are well suited to each other.

If both are in the same field, it often is difficult and sometimes impossible for them to get appointments at the same institution, or even in the same general area. If one spouse gets an offer from a good school and the other does not, they have to decide whether to take the good offer and live apart, or both accept offers from a less desirable institution and live together. Neither alternative is likely to be appealing. The partner who forgoes the desirable appointment may be resentful, the other spouse may feel guilty, jealous, and like a failure. To avoid this dilemma, more couples today choose to live apart, hoping that with one spouse on the scene the other will be able to get an appointment at the more desirable institution. My experience suggests that young couples are likely to underestimate the difficulties and resistance that usually ensue from such a course.

The dynamic of appointment for a spouse of an existing faculty member is almost always complex. It places strain on the faculty that has to consider the other spouse. The desire to be of help to a colleague is likely to be in conflict with the principle that each person should be judged on his or her own merits and on the complementary concept that academic appointments should not be made on the basis of friendship or accommodation. The power of these concepts may lead faculty to be extra critical when judging the merits of a spouse. And sometimes the process of evaluating a spouse brings out resentment or jealousy toward the existing faculty member, even (perhaps especially), if the person is distinguished. Such attitudes made it more difficult than it should have been for such

distinguished women as Susan Rose Ackerman and Barbara Black to receive tenured appointments to the Yale Law School faculty. Each is married to a distinguished scholar, Susan Rose to Bruce Ackerman, a noted
legal theorist, and Barbara to Charles Black, who for many years has been
a preeminent constitutional law authority. Although Barbara Black was
ultimately voted tenure by a large majority, the grudging attitudes of several faculty members, including old friends, were a factor in her decision
to accept a unanimous offer from Columbia University Law School, where
she was shortly thereafter appointed dean.

The position of having one's colleagues evaluate one's spouse is
fraught with possible conflict. Those faculty members who must decide
on appointments are likely to resent being placed in such positions. The
spouse is likely to resent opposition or lack of enthusiasm. Although votes
are supposed to be confidential and the faculty spouse will absent himself
or herself from participation, the couple is likely to find out how each
member stood. This inevitably leads to further division within the faculty.
Even if an offer is extended, there is almost certain to be a period of resentment afterward. I have known of many situations in which the effort
was made to find a faculty position for a spouse. The couples have been
young, old, distinguished, undistinguished, straight, gay. In no case has
the issue been resolved easily. Thus, a couple's decision to live apart frequently means a longer separation than the couple first realized.

The academic couples that I know who have chosen to live apart have
not been people who use the situation as an excuse to separate. They are
couples eager to live together, who believe that their marriage is strong
enough to bear the burden of living apart. Nevertheless, living apart inevitably places strains on a relationship.

When young couples begin teaching on the same faculty, they are
spared the trauma of separation, but the situation of both being judged by
senior colleagues places them in a competitive position vis-à-vis each
other, and this, too, inevitably places strains on their marriage. Thus,
though marriage has changed and life-styles are more flexible, these positive changes have not yet led to the happiness sought by people entering
academic life.

The Experience of Older Female Students

When women first began entering graduate and professional schools in
large numbers, they tended to be older than typical students. Many had
abandoned and then resumed their educational careers. These women

were often angry at the academic system and resentful that they had once been discouraged from careers. Those who studied in the social sciences were generally disappointed by the lack of attention to women's concerns. A great many went to law school, in part because they saw law as an instrument for social change and advancing the cause of women. In the early 1970s in Bloomington, twelve faculty wives attended law school at one time. The women tended to feel out of place and to question the traditional professor-centered system of legal education.

When I visited the University of Chicago Law School, I once witnessed a discussion between a noted male academic scholar and an older female law student. The faculty member objected to the institution of a course focusing on women's rights.

"There is no course in men's rights," he said.

"There is," she responded. "It's called law school."

A long conversation, notable for its calm tone and for the sense of powerful emotion, ensued. At one point, the faculty member claimed that different roles for husband and wife made excellent economic sense and said that he thought the wife's role to be superior in many ways, since it involved much less stress than the husband's role. The woman asked him whether he currently felt fulfilled, and he said he did. She then asked whether he thought he would feel that way if he exchanged places with his wife. He started to say something, paused uncomfortably, and finally said he wasn't sure. She asked how he would feel in having this decision predetermined by birth. He reddened slightly but said nothing. After a few minutes, he resumed the discussion: "The fallacy is that, if I were born a woman, I wouldn't have the same needs and drives which I have now, and I would be satisfied."

She seemed amused. "Then how do you explain the rise of the women's movement?" At that point, an economist remarked in a grave tone that, while he sympathized with the women's movement, he was worried that it would detract from the cause of blacks and other minorities who clearly needed more support.

The woman asked him whether he would consider giving up his own tenured position to advance the cause of blacks. He looked bewildered and said, "Of course not."

"Well, then," she said. "Who are you to judge the strength of other people's anguish?"

The entire exchange was similar to much of my subsequent experience because it demonstrated how difficult it was for leading academics of

The Impact of Feminism

my generation to deal with the emotional and intellectual challenges of feminism.

Older female students helped to shift the mood of the schools they attended from elitist contentment to a more confused and questioning state. In law schools, the women that I knew were generally unhappy with the authoritarian nature of the Socratic method and dismayed by the smugness of the faculty. At many graduate schools, they carefully noted and publicized examples of professorial sexism or insensitivity. At Indiana, when a professor announced in class that students could pick up materials from his secretary upon payment of the costs and leeringly suggested that "if you offer her more, she might be available for private deals," a petition quickly circulated demanding an apology and an open meeting with the dean. In addition, the bulletin boards were filled with letters of protest.

Faculty reaction to the ferment at Indiana, as elsewhere, was defensive and angry. They could understand the anger of minority students but not of the women they had known in an earlier, different setting. In lunch and coffee conversations, they frequently ridiculed the protesting students and told stories to reveal their naïveté and hypocrisy. I recall one luncheon in which a student, Martha West (now a professor and associate dean at the University of California at Davis), whose most notable intellectual trait was her precision, was called a "bomb thrower who shouldn't be in law school" by several faculty.

One result of their hostile reception was that the first generation of female professors entered the academy with fewer positive feelings than the males of my generation. Much of their work has reflected unhappiness with previously accepted conclusions, particularly those dealing with gender. This anger has been a factor in the development of multiculturalism: a point of view that rejects traditional authority figures in general and male intellectual supremacy in particular.

The result in almost every field has been interesting, provocative scholarship challenging traditional notions of excellence. It is not at all clear that this will continue. The female students and young faculty members have come more and more to resemble their male counterparts in background and attitude. Those that I deal with are comfortable with themselves and basically committed to the academic world in which they have been successful. In law schools, I see fewer older students, fewer women with children, fewer women interested in devoting themselves to professional causes. The entry of women into academic life has been marked by conflict, pain, and struggle. The first female scholars and the first female students seemed to present a challenge to elitist values and they were met with hostility. An accommodation is slowly being worked out. Men are becoming less hostile and women less threatening.

Conclusion

The academic life has become increasingly open to women but this change has been accompanied by strife and pain. How the presence of women will change academic institutions is not clear. Will it be possible for female and male academics to combine successful academic careers with family responsibilities? As yet, colleges and universities have not learned to accommodate the special needs of families. It is not clear whether they will.

Another important question as yet unanswered is whether the advent of women will change the balance between elitist and egalitarian aspects of academic life. The evidence thus far is equivocal at best. As Evelyn Fox Keller and Helen Mogler write: "But as the doors to the ivory tower have swung open, as positions of influence and power have become available to women, we have lost both innocence and purity. Recognizing the strategies of marginality to be adaptive . . . we rushed openly to seize the opportunities offered and claim territory in those bastions of privilege from which we had been barred."[40]

Minority Students

Admissions, Affirmative Action, and Traditional Standards

In the mid-1960s, when the civil rights movement was stirring the country, many faculty members and administrators at traditionally white colleges and universities became embarrassed by the small percentage of minority students enrolled at their institutions. Efforts to increase minority enrollment by encouraging applications from minority students were undertaken at a great number of academic institutions.

These efforts were, at first, largely unsuccessful. Colleges and universities found it difficult to recruit minority students with academic credentials similar to those of the general student body. Many elite schools responded by utilizing different standards than those generally applied to admit an adequate percentage of minority students. This practice quickly became widespread but it has always been controversial. Opponents argue

Minority Students

that it is "reverse discrimination"—the abandonment of the basic principle of individualized judgments.

At the heart of the controversy is the fact that affirmative action generally involves ignoring or giving only limited weight to standardized test scores. For many faculty, objective test scores are synonymous with ability, and any effort to abandon them, or to apply them selectively to achieve racial balance, is itself a form of racism.

This position cannot be easily dismissed or conveniently labeled as an unconscious expression of racism. Objective tests were developed to achieve a more equal and meritocratic policy. The decision to rely on such tests was made only after a long struggle to open up universities to previously excluded groups.

Prior to World War II, admissions programs involved broad discretion and the granting of preference to some groups over others. Whites, Christians, and males were all regularly preferred, as were the children of alumni, the wealthy, and the powerful. Jews were the group that most overtly challenged this system, arguing that quotas should be dropped and admissions decisions should be made regardless of race, creed, color, or religion. Universities and colleges did so gradually and reluctantly, moving from total exclusion to explicit quotas, to indirect quotas, and then finally to credential-based admissions with preferences given for limited categories, such as children of prominent alumni.

In order to facilitate credential-based admissions, objective aptitude tests for colleges and graduate and professional schools were developed. The Educational Testing Service, of Princeton, New Jersey, which developed and administered those tests, became a major factor in the admissions process at all levels of higher education. Many of the students admitted to elite universities during the 1950s, myself included, were beneficiaries of the move to objective tests. When quotas were eliminated, Jewish students began to enter elite academic institutions in large numbers. The same process is being used today by Oriental students. By the mid-1960s, when affirmative action programs were first developed, belief in the fairness and objectivity of relying on test scores together with grades as the standard for admission was ubiquitous. Even granting preferences to the children of prominent alumni came to be frowned on and largely eliminated at many schools. While I was a teaching fellow at Harvard Law School, the son of a Harvard-educated Supreme Court justice was denied admission, and the only concern was that the justice was not notified before the denial letter was sent to his son.

The Struggle for Change

When I first entered teaching in the 1960s, it was generally true that the more complete the reliance on academic credentials, the more pleased the faculty was with the admissions process. There was little discomfort or awareness of the fact that the entire process, from recruitment to admissions, disfavored minority students. Only when faculty began to be concerned with diversity did they become aware that, in general, black and Hispanic students do not score as well as whites on objective tests.[41] The reasons why are subject to continuing debate.[42] Many attribute the lower scores to the cultural bias of the tests, some to the generally inferior educational experiences of minority students. A few argue that the tests suggest innate racial differences in intelligence.[43] Some, including myself, believe that test results correlate more with intellectual self-assurance than ability.[44] The proponents of affirmative action in the 1960s not only questioned the validity of tests as applied to black and Hispanic students but also argued that it was hypocritical to give the tests such importance. They pointed out that it was common to admit athletes and others on the basis of lower scores and took the position that the use of objective criteria was not more important than overcoming the harmful effects of prior segregation and discrimination.

Concern about the paucity of minority students did not lead to agreement on steps to be taken. Academic debate has regularly arisen concerning admissions standards, teaching techniques, and the legitimacy of special programs. I have dealt with all of these issues in my professional career.

When I served as admissions officer and chairman of the admissions committee at Indiana University from 1968 to 1969, one of the first actions taken by the committee was to establish an affirmative action program. Our plan called for us to search out qualified minority students and urge them to apply. Even though I visited colleges with large minority enrollments throughout the country and met with scores of black students thinking about law school, our efforts brought few results. Minority applicants with academic credentials similar to those of our student body were generally being recruited and admitted to elite law schools, where attractive financial-aid packages were being offered them.

To increase the number of black students, we decided to apply generally different standards and accept students with lower LSAT scores. The realization that effective affirmative action with regard to admissions would require accepting students with lower scores on objective tests was made by admissions committees at virtually every level of higher education at this time. In the late 1960s, some saw affirmative action as a departure from merit-based selection, some as an effort to achieve a more inclusive meritocratic standard.

The decision to utilize differential admissions standards did not determine how the minority students were to be selected. Some schools continued to rely on the traditional criteria, admitting those minority students who had the best combination of grades and test scores. I.U. was among the schools that tried to develop alternative criteria, admitting students who, one way or another, showed promise of being abler than their test scores suggested.

This new method of selection forced me to pay close attention to the application forms, looking for special achievements, examples of academic successes, and convincing letters of recommendation. One young woman from New York, Sanita Porter, had included an eloquent statement about her reasons for wanting to study law. The statement was brief, well-organized, and elegant, totally inconsistent with her LSAT score, which was the lowest I had ever seen. Exercising my prerogative as an admissions officer, I admitted her as a wild-card selection. My action so upset one of the committee members that he insisted that the minutes of the meeting show that he took no part in the decision. When I pointed out that we kept no minutes, he was unamused and shortly afterward sent me a formal memo recording his abstention. Several other members of the faculty registered similar disagreement with my decision and reservations about affirmative action.

Early in the fall of 1969, minority students at the law school met with several faculty members. The students had a series of complaints about their treatment. The faculty responded defensively; the students seemed angry and disheartened. After a series of barely civil exchanges, a dignified-looking black female student, who had been quiet, undertook to sum up the debate. She pointed out that we had to differentiate those things which the law school could control from those "that are inevitable when a group of minority students come into a community such as this." She also acknowledged the confused, contradictory nature of the students' position; described the fear, alienation, and self-doubt which it expressed; and suggested an intelligent policy for remedying those problems that stemmed from lack of understanding between the black students and the faculty. She was calm, eloquent, and rational. Her statement provoked head nodding from the faculty and exclamations of "right on" from the students. When one of the students announced that "Sanita is a beautiful sister who just spoke for all of us," I realized that this lawyerlike statement—organized, insightful, and articulate—was made by the woman

The Struggle for Change

with the lowest LSAT score I had ever heard of. Sanita was a fine student and a decent, sensitive, intelligent person, someone whose contribution made me appreciate the liberating potential of affirmative action.

The affirmative action program influenced our entire admissions process. Utilizing a more discretionary standard, we admitted a substantial number of whites who did not have the academic credentials but whose references or personal statements hinted that they were better students than the record suggested. Thus, one of the first effects of affirmative action for minority students at Indiana University Law School was to open the process to white students who might otherwise have been denied admission. Of course, every admission of someone who would previously have been denied meant the denial of someone who would previously have been admitted. The new approach inevitably became a source of controversy both inside and outside of the university. Since that time, differential admissions and greater use of discretion have become widespread, but the controversy about their legitimacy has continued. At the moment, most academic institutions have some form of special admissions process that takes credentials into account but also ensures the admission of a significant number of minority students.

The special admissions (or compromise) system has its detractors in most institutions but has remained in effect. In state schools, affirmative action is partly held in place by the increased political power of minorities. It would, for example, be very difficult politically for a state university in Texas, which has a large percentage of Mexican-American and black voters, to suddenly move away from special efforts to recruit minority students. The current Texas governor, Ann Richards, and attorney general, Dan Morales, would likely be outraged. At elite schools, the process of affirmative action is kept in place by a strong sense on the part of many faculty of its importance. Faculty are aware that the minority students they educate play a very important role in society, and very few would willingly return to the days in which the student body was almost entirely white.

This is not to say that all minority students are admitted through differential standards or that the minority students admitted are not qualified for the study or practice of law. An increasing number of minority students would be admitted to any institution without the need for special considerations. And the goal of all affirmative action programs is to achieve diversity while selecting from those candidates who are obviously competent. At Yale Law School, for example, the minority students selected with diversity in mind almost invariably have far better credentials,

Minority Students

in every way, than most of my fellow students or I had when I was admitted to both the Yale and Harvard law schools in 1953.

The Impact of Increased Minority Enrollment on Educational Institutions

In the fall of 1969, by far the greatest number of black students in Indiana University Law School's history enrolled—seventeen. Many of the first group were insecure about their academic abilities. They had typically gotten high grades at small, primarily black colleges, but generally they had low LSAT scores. They were reminded, in both subtle and obvious ways, that they were specially admitted as a matter of social policy through administrative grace. At the first meeting of the 1969 entering class, the dean spent about five minutes describing the improved credentials of the students generally, and then added, "We are simultaneously, through our affirmative action program, increasing our efforts to upgrade the quality of legal services available to the deprived citizens of our inner cities." No one laughed or protested.

At first, the black students seemed to meld into the general student body, but early in the fall I heard rumors of their unhappiness. We received notification that the Black Law Students' Association had been formed, and sometime in October a meeting was called in which some faculty, myself included, met with the newly formed association. The first half hour we heard a litany of complaints from the students. They were rarely called on when they tried to speak in class. When they did say something, the white students almost always ignored their comments. The professors never responded except to patronize. The black students pointed out that the only picture of a black person in the law school was of a former caretaker of the law school, identified only by first name and wearing a vest rather than a suit. During the next fifteen minutes the faculty and dean responded defensively. One unstated but clearly present feeling was amazement that a group of students admitted by grace should undertake to criticize the faculty who had made special efforts to admit them. The meeting ended with no resolution and little agreement.

Surprisingly, however, this initial expression of discontent had impact. It caused considerable faculty discussion and led many of us to reconsider previously unquestioned teaching methods. Some of us gradually became convinced that the techniques developed in the name of rigorous professionalism were beneficial to neither black nor white students. In the early 1970s, the law school of Indiana University in Bloomington experienced, thanks to the black students, a period of creative pedagogic experimentation. Similar confrontations and meetings took place around the same time at many universities and colleges but with varying results. At some schools, including Indiana, the black students became better integrated into the university, and at others, such as Cornell, the estrangement deepened.

The impact of minority students on pedagogy was attested to in an interesting way at my twenty-fifth-year reunion at the Harvard Law School. We were lectured to on the current state of the institution by a brilliant and intense young faculty member. He pointed out that the affirmative action program had made teachers more self-conscious. "In the old days," he said, "the great Socratic teachers could point their fingers menacingly at a student and demand an answer. If they didn't like what they heard, they let you know promptly and unforgettably. But when we started admitting large numbers of minority students, many of us felt that this style would be unfair to them and we became less demanding. Then I started thinking, if I can't point my finger at the black students, is it fair to be so demanding of the white students? And lots of us have felt it necessary to change our teaching style because of affirmative action. I'm still in favor of it, but it has its costs." During the question period I suggested that the process of reasoning he had described was a contribution that the black students had made to the institution. I argued that too much finger pointing and ridicule had previously been employed and that students in general were entitled to be treated with more respect.

He looked at me aghast. "I disagree with everything you say." This caused a derisive laugh that made me realize how much lingering anger about the pedagogic use of fear existed among my now-successful classmates.

Working with Minority Students

I believe that minority students are more likely than white students to battle the educational system in self-defeating ways. Because I acted similarly during my days as a student, I understand as some of my colleagues cannot why students who know that they should concentrate on their studies find themselves unable to do so. I can empathize with those for whom just entering the law building becomes an emotional chore.

I am the director of the summer Minority Orientation Program, known locally as MOP, at the University of Texas Law School. The program that I developed with the help of some colleagues lasts for seven to ten days just before regular classes begin and involves fifty entering minority students. About 50 percent of the students are black and about 50 percent are Chicano. The course of study, which is largely modeled after the long-abandoned teaching-fellow program at Harvard Law School, introduces the students to case reading, statutory analysis, legal writing, and Socratic teaching.

When I taught a model class on the first day of the program in 1989, having been counseled by an educational psychologist to avoid provoking anxiety, I was prepared to go easy on the students. I changed my mind at the very last minute and decided to be as demanding and analytically complex as I would have been if I were teaching a first-year class at Yale. It was a good decision. The students reacted to the class enthusiastically. They got the point of my questions and comments, laughed in the right places at the hypotheticals, and responded with thoughtful, imaginative answers. The entire discussion was on as high a level as any first-year class could be. The next day my colleague, Gerald Torres, was even tougher, demanding that all the students speak and giving them little time to think about their answers. They responded with delight, obviously enjoying the intellectual challenge of the class and taking pleasure in dealing with complex issues. The Chicano students particularly seemed to revel in Gerald's quickness and his no-nonsense demeanor. He was as impressed with the quality of the class as I had been the day before. The same dynamic, causing far less faculty surprise, occurred in both 1990 and 1991 when the program was offered again.

The caliber of the students' responses and their pleasure in the classes have made all of us involved wonder why these same students have not been as willing to participate in their regular classes and why many who demonstrated both insight and analytic ability during the MOP program did poorly on their exams. One answer stressed by the students is that when minority students spoke up during the orientation program, they did not feel the pressure of representing all black or Chicano students to a judgmental or hostile Anglo audience. Minority students in their regular classes often anticipate rejection in the form of unfavorable student and faculty response to their contributions. In part this anticipation is based on experience, but in part it is based on the students' own doubts about their abilities.

There is a widespread belief among law school students and faculty that the LSAT measures raw intellectual power. Many black students who do not have good scores believe this to be true. Not infrequently this belief leads them to anticipate failure and behave as though they are indifferent to success—not preparing for class, not participating, and writing exam answers meant to sound like legal treatises instead of dealing with the question actually asked. For a professor to deal effectively with such self-defeating attitudes and behavior is a major pedagogic challenge. Success requires a mix of toughness and empathy that is difficult to achieve or sustain. When I have succeeded, I have felt elated; when I have failed, I have felt depressed.

My first insight into this process occurred at Indiana University during the early 1970s. The student involved, whom I will call Bill Randolph, had a poor record and an ostentatiously indifferent attitude toward his studies. Bill was usually found in front of the law school trading jokes with another black student. He had a sharp, insightful edge to his humor and a quickness and originality to his casual conversation that were totally absent from his work as a law student.

I had organized a seminar to work with various administrators in developing an affirmative action plan for the university. I limited the group to fifteen students and Bill was not among the group who had signed up. But he came to my office later and pleaded with me, telling me how important this area of law was to him, and I relented. His assignment was to draft a paper on legal issues relating to scholarship assistance. His attendance was irregular, his participation perfunctory and disappointing. His paper, submitted late, was short, badly written, lacking in originality, completeness, and analytical rigor, and poorly typed to boot. I put up a note on the bulletin board asking Bill to come see me, which he failed to do either of the next two days.

During the weekend, I was playing tennis at the university courts when I noticed Bill running around Woodlawn Field, which adjoined the courts. It was a clear, hot day and so humid that I was having trouble gripping my racket. The field was about half a mile around. Bill was alternately jogging and running half miles, in a long, graceful stride that filled me with envy and admiration. I was even more impressed with the powerful effort he was making. He leaned forward, his face contracted with pain, pushing himself to the limits of exhaustion. I estimated that he must have been running some of his half miles in close to two minutes.

My companion noticed me watching. "That's Bill Randolph, the former Big Ten quarter-mile champion. He works out like this all the time. Beautiful, isn't it?" I knew from my own high school track-team experience that no one could be a first-class runner without possessing discipline and determination. I determined to confront Randolph with this paradox as soon as possible.

The following Monday, Bill sauntered into my office and offered me a high five. "Hi, there, Professor Getman. What's happening?"

"Your paper is disappointing," I said severely.

He smiled at me in a friendly manner. "You know, it took more work than it looks like to do this paper."

"Bullshit," I said. "There's hardly any work involved and it's in late. After telling me how important it was to you to be admitted to the seminar, you have done essentially nothing."

He sighed as though caught. "You're right. I just can't bring myself to work. That's the kind of guy I am basically—happy-go-lucky, sort of lackadaisical."

"Maybe you could have gotten by with that last week, but I saw you working out at Woodlawn Field on Saturday. I was a runner myself in high school and college. I know a little about what it takes to become as good as you are. So don't give me this 'lackadaisical' crap."

I saw a momentary look of annoyance, then his face softened. He stared at me, started to speak, smiled. "You want to know the truth?"

"That would be nice."

"I began to really work on this paper several times and then I got to thinking: I'm going to do my best and hand this in to Professor Getman and he won't like it. He'll see everything wrong with it and I'm just going to have another defeat, and in the one area of law where I have no excuse." He looked at me, his face a mixture of resignation and shame.

"You know what the main difference between us is?" I asked, speaking with feigned assurance. "I have confidence in your intelligence and you think you're stupid."

He smiled, looking embarrassed but also relieved. "It's hard to have confidence when you know you were only admitted because of affirmative action, that almost every white student has a higher LSAT than you do, and that all the people around here, including the other black students, are expecting you to fail."

"If you think the LSAT measures intelligence or ability, you're wrong. But thinking so will make it so," I said. He looked at me doubtfully. I felt I was being too abstract. "Listen, Bill, two women I know, close friends, have LSAT scores as low as yours. They're two of the smartest people I know, but they have the same problem you do. They believe the LSAT, and they've never done the work they are capable of doing. What makes someone a good law student is self-confidence. There's no one here who isn't smart enough. Look at Barbara Kennedy. When she thought she couldn't do it, she couldn't. She is one of our best students now and everyone knows it. Your problem isn't intelligence; it's fear." I could sense that he was listening. A slight smile of relief showed briefly on his face but it quickly disappeared. "Take a chance. Work as hard as you can on this paper. If you do badly, I promise to tell you and then you can believe the LSAT."

I went on in this way. His expression alternated between hope and disbelief. When I finished he got up. "Thanks a lot, thanks a lot, Professor Getman. I'm going to try it." But his face showed doubt and confusion.

I was depressed, convinced that his lack of self-confidence was too powerful to be dealt with in this way.

About five days later, I got a call at home about 10:30 P.M. "Professor Getman?"

"Yes."

"Bill Randolph here. I think I've got it. You're going to like the next draft a lot better than the last one."

"That's fine," I said, slightly confused about the purpose of the call. "Do you need any help with it?"

"Oh no," he responded quickly. "I'll probably have it in to you by the end of the week."

He delivered it the following Friday. It was neatly bound in a manila cover. The front page had the title sentence and "Submitted by Bill Randolph for the Affirmative Action Seminar" typed in at the bottom. We made an appointment to meet the following week. I read it over immediately. It was excellent, well written, carefully thought-out and researched. He must have worked on it almost continuously since we spoke. At our meeting, I was eager to give him the good news. "This is excellent, Bill."

He smiled briefly. "I'm glad you like it, but what would it take to make it really good? I mean, how far is it from being an A paper?"

"It's an A paper now," I told him.

He looked surprised. "But it's not as good as I can do. Tell me what's wrong with it."

"Well, you could develop the equal-protection analysis more and your conclusion could be expanded."

He wrote down my criticisms and returned with a significantly improved report in another week. It was by far the longest and the best paper

I received that semester. The experience was equally meaningful to Bill. When he introduced me to his father at the graduation ceremony, he put his arm around me and said, "This is the guy I wrote my paper for."

Over the years and after many similar conversations, I have learned how typical Bill was. Many minority students and a significant number of white students who do not have outstanding records affect a facade of disinterest to protect themselves against expected failure. Making contact with them requires dealing with the fear that the facade seeks to hide. I recently had a similar experience with a black student at the University of Texas. We spent two hours arguing about her exam paper and why her most erudite sentences were expressions of insecurity rather than formulation of her ideas. She came back two weeks later to show me a first-rate paper she had written for another course and said, "Suddenly, everything we talked about made sense and from then on it was as though you were sitting on my shoulder."

On the other hand, I have spent many hours over the past two years with one of the recent MOP graduates, using every strategy I could think of to no avail. We have talked basketball, law, jurisprudence, pedagogy. In each area he has something original to say, but he has not applied his intelligence to the study of law in a systematic way. He has recognized that he finds dealing with failure easier than having limited success, which would stimulate his powerful ambition. He understands his problem but seems unable to deal with it.

Ultimately, the student must take responsibility and be willing to risk either failure or success. This is never easy to do, and the professor rarely knows in advance when a student will act upon an exhortation to intellectual risk-taking. When William Randolph left my office, I was not at all sure he would make the effort. I suspect he did not know himself.

Minority Student Performance: Elitism, Egalitarianism, and Voice

Issues of elitism and egalitarianism arise internally for almost every minority student and scholar. They focus on maintaining or developing identification with the exploited and downtrodden members of the student's racial or ethnic group. The nature and intensity of the struggle varies with the background of the students. It is particularly difficult for those coming from inner-city ghettos and barrios. The struggle is likely to affect the student's dress, choice of friends, career goals, and the "voice" in which the student speaks and writes.

The Struggle for Change

Developing an effective voice is particularly important for achieving academic success. Exams and papers are inevitably graded for writing style and fluency, as well as for the ideas being put forward. Indeed, the process of education can accurately be described, in significant measure, as learning the language of discourse in the academic disciplines studied. Typically, of course, academic voice is a combination of standard prose and special disciplinary phrases. This makes it especially difficult to adopt by those who grew up using ghetto or barrio speech patterns. They must simultaneously learn to utilize standard English and the particular variation employed in whatever field they are studying. It is rare for inner-city minority students to have developed the ability to do this easily in their precollege educational experiences. For many minority students, learning to use the type of language necessary for academic success requires abandoning the style of discourse that identifies them with their own backgrounds. Attempting to develop a professional or scholarly voice may seem difficult, pretentious, and disloyal.

It is a difficult problem. An effective voice for academic discourse cannot be attained if the student attempts to limit its use to exams and papers. When the student tries to change his or her style of discourse just for examinations, the result is likely to be pretentious and lacking in precision. Donald K. Hill, a professor at Thurgood Marshall Law School, a predominantly minority law school affiliated with Texas Southern University, believes that being unwilling to make the effort to adopt professional language is what causes minority students their greatest difficulties in legal education. Professor Hill makes the point in carefully reasoned academic voice: "The difficulty Black students have with the study of law and the taking of bar examinations may have more to do with their culturally dictated linguistic responses to the discipline of law than to either their intellectual or skills capabilities." [45]

The comedian Franklyn Ajaye, who attended law school for a year, makes the same point less academically in a comedy routine. He says that one of his discoveries in law school was that white and black students talk differently. According to Ajaye, a white student might say, "I believe the plaintiff has enough evidence to substantiate his case. The defendant cited provocation but I do not see how that will mitigate his culpability in any way, shape, or form," while a black student would make the same point by saying, "Man, the way I see the shit, the motherfucker is guilty. He's lucky he doesn't get his ass kicked." [46]

Of course, this distinction is not universally true. I have had many minority students at Yale and elsewhere who grew up familiar with academic and professional prose. Randall Kennedy, now a law professor at Harvard, entered law school able to write traditional English prose better than almost any of his fellow students and most of the faculty. Steve Carter, now a professor at Yale Law School who has written a fine book on his background, was similar to Kennedy in this respect. His father taught English at Cornell University before becoming a university president. The fact that both Kennedy and Carter knew from early in their careers how to use academic voice helps to account for the fact that both were outstanding students and that both are now highly successful and prolific academics.

The problem of voice is not limited to blacks and Hispanics. For many previously disadvantaged groups, success in school required adopting the style of discourse of the dominant Anglo-Saxon culture. This was true of my family and thousands of other working-class Jewish families. A few years ago I had dinner with someone from my old neighborhood who graduated from Harvard Law School second in his class in the late 1940s. My friend went on to become the first Jewish associate in a distinguished Wall Street law firm. He made partner quickly and was quickly integrated into upper-class New York society. He told me that he achieved his initial success in part because, as he said, "I was a parrot. I listened to the way my teachers, professors, and senior associates spoke and I spoke exactly the same way." There was, of course, a price to be paid for such success. At one point he used to sign letters to his sister, with whom he always had a loving relationship, "Warm personal regards." He stopped only when she finally wrote back and told him that one more instance of "warm personal regards" would be the end of their correspondence.

When I was a child I was envious of him. But now I have nothing but respect for his achievement. He was one of those who made it possible for the next generation of Jewish associates to enter the practice of law with little concern about the correctness of their style. And later in his career as managing partner of his firm, he insisted that Amalya Kearse be hired as the firm's first black associate. She is now a distinguished judge on the United States Court of Appeals for the Second Circuit.

I had a more difficult time. When I was in law school, I felt pretentious and silly when I tried to "speak like a lawyer" using a grammatically correct prose style and appropriate legal terminology. That is one reason I was not an outstanding student and one reason why I can relate to the struggles of some of my minority students.

Evaluating the Impact of Affirmative Action

Affirmative action has enriched academic life by bringing in students whose experiences, attitudes, personalities, and life-styles might otherwise have been absent or in short supply. It has given me the opportunity to teach many of the students with whom I have most enjoyed working. Because minority students often have outsiders' perspectives on official behavior and powerful institutions, their presence makes the easy assumption of the system's benevolence (something that was quite common when I was a student) less likely. Since many have had to battle aspects of their own cultural environment, they tend to be iconoclastic and doubtful of the truth of widely shared beliefs.

In states like Texas, California, and Florida, all of which have large and growing minority populations, working with minority students is the most important task in which the faculty engages itself. We are training a new cadre of political and cultural leaders. If the teachers do it well, their students will be more technically able and will have a much more positive view of the value of working together with other groups—whites, academics, women, and minorities. In addition, the presence of minority students forces faculty to reconsider credentials, standards, the concept of academic success, and the costs and benefits of the pedagogy we employ. When students like William Randolph do outstanding work, that reminds us that test scores and predictive indexes are only guesses that frequently fail to capture the potential of those whose ability they purport to evaluate.

Older Students and Workers' Education

The field of adult education is varied and growing. It involves several million older students in different parts of the educational system. Much adult education takes place away from college campuses, in offices, factories, continuing education centers, and public schools. Some of it takes place in local community colleges and some on university campuses.

A fair number of colleges have adult-education programs that are designed to help educate workers, retirees, homemakers, and other people not able to devote full time to their education. These programs vary in scope. Some involve study for a degree; most do not. Adult-education programs have little status and are generally not well funded. Faculty with choices rarely enter adult education, which tends to be poorly paid, housed, and staffed. It often involves dispirited faculty teaching simple material to poorly prepared students. The programs rarely fulfill their potential. Adult-education programs have not had a significant role in shaping higher education in the United States. Yet adult education has great promise in many areas.

Labor education is a field that gives insight into the problems and potential benefits of part-time programs for older students. Labor education (sometimes referred to as workers' education) has been defined by Everette J. Freeman and Dale G. Brickner as "a specialized branch of adult education that attempts to meet the educational needs and interests arising out of workers' participation in the union movement."[47] Labor education involves roughly 600,000 students in a variety of different programs.

The Historical Background

Labor education is essentially a product of the twentieth century. It began as a way of "educating European immigrants and politicizing native-born workers about the perils of industrialism."[48] Early programs were political and class-oriented, but gradually they began to focus on helping immigrant workers to cope with American society. The garment-industry unions, which had a high percentage of foreign-born workers, took the lead in this area. They developed programs that taught workers to speak and write, introduced them to literature, and developed political and class consciousness. My father had his only formal educational experiences in such a program; they led to a lifelong interest in books and culture.

Colleges and universities came into the field of labor education in the 1920s. Their entrance was delayed and their role hindered by mutual distrust between academics and trade unionists. This problem remains a major hindrance to the development of labor education programs. Interest in labor education developed rapidly after World War II. Universities were ill-equipped in structure and in expertise in subject matter to develop such programs. Those universities that decided to develop programs had to organize special units and hire new faculty to do so. As Freeman and Brickner report, "Labor education centers had to be discrete units within the university, regardless of the academic structure to which they were attached. The faculty and staff had to know the subject matter of labor relations, not just how to administer a program. Experience in the trenches of unionism was as important as academic credentials. Advisory committees composed of prominent members of the state's labor movement were an absolute necessity. And tuition fees and other charges were typically minimal.[49]

As Freeman and Brickner indicate, by the late 1960s and early 1970s labor education was established as a special academic field with its own faculty chosen on the basis of unique criteria and with its own administrative apparatus. The fact that labor education programs were in part controlled by academics and in part by organized labor inevitably created tensions with respect to subject matter and approach. Its faculty inevitably pushed toward greater academization—research and degree programs. The labor movement was more interested in short programs to teach basic union skills—collective bargaining and grievance handling. The participants wanted each of the above and basic educational tools as well. This diversity of approach led to a proliferation of widely different approaches to labor education. Some unions developed their own educational programs and others concentrated mainly on university or college-administered programs. University-sponsored labor education programs vary greatly in approach, but all reflect the tension in their orientations between academic achievement and union-oriented skills. Perhaps because of this tension, or perhaps because of funding and status problems, labor education as yet has rarely been able to tap the great reservoir of unused intellectual interest and ability of those served by the programs.

The Promise of Labor Education

The promise of workers' education is multifaceted. Experience in other countries has demonstrated that workers' education can be a significant aspect of higher education and a source of important research. It can change the lives of people who, for financial or emotional reasons, leave the educational system early and whose intellectual potential has never been realized or even recognized. Such employees are often locked into limited Tayloristic[50] jobs. Higher education can improve their lives and simultaneously increase the productivity of American industry.

Labor education could also play a key role in revitalizing the American labor movement, adding new ideas that are badly needed and extending its scope to issues and causes well beyond its current limited focus. More dynamic workers' education programs would also contribute greatly to the educational institutions that develop them. The voice and perspective of workers could enrich higher education generally.

Despite its promise, meaningful workers' education programs are difficult to establish. For one thing, such programs require cooperation among universities, labor unions, and industry. Labor is suspicious, resentful, and jealous of universities. University faculty and administrators, in turn, are frequently patronizing or hostile toward labor unions and contemptuous of the intellectual potential of their members. In general, hostility between unions and employers has grown greater in recent years.

The 1960s—Opportunity Lost

Labor education, like the labor movement itself, had a period of great expansion and experimentation during the 1960s, particularly in the Northeast and Midwest, where the political power of labor at the state level was considerable. The state of Indiana was typical. The elections of 1960 and 1964 brought union supporters and members into the state legislature in record numbers. Indeed, after the 1964 elections, union members were the largest single group in the legislature, more numerous than either lawyers or farmers. The president of the state AFL-CIO, Dallas Sells, became important to state university lobbyists seeking funding for their institutions. During this period, Indiana University set up a system of collective bargaining for its staff. During this period, labor education programs were expanded and new staff members were added to the Bureau of Labor Education. During this period, the United Steelworkers of America, or USWA, the largest union in the state, expanded its educational focus and negotiated for paid leaves for its members. The combination of these factors led to the establishment of a residential program for union members on the campus of Indiana University at Bloomington.

This program was described by Freeman and Brickner: "In 1962 the Steelworkers' Union, with its newly negotiated sabbatical leave program in basic steel, induced the Ford Foundation and Indiana University to participate in a three-year experiment in resident study. The basic construct of these programs was their emphasis on taking workers away from the pressures of their work environment and relocating them to a university campus for ten to twelve weeks of intensive study. Participants were carefully screened and selected."[51]

I became involved in what was called the Resident Labor Education Program accidentally when the person who was to teach the labor law segment quit suddenly and I agreed to take his place. The first task was to choose the participants, who would later be known as the fellows of the program. More than 250 steelworkers applied. The fifty who seemed the most promising were invited to Bloomington for interviews.

The Struggle for Change

The selection process took two days. Three selectors (two political scientists and myself) interviewed the applicants individually. Our first applicant was Charles Ellinger from Diamond Chain Company in Indianapolis. The form indicated that he was the vice-president of his union, the grievance chairman, a member of the bargaining committee, and a high school graduate who had never attended college. He had sandy blonde hair and smooth pale skin, which made him look very young, and the powerful chest and arms of a person who had spent most of his working life lifting heavy objects. His demeanor was shy, almost diffident. He was obviously embarrassed by his lack of formal training, but he told us that one way or another he would return to school some day. "When I was chairman of the union's bargaining committee, I began to realize I needed to know about all sorts of things—economics, political science, law—to represent our people effectively. I started reading seriously, and it made me a better union official and a better person. I set up an education program for our local but I didn't get support from the international union. They don't realize how important education is to the labor movement."

His earnestness was evident as was his disappointment with the union. He described himself as a "union man since I was old enough to think," but he claimed that the unions were not doing enough to support the civil rights movement. "People complain about sit-ins. Hell, if I was a Negro, I'd do more than that. I am amazed that they're so peaceful, that they can control their tempers and remain nonviolent." He spoke while staring down at the floor as though it pained him to state his ideas so forcefully.

We questioned him about the attitudes of his coworkers toward their jobs, unions, and the civil rights movement. He had interesting things to say on all these topics, as he did on national politics, the problems of the cities, and the role of the universities. By the time the interview ended, I felt as though I were in the presence of a unique, thoughtful person—someone who had molded his own life to bring together his experiences as a worker with the world of ideas. I was impressed by his decency and thoughtfulness, intrigued by the mixture of certainty and tentativeness with which he stated his views, and curious whether this likeable, well educated, and committed person was typical of the applicants.

He was typical only in being more interesting and better read than I had anticipated and more committed to the union. In terms of style, ambition, and philosophy, the applicants were diverse, frequently at odds with one another. Bill Baer, a stocky, round-faced, young high-school dropout who spoke with a marked rural twang, was far more outgoing, cynical, and combative. He told us proudly that he had read over a thousand books in the last five years, including "virtually every novel by any writer of consequence." He enjoyed our surprise. He seemed to get particular pleasure from referring to books with which we were unfamiliar. Sometimes I felt that he was striking a pose, taunting us with his bluntly stated no-nonsense working-class judgments: "Mailer is full of shit; Baldwin is an overrated fairy." But sometimes I felt that he was talking of things important to him, which were made painful by his ambition, yearning, and frustration.

Dick Cobb was over fifty, a pleasant-looking man with close-cropped gray hair, who had been active in his local union for many years, holding various offices and having taken part in several short educational programs. He spoke in a calm Hoosier accent, with little obvious emotion, but the strength of his desire to take part in the program was as evident as his pride in his two daughters, both of whom had graduated from Indiana University some years earlier.

All three were among the group of twenty men selected. Cobb was the oldest at fifty-one, and the youngest was just twenty. The program involved college courses in economics, government, politics, literature, and labor studies, as well as a variety of special educational experiences that included a seminar series with distinguished speakers as well as opportunities to attend plays, concerts, and museums.

I prepared a special set of materials for the steelworkers, setting forth the basic legal rules, and each day in class I would teach them much as I taught the law students, using hypothetical problems. The fellows knew very little about labor law, which made it easy for me to stimulate, confuse, infuriate, and intrigue them. They did not resent my approach. They welcomed it, and I could see quickly that they reveled in and overestimated my technical competence.

The fellows were excellent students. They did their homework scrupulously, responded to my questions enthusiastically, and raised interesting questions based on their experiences. I was as ignorant of labor relations and the reality of factory work as they were of labor law. Their questions provided a bridge for me to the people about whose rights and interests I regularly taught and wrote. Frequently the situations they described provided a factual context for a legal rule which I had previously understood only as a verbal formulation. It is a rare experience for a professor to teach people far more experienced in the practical aspects of the subject than the professor. Such an experience is inevitably educational and humbling.

The fellows came with their own ideas and values. They not only resisted indoctrination but also formed their own, sometimes severe, judgments of the academic world to which they were exposed.

When Terry Connors, a member of the Bureau of Labor Studies who had been a shop steward when he worked in the auto industry, once asked them how their ideas had changed because of the program, they almost all said that they had developed a greater sense of the complexity of problems and a greater awareness that academic experts were frequently as baffled as they. Bob Earl, one of the most practical of the group, stated, "We realized that the experts are groping for answers the same as us."

Many were surprised at how rarely academics were willing to listen to them. One of the fellows said, accompanied by general head-nodding, "It seems that a certain egotism goes with formal education."

Several others expressed the thought that the world of ideas was not beyond them and that academics were not their intellectual superiors. They pointed to their own leaders who lacked formal training, and concluded, as one of them said, "You don't have to be an intellectual to have ideas."[52]

The fellows often referred to themselves as "college boys," half sarcastically, half proudly. The desire to feel a part of the university, which this reflected, was very strong for many of them. Several made a point of mixing with the regular students, against whom they constantly tested themselves.

They argued fiercely about unions, civil rights, and workers' attitudes with the business school students, whose snobbery and conservatism genuinely shocked them. Charlie Ellinger was thrilled when he was shown a letter by a business student which stated that mixing with the fellows "was the most rewarding and stimulating educational experience I have ever had."[53] The writer stated that the fellows "brought a refreshing and stimulating attitude to the campus." He acknowledged, "I have been in school for seventeen years, and have never really known a union man." The letter ended by praising "the opportunity for the residents of the Graduate Residence Center to make new friends, broaden our education, and see labor's point of view in the flesh."[54]

The fellows were interested in everything. They attended operas, concerts, and plays and heard lectures from some of the most distinguished members of the faculty. English literature was the course that most excited them and caused them to argue with each other and the professor, to experiment with writing, and to compare themselves and their lives with the insights derived from literary imagination.

At the closing banquet held in late December, the sense of camaraderie, pride, and achievement evident in the fellows' small talk and teasing was in marked contrast with the formal speeches filled with homilies and the general tributes to education by union and university officials that followed one another in a seemingly endless progression. After dinner, the fellows put on a series of skits that teased the faculty, themselves, the union, and the university. They had put considerable time into the skits, and the inside jokes about the program and the faculty were received with knowing laughter and applause.

The graduation ended with the singing of the United Steelworkers' anthem, "Solidarity Forever." The fellows sang loudly and with considerable emotion. Jim Bruce, whose powerful build and sharp, handsome features made him resemble the worker on union posters, ostentatiously loosened his tie and shirt collar with both hands during the singing, as though eager to emphasize his working-class loyalty.

The resident program was repeated twice more as planned, and I had similar reactions to it each time. Like all of the faculty who participated in the program, I found the teaching challenging and rewarding and the fellows immensely likeable, talented, and hardworking. In each program, I felt moved and inspired at moments by the fellows' dedication and progress. I was sure I was in on the start of something big, yet the program was not extended and has never been duplicated. A variety of factors combined to limit the programs' effectiveness—academic snobbery, internal union problems, and university indifference.

ACADEMIC SNOBBERY

The evaluation of the Resident Labor Education Program by an educational service was not nearly as positive as I had expected. In recently rereading the reports, I was struck by the class bias of the faculty evaluators and by the condescending quality of their efforts to compare the fellows with each other and with idealized images of working-class scholars. For example, one of the evaluators commented about Charlie Ellinger, "Charlie has not simply been sold on racial equality, he really believes in it. For reasons unknown, however, I am drawn to a student with a flair for nonconformity. Although I like Charlie very much, he just doesn't strike the responsive chord."[55] The woman who coordinated the evaluation criticized the fellows for their "failure to understand academic society," their preference for "discussion over lecture," their "simple patriotism," and their "conservative views."[56]

Another evaluator stated that the most significant failure of the program "at the end of the twelve weeks of exposure to the academic life was the fellows' lack of appreciation for the contribution of scholars and/or specialists." As proof, the evaluator cited the following discussion. "When I said maybe [Charles] Hyneman's book on the Supreme Court ought perhaps to be supplemented by one that takes another view of the situation, Bob Earl told me not to worry—there would be at least twenty other points of view (the students). When I explained that I wasn't thinking of just lay opinions, but rather a scholarly counterpart, this difference didn't seem significant to him." The same evaluator criticized Jim Bruce for saying that the paper that three of the fellows wrote in sociology "was just like the ones written by the regular students, except they used different words."[57]

The gap between the evaluators and the fellows was most sharply illustrated by the questions, "Who do you think got the most out of the program? Who do you think got the least?" To the evaluators, the questions were a way of determining the basis for group interaction; to the fellows, they were an assault on their privacy and solidarity. Not a single fellow answered this question seriously. Most of them wrote simply, "No comment." A few explained their positions. Bob Costa wrote, "I can't honestly answer the last two questions and I don't see how anyone else could." Charlie Ellinger responded, "I don't think I can answer the question or the following one accurately enough to be of any value." Dick Cobb, always a diplomat, wrote, "This would be hard to ascertain at present time. I couldn't truthfully determine at present because all have shown they have gotten benefits. The determination of this will come after an opportunity to see the results of activities of the fellows in the future." Bob Sanders wrote, "I don't know what the other men got from the course, but I received much from it." Several wrote "myself" for both the person who got the most and the person who got the least. And some overtly objected to the question. Gregg Forrest wrote, "I don't think this is a fair question," and Terry James responded to the second question, "I don't know. This is very unfair and also a discriminating question. Do your own spying. I didn't have time to sit around and watch the other fellows."[58]

INTERNAL UNION PROBLEMS

The consequences of the resident program were not all positive for the union or the fellows. When the fellows returned to their factories, they were received with considerable suspicion and resentment by union staff and some of the rank-and-file members. For some, relations with coworkers became strained almost immediately. Dick Brimmer, a fellow noted for his aggressiveness, got into an argument with a staff representative about whether the union could strike if the company engaged in a breach of contract. Brimmer quoted me erroneously as saying they could. He accused the staff man of "not knowing anything about labor law." The staff man responded by telling Brimmer that there were already too many lawyers around and he didn't need another.

I received a telephone call from Brimmer seeking support and shortly thereafter one from the director of the Bureau of Labor Studies, who nervously suggested that I call the United Steelworkers' staff man to disavow Brimmer's position. I called the staff man. Brimmer was right; the staff man did not understand the issue. He did not seem eager for my help and told me several times that Brimmer had "become a pain in the ass ever since somebody in the university had convinced him that he knew something."

This problem of having rank and file more knowledgeable than the staff was not a minor one. My worst experience in workers' education involved teaching the Steelworkers' staff at a leadership-training program. The students were all high-ranking union leaders. The most powerful of them was Jim Robb, the district director of USWA District 30. He was probably the least interested and most opinionated of all the students I ever taught in workers' education. He was unwilling to listen or learn. Robb believed that the employees should look to the staff for answers and not the other way around. After the first year, he insisted that he and not the faculty pick the students for the program.

Many of the fellows had hoped that their selection to the program meant that they were being prepared for positions on the district staff of the union, positions that were eagerly sought. The one black fellow, Bob Sanders, was young, inexperienced, and unsophisticated and was particularly open about his ambitions and his feeling that he was almost certain to be chosen because the union was seeking to add a black to the staff. This certainty, with its racial overtones, articulated by Sanders well before the era of affirmative action, was not very well received by the others, although Sanders' openness prevented the development of any real hostility. Nevertheless, several of the fellows who were his rivals teased Sanders about it regularly and openly and not always with complete good nature. After graduation, their jockeying for selection became intense. Finally, Bob Earl, a quiet, sensible man who had much union experience, was chosen, and several of the others, particularly Bob Sanders, felt angry and aggrieved. A short time later, Jim Bruce, one of the most promising and appealing of the fellows, accepted a position with management.

Bob Earl would probably have become a business agent without the program, although the experience made him feel more secure about his abilities and helped him to perform better. For him, the resident program constituted a bridge to a new and more satisfying career. For many of the others, the experience was enriching, but it also stirred up ambitions and therefore made sharper the regrets and unhappiness that first led some of them to apply for the program.

When the time came to seek renewed funding, the union was not as vigorous in its support as it could have been. Other unions declined to join in. Their refusal was understandable, even if shortsighted. They were concerned that the United Steelworkers would dominate the program. All of the other unions had their own agendas, leaders, and education directors. They wanted control over course selection, curriculum, and faculty. They also were concerned that the resident program was less economical than traditional, more narrowly focused labor education programs. Several were worried about the role of the graduates, having heard stories about the problems created when the District 30 fellows returned to the steel mills and their local unions. Expansion of the program beyond the United Steelworkers was crucial to the Ford Foundation, which refused to renew its grant after the three-year experiment was concluded. No other foundation could be found that wanted to finance the program.

UNIVERSITY INDIFFERENCE

Some of the problems of participation and funding might have been solved if high university officials had a strong commitment to the program. That they did not was in part a function of lack of knowledge and interest and in part a function of the delicate political balance in the state. They did not want to seem to be too favorable to organized labor. In addition, the program was seen as peripheral to the university's main concern. The administrators of the program were members of the university's Bureau of Labor Studies. They had little academic prestige and little access to top university officials. Aware of their low status, they were careful not to be too aggressive in dealing with the administrators who decided upon their budget and passed on suggestions for new programs. The net result was the complete termination of the best educational program in which I ever took part.

The Administration of Labor Education

After the first resident program ended, I was appointed a member of the university's Labor Advisory Committee. My experience on the committee was invariably frustrating. The committee was made up of labor leaders, university officials, and an odd assortment of academics, most of whom had only the remotest connection with labor courses. The union officials who served on the committee were defensive about their lack of education, contemptuous of anything removed from their experience, and concerned more with internal union politics than with the education of their members. They wanted the Bureau of Labor Studies to limit itself to conveying technical information about collective bargaining and union structure to people designated by them. They were suspicious of any ideas that deviated from the basic positions of the union movement. They treated members of the bureau's staff like hired hands.

The academics on the committee acted similarly, scorning bureau staff because they either did not have Ph.D.'s or else they did not earn them from prestigious schools. Bureau members rarely did research and the bureau itself did not award degrees or have a graduate program. D. W. "Whit" Murphy, the director, had a doctorate but little practical experience. It was apparent that Murphy, a basically decent, unaggressive man, felt his lack of experience and credentials keenly. He rarely opposed any of the ill-considered ideas proposed for his program or offered any ideas of his own. The committee meetings were a constant reminder of the low status of labor education. The ideas of the bureau staff were rarely accorded respect by either the academics or the union leaders. The director spent his time attempting to appease both his academic critics and the labor leaders and in trying to mediate disputes between the two groups. This posture made it difficult to be innovative and difficult to attract faculty who had other choices. Such problems were not uncommon in states like Michigan, Ohio, and Pennsylvania where organized labor was powerful—the only states in which labor education was taken seriously.

Traditional Labor Education Programs

The resident program was taught by selected faculty under nearly ideal conditions. More typical of labor education were courses I taught one year at the Indianapolis campus to two different groups of lower-level union leaders, an afternoon group and an evening group. I had to leave Bloomington right after my law school class. I would generally arrive in Indianapolis late, breathless, and unprepared and then compose the class as I went along.

Pedagogically, everything about the classes was wrong. I was unprepared, exhausted, and had little idea of the students' personalities or interests. The students, who were usually tired, had varied educational backgrounds and labor experiences. The materials I used were not well suited to the class, and many of the students had no time to prepare. Yet almost every class had moments of intellectual excitement and a feeling of significant progress. Sometimes, particularly when disagreements arose, I could sense the students' pleasure in exchanging ideas. Among the students was an organizer for the International Union of Electricworkers whose quickness, intellectual thoughtfulness, and sensitivity made her a match for the ablest students I have ever taught. She was always able to understand the relevance of what we discussed to her experiences and quick to point out the inaccuracies and naïveté of some of my assumptions, although no hint of malice was to be read in her statements. By the end of the semester, I found to my astonishment that I was looking forward to the day of the class despite the long drive and poor accommodations.

I taught in the labor education program for a period of about five years. I never turned down a request to participate and never missed a class. I would have continued teaching such courses if Whit Murphy, the head of the bureau, had asked. I do not know why he did not. The absence of such a request could not have been based on student dissatisfaction, for I know that my classes were well received. Perhaps my growing status within the university made him uncomfortable about continuing to ask me. He once described me as an "NR" (which, he explained, meant "nationally renowned") to a group of union leaders. Perhaps he was satisfied to let the relationship end because I was constantly pushing him during meetings of the Labor Advisory Committee to take firmer positions in support of the bureau and its program. This must have been particularly galling to him, a constant reminder of his lack of status and influence.

The Restructuring of Labor Education in the 1970s and 1980s

THE EMERGENCE OF COMMUNITY COLLEGES

In the early 1970s, some of the major unions, such as the United Steelworkers and the UAW (United Automobile, Aerospace, and Agricultural Implement Workers of America), negotiated tuition payments for their members in their collective bargaining agreements. This made union members an attractive target for community colleges, and labor-education programs were developed in a great number of such institutions. In order to qualify under the agreements and to compete with more established programs run by larger institutions, these programs typically gave credit. They also had the advantage of being on campus in the communities in which the employee-students lived. According to Lee Balliet, former president of the College and University Labor Education Association, the period of mutual infatuation between unions and community colleges was brief. The community colleges did not have the personnel, the experience, or the understanding of the labor movement that would have been necessary to run effective programs. In addition, tuition money became more difficult to obtain as union jobs and members were lost in the major industries. Most community college programs have been dropped or substantially reduced.

NEW UNIVERSITY-BASED PROGRAMS

Inevitably, the community college effort stimulated response from the universities that historically offered labor education programs—Rutgers University, Wayne State University in Detroit, and Indiana University. Indiana was typical of the schools that battled to maintain their programs. A new director was hired who was academically impressive, trained in labor education, and knowledgeable about the labor movement. New staff members with a variety of relevant skills were also hired. In the early 1980s, the bureau acquired independent degree-granting authority. It became possible for workers to acquire either an associate in arts degree in labor studies or a B.A. or B.S. degree with a major in labor studies. As was true when the resident program was instituted, the hunger of workers for learning and higher education quickly manifested itself. More than a hundred worker-students obtained degrees working through the required curriculum on a part-time basis. It took them, on average, five years to obtain the associate in arts Jegree and ten years to obtain the baccalaureate degree. The employees who entered the new programs were dedicated and persistent. Quite a few went on to study for advanced degrees after finishing. A few went to law school, some studied political science, and several went on in labor studies and became labor educators. They made significant contributions to the state's labor movement, improving its legislative, bargaining, and educational capabilities and generally adding new ideas to what had become a staid and unimaginative enterprise. The current head of Indiana's AFL-CIO is a graduate of the program, as is the president of the largest UAW local in the state.

Despite these achievements, the future of the program is in doubt at Indiana, as it is everywhere. Several universities, including Michigan, have already dropped or severely reduced their labor education programs. The cause of the difficulties is a traditional combination—financial problems and academic snobbery. State universities are in financial difficulty, and labor unions have neither the resources to contribute significantly nor the political power to influence legislatures to support universities at a higher level. The past and potential contributions of labor education are typically undervalued at major universities. At a time when complex, theoretically oriented research is in vogue, labor education, with its limited research programs directed to practical problems, seems almost anachronistic. Within labor education, some are moving toward more academically oriented research, but that pressure is being fiercely resisted by traditionalists and by the labor movement itself. In addition, the weakness of organized labor has led opponents of the program to revive the charge that it is inappropriate for state universities to be allied with labor or to give labor a major role in developing adult-education programs.

People outside of labor education and a few within it argue that since organized labor represents only a fraction of the work force, its concerns should not dominate the educational mission of a significant university program. Opponents of traditional labor education programs argue that university-based adult education should be geared to developing professional and academic competence and should ignore the traditional staples of labor education, such as collective bargaining and grievance handling.

At the moment, the financial problems of state universities and the weakness of organized labor likely mean that labor education will either change or will gradually disappear. One possible change is to bring unorganized workers into the programs. Such an approach could help both labor education and unions. Labor education would provide an opportunity to teach such employees something of the history and function of organized labor. Programs geared to unorganized employees might encourage more creative thinking by organized labor and its proponents about what unions can and do offer. But that is all in the future. At the moment, labor education, like organized labor itself, is struggling to survive.

The Educational Cost of the Current Situation

The general absence of creative labor education programs has been harmful both to the labor movement and to the universities. For the labor movement, it has meant unfortunate separation from the world of ideas and the loss of opportunity to inspire new leadership. For universities, it has meant separation from the lives of an important segment of the society and reinforcement of the idea that higher education is only for the academically select.

The lost opportunity may partly be appreciated by looking at other countries where workers' education is typically much more an integral part of the educational system. In England, for example, Ruskin College, modeled after and affiliated with Oxford University, has trained numerous academics, politicians, and labor leaders. Its graduates include Allan Fox, the novelist; George Woodcock, former general secretary of the English Trade Union Council; and the late Tom Mboya, political leader of Kenya, who once wrote that Ruskin stimulated him "to take part in intellectual discussion, sometimes of a very provocative nature."[59]

This is not to say that the conflict of loyalties and the push of ambition which marked the resident fellows experience is unique. It happens everywhere.

The pleasantness of life at Ruskin, however, is said to be at contrast with the reception many students have received when visiting their friends, former shopmates, and union colleagues between terms or after having received their diplomas. They were accused of having "lost all interest in the struggles of their old workmates." According to Nash, "the reaction of the students once they attend school suggests a 'push-pull' system scheme for interpreting their behavior. The 'push' of their former shopmates makes it difficult for them to return to their former jobs and the 'pull' of their newly acquired education motivates them to seek new goals and new jobs."[60]

In Europe generally and in Sweden in particular, workers' education is an important part of a university. Workers' education faculty are often distinguished scholars who have contributed much to Sweden's economic and industrial relations policies. It is not surprising that Sweden has pioneered in replacing traditional hierarchical organization of the workplace. Sweden's experience underlines what many American companies are beginning to learn, that better educated workers mean greater productivity, efficiency, and receptivity to new ideas and methods. Workers' education also offers the promise of greater interaction between workers, union leaders, and intellectuals—interaction that should benefit all these groups, as the Polish Solidarity experience shows. Improved workers' education would broaden the vision of unions and provide practical understanding and new insights to faculty in a variety of fields, from economics to industrial relations to political science. Yet colleges and universities are generally indifferent to such programs. Yale University recently established a School of Organization and Management to train business and government leaders. A labor education program could easily fit into its mission, but the idea never even surfaced. It is not easy to know why. Class bias and snobbery are almost certainly important parts of the answer. Also,

The Struggle for Change

many of the faculty would feel uncomfortable with students with practical experience. As far as I know, the labor movement never pushed for such a program, perhaps because its members were in awe of the institutions and not sure whether they would have adequate control. Labor leaders prefer to run their own programs that teach a limited curriculum from a purely partisan perspective. Thus, two institutions—unions and universities— that should be advancing the interests of working people have combined to defeat them instead.

THE STRUGGLE PERSONIFIED

Of all those people I taught in workers' education classes, only one entered academic life—Charlie Ellinger. He is a full-time staff member of the Bureau of Labor Studies at Indiana University. He teaches in union-leadership programs. I interviewed him in 1987 for this book. His face was still boyish, his hair blonde, and his blue eyes as youthful as ever. Only faint lines around his eyes and mouth suggested that he was over fifty. It was a long struggle from the factory to the academy.

It took Charlie nine years after the Resident Labor Education Program to graduate from college. In the meantime, he and his wife raised six children. During most of this period, Charlie continued to play an active role as an officer at the local union.

I asked him about his experiences as an academic and how the people in the university compare with the people in the factory. He smiled to himself, as though thinking back at his own naïveté. He started speaking rather tentatively, as though afraid to hurt my feelings, but his views came out sharply. "Professors are not that much removed from ordinary people in terms of intelligence. Of course, they have a certain narrow range of expertise, but their judgments, their general abilities, are often lacking. Many of the people I dealt with in the shop were extremely capable. The people in the factory rarely recognize their own talents."

I asked him how he found them as students. "When they come into this environment, they feel awed, but they can learn from their experiences. I think they're more open, more eager to learn, and more willing to change. You don't see that in faculty members. They're so locked in, resistant to change, afraid to concede they were ever wrong. Working people are wonderful to teach. You get them in a dialogue and they start out a little uptight, but you talk to them long enough and exchange ideas and these people change. It's a very rewarding kind of thing to see," he replied.

I asked why he thought so few people at the university are interested in labor education. "One thing: labor's image is not good," he answered. "Most university people haven't really looked at labor and its role in the social order. They're fearful of it. Another problem is that no one has ever really spoken up for us."

I asked him whether he thought union leaders place a high enough value on education; his sense of anguish was evident. "I have always felt strongly that my main function should be to excite the union's top leaders about education, to show them how important it is for workers to expand their knowledge, but they don't recognize its importance. I know that we can change the labor movement through education. Working people love to learn, but they feel put down by their school experiences. They see themselves as not being good students or not being intelligent. That's the real problem. They'll come and tell you they're dumb. And you have to say, 'Who the hell told you that?' and they look surprised, as if everyone knows that."

I asked him if he ever had the feeling about himself, and he answered quickly, "No doubt about it. I had a hell of a time with it. I don't think it will ever come completely easy to me to deal with highly educated people. At the university they don't let you forget your background."

Charlie represents the best part of the labor movement; he is the very sort of person universities and unions should seek out, although they rarely do so. He has been able to withstand the snobbery of the academic world and the venality and indifference of high union officials in order to achieve a place in the world of education. He has won out over great odds, although his achievements have been hindered by those who should have been his allies.

Conclusion

Labor education has the capacity to enrich higher education and provide a sense of meaning to its faculty while simultaneously improving the quality of organized labor. In labor education, as in general adult education, one can have the experience of helping someone to feel at home in the world of ideas while obtaining a fresh, often perceptive, critique of the institution, its methods, and its values. As Leonard Kriegel, director of the Center for Workers' Education at CUNY, has noted: "[Workers' education students] tend to see higher education not simply as the passport to economic success, but as the confirmation of adulthood. To become educated is to become literate, and I use the word in its traditional sense: to denote the capacity to hold, analyze, and express ideas. Education offers

The Struggle for Change

one the chance to claim intellectual currency and it is precisely here, it seems to me, that CWE students affirm an intellectual tradition that many university teachers simply pay lip service to: the centrality and worth of ideas."[61]

A powerful criticism of the academic world is that workers' education and the people who engage in it are so little respected. I believe the most valuable change that could be made in higher education today would be a vastly increased emphasis on adult education in general and labor education in particular.

FIVE

Special Features of Academic Life

A number of special features shape the nature of academic life. These include engaging in work outside the academy, the chance to travel, and the nature of the community in which academic institutions are located. All of these features are influenced by and, in turn, affect the basic tension between elitist and egalitarian values in academic life.

Outside Activity

The Lure of the Nonacademic

One of the ironies of academic life is that it creates opportunities to engage in interesting and often financially rewarding activities that compete with the life-style that made one want to be an academic in the first place. Despite the inherent conflict, most academics welcome opportunities to consult with corporate officials or undertake other remunerative professional activities related to their fields. Bowen and Schuster report that "half of all faculty earn income from services rendered outside their institutions."[1] Outside activity involves faculty from diverse disciplines at every level of academic eminence. Professors of English consult with corporations about writing and communication skills; business school faculty advise about personnel and entrepreneurial and marketing strategies; musicians play concerts and give advice about the design of instruments; and law faculty work at criminal defense, argue constitutional cases, appear as expert witnesses, design alternative dispute systems, and act as political campaign managers.

Indiana University, because it is located in a rural setting, provides less opportunity for such work than most major institutions. But when I first arrived in 1963, Ralph Fuchs was president of the American Association of University Professors; Bill Oliver served as tax advisor to various state agencies; Howard Mann was a labor arbitrator; Henry Pratter acted as a consultant in commercial law cases; Reed Dickerson advised legislative committees about drafting; and Austin Clifford was "of counsel" to a local law firm. Since then, the amount of outside activity has increased. At the most prestigious institutions, the amount of outside activity is greater, more lucrative, and honorific. At the University of Chicago during the early 1970s, many of the faculty advised the president, cabinet members, and major businesses. Yale University prides itself on the academic focus and achievements of the faculty, but, during the period I taught there, from 1978 to 1986, almost everyone I knew in or out of the law school was involved in a significant amount of outside activity. The widespread nature of the practice suggests both that opportunity to utilize academic expertise is common and that total involvement in academic life fails to satisfy many professors. In some cases, the primary lure of outside activity is money, but money is rarely the sole attraction. People whose primary desire is for money rarely become academics. Professors who engage in outside activity do so to test their ideas, affect reality in a meaningful way, bridge the perceived gap between themselves and the outside world, and obtain additional evidence of their importance. A fair amount of academic discussion involves professors suggesting the importance of their outside activity while complaining about the time it takes and its interference with their teaching and research.

Outside activity has an immediacy and sense of excitement often missing from basic academic activities. I learned this in 1964 when the maintenance employees at Indiana University formed a union to bargain with the university. The university president, Elvis Stahr, asked for my advice about how to proceed. In this work for the university, I functioned as an outside labor consultant, not as an academic. I urged him to be generous and suggested a workable plan modeled on the federal government's program that I was sure the union could accept.

This advice turned out to be highly controversial among his advisors. The university's labor relations managers were strongly resistant and convinced President Stahr that I did not understand the practical problems they faced. A series of technical obstacles to collective bargaining were established by the university administration. The union then called a strike, which was supported by a surprisingly large number of employees, other unions, students, and faculty. For a time, the strike threatened to close down the university. President Stahr called upon me again in a state of near panic, not knowing how to handle the matter. I was able to quickly develop a compromise acceptable to Stahr and the union's leader, whom I had met through my work in labor education.

Because neither President Stahr nor I were experienced in negotiations, we simply assumed that what would be acceptable to the union leadership would be acceptable to the bargaining committee, which was made up of rank-and-file university employees. We did not anticipate that their anger toward the university, combined with their sudden feelings of power and importance, would make them willing to continue the strike until the university capitulated totally. In the end, after a long, stressful midnight meeting, the compromise was accepted. Implementing the new plan turned out to be difficult. Feelings ran high on both sides, and, for about a week, I was fully occupied in convincing militant union leaders and nervous university administrators that it was necessary for them to make difficult compromises to implement our agreement. The chore was demanding and totally involving, and the final outcome was in doubt for some time. When the program was instituted, the university, at my suggestion, hired an outside law firm to provide it labor relations counsel. Instead of relief, I felt letdown. I realized how much I had enjoyed being an active participant in the university's labor relations. I enjoyed the excitement of the meetings, the sense of being important to the university, the challenge of reducing animosity in a situation fraught with traditional antagonisms, the ebb and flow of success and failure, and the heightened sensibility that the situation called forth. The mix of these emotions had given me a sense of exhilaration normally lacking in my academic life.

Dealing with the university's labor problems simultaneously raised my status and deepened my understanding of the human dimension of labor relations. I never again made the mistake of equating the views of union leadership with those of the rank and file, even when the leadership was dedicated and honest.

Because of the status and presumed expertise of professors, much that we get to do is prestige-oriented, both in terms of how we are selected and how we are employed. Political scientists advise legislative committees and foreign governments; economists and tax experts advise major corporations. People in labor relations, like myself, often get the chance to arbitrate disputes between unions and employers. I did this sporadically for many years. Periodically I would get a letter from the Federal Mediation and Conciliation Service. The envelope's plastic window tipped me off to its purpose—notification that I had been selected by the parties to arbitrate a labor dispute in the Midwest, usually somewhere in Indiana. Each notification letter, certifying outside recognition, was a cause for inner celebration because it certified my status in the field of labor relations. I did not, however, enjoy the process.

Being a labor arbitrator is much like being a judge. I frequently found the process of deciding the case painful. My prounion sympathies would conflict either with my responsibilities as arbitrator or with my desire to remain acceptable to both sides. I was continually faced with the decision of whether to step outside the traditional arbitrator's role, particularly when I thought the union's case had been badly handled and felt that an employee's job might be lost as a result. Often I succumbed to that temptation, thereby angering both the company lawyer and the union representative, who sometimes felt that I had shown him up.

Despite these problems, being an arbitrator was, for a time, an excellent financial supplement to my teaching and a source for several articles. When I taught about arbitration in my labor law course, I was able to give the students a sense of how the process of labor arbitration works. The marginal value of each case for pedagogic or scholarly purposes, however, rapidly diminished, and after a while I was learning little, if anything, to supplement my basic understanding of the process. I continued to arbitrate long after its help in my teaching had disappeared. I did so because I liked thinking of myself as an arbitrator and enjoyed the sense of continuing contact with reality. I also did it for the money. Being an arbitrator should have been a humanizing experience, because I came into contact with employees coping with their jobs and with union officials at various levels. However, because I was judging them, deciding whether they were entitled to their jobs, vacation, or pay, and because I was treated with constant deference, arbitrating was more a reminder of the difference between them and me.

The Impact of Outside Activity on Research and Teaching

It is true that outside activities frequently inform teaching and research, but they also often conflict with it. Arbitration is an excellent example. The most significant writing about the process has been by professors who are also arbitrators. The lecture and article, "Reason, Contract, and Law in Labor Relations," by Harry Shulman, former labor law professor and dean at Yale Law School, was cited repeatedly by the Supreme Court when it held that federal policy was to encourage the use of arbitration.[2] Shulman had been permanent umpire under a collective agreement between Ford Motor Company and the UAW. His lecture reveals his intimate first-hand knowledge of the subject. But Shulman wrote about very little else other than arbitration awards. Many labor relations professors who are also successful arbitrators have written even less to vindicate their outside involvement. Inevitably the demands of arbitration also reduce their availability for students. Moreover, even Shulman's piece was somewhat distorted because it was an account based almost exclusively on firsthand experience. Shulman generalized from his own experience, which, because he was a permanent umpire between a large, powerful union and a major company, was not at all typical of the great run of arbitration cases involving small disputes, weak unions, or uninformed arbitrators. Shulman is full of praise for the process of arbitration, as are most pieces written by academic arbitrators. Some of the literature reflects more than anything else the notion that any process which bestows power on someone like the author must be a good one. Indeed, to some extent, the experience of power as part of an orderly dispute-resolution process is likely to color the professor-arbitrator's view of the entire labor relations system. It appears more rational and evenly balanced than it might if the professor was regularly involved in the organizing process or viewed it from the prospective of a striking worker. It is noteworthy that professor-arbitrators rarely undertake basic criticism of the industrial relations system from professor-arbitrators. Another way exists for arbitration to corrupt scholarship. In order to maintain one's practice, an arbitrator must appear neutral between labor and management. This may prevent the professor from speaking out on issues in ways likely to damage his or her reputation for impartiality. I felt this impulse myself during my early years; its impact is one reason why my early writing is marked by a lack of commitment and passion. I have also experienced the impact of this sentiment from other professor-arbitrators. Several have refused to become members of or visibly active in the AAUP because they feared that it would make them appear to be union sympathizers. The risk involved in AAUP membership or activity is so small that professors who are motivated by it must certainly have acceptability in the forefront of their minds; it is naïve to think that this sentiment will not affect what they are willing to write, since that is much more clearly identified with the person than membership in a mainline, traditional academic faculty association. The very fact that the arbitrator is neutral and hands down impartial judgments, treating the claims of management and labor equally, also sets a bad precedent for scholarship. A professor who approaches scholarship as he or she approaches arbitration has inevitably lost much of the zeal and openness and concern for justice that marks first-rate legal scholarship.

I have focused on arbitration, but only as a model. Many forms of outside employment may conflict in a variety of ways with the scholar's role. Being an expert witness, a business consultant, or an advocate all produce valuable real-world experiences, but all may conflict with the openness and willingness to engage in critical analysis that scholarship requires.

This is not to say that practical involvement in the day-to-day operations of a field that one studies is undesirable. Such involvement has the potential to humanize scholarship and teaching. For those who do not enjoy or find themselves emotionally blocked by scholarly writing, outside involvement may provide the only way to keep one's thinking current and one's mind open, and thereby enrich teaching. For those who do scholarship, day-to-day involvement may suggest new and more meaningful lines of inquiry.

My work with the Connecticut State Police Union is an example of the delicate balance between aid and hindrance of the academic enterprise that outside involvement frequently involves. I had already decided to study the impact of police unions on collective bargaining when in the fall of 1977 I serendipitously received a call from the police union, which was seeking a lawyer to help the union with its upcoming negotiations with the state. I agreed to meet with members of the union's bargaining committee at the bar of the Sheraton Hotel. When I arrived, I had no trouble picking the police union members out from the groups of business and professional people in their professional-looking business apparel. The police wore leather jackets, bright sports coats, and shirts opened at the throat. Their manner was boisterous. Despite the laughter and drinks, their posture suggested wariness rather than relaxation.

They told me about their union, which had only recently been organized when the troopers had become dissatisfied with the traditional role of the Policemen's Benevolent Association. They had negotiated a contract once before but felt that their lawyer was not a match for the tough professional negotiator who had represented the state. The troopers were still unhappy with "things," they said.

"What sorts of things?" I asked. This set off a flood of complaints. The department was rife with favoritism. Assignments were based on getting along rather than on ability. Police were punished unfairly on the basis of unproven allegations. Senior people were denied legitimate op-

Outside Activity

portunity. No career ladder existed, and training was inadequate. The police were subject to arbitrary discipline. The police auxiliaries they had to work with were a joke and a menace. Each accusation was illustrated with stories that brought forth knowing laughter, expressions of anger, and a series of similar anecdotes. Their stories resembled those told me by steelworkers and autoworkers in Indiana, although the injustice seemed starker and the cops angrier and more cynical.

I had never thought of cops as victims before, but, then, I had never really thought about the conditions under which they worked. I asked what sort of help they wanted. They hemmed and hawed until it became clear that they wanted me to actually conduct the negotiations, to draft the proposals, and to speak on their behalf. The offer was tempting. It seemed a wonderful way to learn both about police and about the intricacies of collective bargaining, something about which I had taught but had never done. Also, the group was surprisingly appealing with their camaraderie, toughness, and cynical humor. They were far less hierarchical than I had expected.

I spent at least a day each week during the next few months meeting with the troopers and learning about their jobs, concerns, and attitudes. I got a sense of how the world looked from the vantage point of those compelled to deal with human beings at their worst and who confront violent death, tragedy, hostility, and deception on a regular basis. They saw themselves as guardians of a society that did not appreciate them and as workers for a government that underpaid, scorned, and regularly mistreated them. I was impressed by their commitment to their job, their sense of its importance, and the air of camaraderie that prevailed whenever the formal part of our meetings ended and the drinking and storytelling began. But I was appalled by their social and political views. They had contempt for civil liberties, were furious at "bleeding-heart liberal judges," disdainful of the entire political system. I made up my mind not to lecture them but to take them as they were.

As they became free with me, their humor became more and more tinged with un-self-conscious bigotry. They told anti-Polish jokes, anti-Jewish jokes, anti-Negro jokes, and anti-Puerto Rican jokes. The best jokes were those that offended the most people. The one Jewish trooper among them, Jerry Markowitz, joined enthusiastically in trading ethnic insults. He was known as a "radical," which in police parlance meant someone willing to strike or engage in job actions to get more money and better working conditions. He had a bull neck, small dark eyes, and a broad face that always looked as though he needed to shave. He did not drink or curse and had insisted on kosher food while at the police academy. He had great status within the group and a reputation for being tough, willing to take on anyone. He was the only one who could effectively rebut the head of the negotiating committee, Dan O'Neill. Jerry was later elected president of the union.

The day negotiations began I was nervous and eager to demonstrate my skill to my clients. We first began by discussing the ground rules for the negotiation. The troopers wanted the state to put the negotiating committee on a special schedule so that all members could attend each negotiation. Allen Drachman, the state's able and experienced lawyer, said, "It should be no problem, although we have already worked out the rotation. Just get the people on the negotiating team to work out trades with the people on the shift they want and we'll approve it." It seemed reasonable to me and I was about to agree when Mike Castellano, the president of the police union, leaned over and whispered sharply, "Tell him to stick it up his ass." I could not understand Mike's totally negative reaction and called for a caucus. When we reached the caucus room, I asked Mike why he was upset. "We'll have to bust our asses to do something they can do easily. The guys will get pissed off and will look like assholes," he replied. I nodded, ashamed at myself for missing the point.

When we returned, I told Drachman his position was unacceptable because it was "demeaning, divisive, and administratively burdensome." Mike nodded happily, and afterward the committee members seemed pleased. "You sure told him," Mike said happily. I was appalled at how close I had come to making a stupid mistake. Over the next few months I witnessed several other examples of the quick intelligence of my clients. Indeed, the more closely I worked with the troopers, the less clear it seemed that I was dealing with people whose intellect was inferior to my colleagues at Yale. They were less intellectual, less pretentious, and less able to articulate their views in a systematic fashion, but they had great capacity to understand the subtle emotional dynamics of dangerous situations. They were far more tuned in to the nuances of language than I had expected.

I became totally engrossed in the process. The easy part of the proceeding was when I argued with the state negotiator. The troopers loved to hear me best Drachman in the give-and-take of argument. I do not think Drachman tried to win in our verbal confrontations. He wanted the troopers to feel satisfied with me so that they would accept any compromise I later suggested. The harder task for me was to hear the possibility of a compromise in what Drachman did not say, and the most difficult task of all was convincing my clients that compromise was sometimes a necessary part of the negotiating process. Conveying that basic insight was rarely easy. During the early weeks of the negotiation, I would state my opinion to the negotiating committee early in the debate, explaining why they had to make some concessions. They would promptly ignore my advice and get into a macho contest, which led to unreasonable positions and no agreement.

The members of the bargaining committee were constantly fearful that "the guys" would accuse them of selling out if they compromised on key demands. I learned to wait patiently while the bargaining committee's own process of decision making went forward. When the question of accepting a compromise arose, the troopers never accepted it right away. They argued, cursed, insulted each other's ancestry, called one another "pussies" or "chickens," and often seemed on the verge of blows. But generally they would become reasonable after a certain amount of conflict had set the stage. When my opinion was sought by the committee at the end of such a process, they would pay attention and generally accept it. The person who was the most likely to understand the importance of compromise, and whose style was ideally suited to achieving it, was Tom Weller, a huge, barrel-chested man whose arm muscles bulged out through his uniform. Once, when the group was being recalcitrant, he exploded, "We're not fucking biting the fucking bullet and we won't get a fucking contract. I may be dumb but don't piss on my shoes and tell me it's raining." This, followed by a few short words from me, led to the necessary compromise. I learned much from Weller and the other cops about techniques of persuasion in bargaining situations. The lessons enriched my teaching and permitted me to deal with the nonlegal aspects of collective bargaining more confidently than before.

The more I worked with the members of the police union, the more I liked them, and gradually I began to see another side of them, a more thoughtful and deeper one. We talked about relationships, power, and the problems that came with being a cop. One told me that he hated giving tickets to people: "Mostly they're people like me and I end up lots of times feeling like the gestapo. I'd much rather deal with criminals than irate citizens." Jim Kerry, who graduated in 1990 from Fordham University Law School, told me, "Every cop has worked at least one accident that he dreams about for years." I realized that the police were people whose contacts with people involved anger, danger, or tragedy. Such conversations, however, never came to override the fun and cathartic humor that was a staple of their interactions.

Special Features of Academic Life

I spent a lot of time during the next weeks wondering why I enjoyed having lunch with the cops more than I did with my colleagues at Yale Law School. I never fully worked it out, but I realized that the cops' lives were filled with those elements found most lacking in academia: mutual caring, excitement, engagement, and straightforward expressions of feeling. The police were not removed from the unpleasant realities of human existence, and, perhaps as a result, I found them less hypocritical than academics. They never claimed to be saints.

Working with cops gave me a deeper understanding of law enforcement, the collective bargaining process, mediation, and public-sector labor negotiations. It also meant I had less time to spend on traditional academic activities. It is impossible for intense involvement in outside activities to coexist easily with good teaching and research. During the time I was involved with the police negotiations, I did little writing and no innovative teaching.

Most of my other outside activities, such as being an expert witness, appearing on television, or testifying before congressional committees, were more calculated to appeal to my desire for prestige and recognition. This is quite common. The skills that academics possess are more apt to be of use to elite institutions that can pay well and that provide the trappings of success and recognition. The most skilled academics almost always deal primarily with the wealthy and powerful.

At his Supreme Court confirmation hearing, Robert Bork could not remember a single time when he worked for a disadvantaged client, although he was doing a great deal of outside consulting. This is not because Bork is snobbish or uninterested in people. As a colleague and a person to share a drink with, he is more human than most. As an expert on antitrust law, constitutional law, and economics, his talents are unlikely to be of use to troubled individuals. As Bork acknowledged in his testimony, this is unfortunate. The elitist impact of outside activity is not a function of political ideology. Liberal law professors writing Supreme Court briefs or appearing on television are thereby likely to be reminded of their special knowledge, talent, and role in the scene of things.

Conclusion

To all but a very limited and special group, total immersion in academic life is deadening and neither necessary nor desired. Eventually, most academics are caught up with the idea of playing and given the opportunity to play an active part in dealing with the issues of their times. I believe that the impact of such an active outside role on academic enterprise is often beneficial but that it also often replaces teaching and research as the activity through which academics find meaning and to which they devote their greatest abilities. Activities apart from the academy may be either a way of making contact with reality and ordinary people or a further reason for feeling separate and superior. Unfortunately, the latter seems to dominate, not because of flaws in the professorate but because of the types of opportunities most likely to arise.

Autonomy and Time

Academics have considerable autonomy. We choose our research topics and usually have considerable leeway in deciding what and how we are going to teach. Teaching and research are isolated, difficult to monitor, and protected against interference by custom, academic policy, and tradition. For many of us, the degree of choice in what we teach and in selecting topics for research is one of the best aspects of academic life. Related to autonomy is the fact that the number of hours that most academics are formally required to devote to their jobs is small. Required class meetings may be as little as three hours a week for senior professors at elite schools. Generally, in academia, twelve hours a week is normal and twenty is considered a heavy teaching load. Even if a professor adds two to three hours a week for committee meetings and an additional three to four hours for meeting with students, the time demands do not seem great to people required to work a forty-hour week, particularly since these requirements exist only when classes are in session, which may be not more than twenty-eight to thirty weeks a year. Even adding in time for composing and grading exams (which is not very burdensome for many professors because of teaching assistants and computers), it is obvious that most academics have large blocks of time that are not committed in advance. Much of this time occurs during the summer break, but holidays, midsemester breaks, and reading periods for students provide unscheduled time for teachers during the academic year.

In addition, many schools offer sabbatical leaves and the possibility of research leaves. At elite schools, a fair proportion of the faculty is likely to be on leave at any given time. Graduate students at elite institutions are aware of this; as a result, most people entering academic life visualize having a great deal of time free for thinking, reading, and exchanging ideas with colleagues.

The reality is far different from the expectation. While it is in fact possible for burned-out tenured professors to devote little time to academic pursuits, most of us live under constant time pressure, trying to juggle a variety of commitments and never free of the feeling that we are behind on our academic commitments. During the time that he was a full-time professor, Judge Richard Posner told me several times that he was on the verge of declaring "academic bankruptcy."

The nature of the time pressures vary with the stage of the professor's career. In the beginning of an academic career, a great deal of time is spent learning the subject matter one is teaching and figuring out how to teach it. Every hour of class is likely to involve three to four hours of preparation. And, increasingly, young professors spend great amounts of their time doing research and writing. Some do it to obtain tenure, some to be recognized, some because there are issues they want to explore. (As tenure requirements become more difficult to meet, more and more time is spent on research, which is increasingly accompanied by anxiety and feelings of competitiveness toward other young scholars.) In the beginning, one must anticipate many hours spent researching, reading, and editing for each page of publication. For me, the ratio has sometimes been hundreds of hours of preparation for each finished page. If one adds in even modest amounts of time for meeting with students; serving on committees; attending lectures, scholarly meetings, and a respectable number of academically related social events; reading drafts of papers by colleagues and finished papers from students; developing research designs; participating in disciplinary societies; and aiding people and firms interested in utilizing one's expertise, all of the time of young faculty and much of the time of senior faculty is used up without any major scholarly effort having yet been put forth. If one is writing a major text or doing significant research, the time commitments may be huge and stretch out over many years. One of the paradoxes of academic life is that we are drawn to it by the lure of free time but discover that by undertaking a single task we may be committing ourselves to years of fairly intense effort. This was the case for me when I decided to work on the NLRB field study, and it is the case for any academic who undertakes a major research effort.

On the other hand, sometimes senior academics who have obtained tenure devote little time to the enterprise. They may be teaching familiar material that they rarely think about, spend little or no time with students, do no research, and avoid committee work by demonstrating that they cannot be relied upon to take it seriously. I know of academics who in this manner have effectively removed themselves from institutional or professional responsibilities. They are to be found at almost every institution. They are, however, almost always miserable people who feel like failures and are disdained by students, colleagues, and administrators. They are paid little, and, in a world where status is the coin of the realm, they have none. Young academics never envy such people and typically enter academic life determined not to be like them. In my experience, those who adopt such a life-style do so out of fear or depression. The problems of "workaholism" and spending great amounts of time turning out large quantities of meaningless research are both far more common.

The University Community

The Importance of Setting

The quality of life in colleges and universities is inevitably shaped by the nature of the communities in which they are located. Harvard exemplifies the variety and cultural richness of Cambridge and Boston and their concern with history, tradition, and status. City University of New York has always mirrored the shifting immigrant population and complex political attitudes of New York. Big Ten universities, with their emphasis on sports and their varied social agendas, reflect the values of the Midwest and its suspicion of unadulterated intellectuals.

Like most young faculty who come from the East to do graduate work at Harvard, I would have liked to stay in the East. I went to Indiana University only because I was turned down for faculty appointments by Rutgers, Georgetown University, and Boston University. During my one visit to Indiana, it seemed a strange place, slightly pretentious and culturally isolated. I was upset at the thought of living in the Midwest when everything with which I was culturally familiar was in the East. When my wife, Bobby, and I drove to Bloomington in the summer of 1963, I felt as though I were entering the unenlightened center of America, passing through communities ever more foreign to my experience in their solid, unpretentious midwestern architecture, flat landscape, and neatly laid-out streets. Bloomington, set in the rolling hills of southern Indiana, was lovely and peaceful, the homes, comfortable, old-fashioned, solid. Everything about it—the easy pace of life, the calm midwestern accents, the pleasant appearance of the houses, the profusion of churches, the Scotch-Irish names of the people, even the unhurried manner of the merchants—conveyed a sense of community, of continuity with values, history, and tradition far different from my own, and all combined to make me feel out of place, isolated, and apprehensive.

Shortly after we arrived at the small, three-bedroom house that we rented for the year, our next-door neighbors, Jim and Pru Eads, came over to visit. Jim was a stocky, serious-looking man. I offered him a beer. "I'm not a beer drinker. We're strict Baptists," he said with a tone of severity. But they accepted coffee and told us a little about the neighborhood, which, they assured me, was made up of friendly, decent, religious people. Pru, a pretty, primly dressed woman, asked about our children and told us about their boys, aged eight and ten. She assured us that they would be happy to bring our sons, Dan and Michael, into the neighborhood games and introduce them around. Later on, Jim asked me about a new course that he had heard was being offered in the law school dealing with Russian law.

"They don't really have a legal system like ours, do they?" he asked.

"Well," I said, "they have rules and judges."

He interrupted. "But if they want to get rid of someone they can just throw them in jail or kill them or something—and they don't have property. The state owns everything."

"They have laws covering most things, even though their system is very different from ours." I spoke calmly but the topic made me nervous.

He looked skeptical. "I can't understand why Indiana students have to learn Russian law."

"Some may need to use it to help American companies trading with Russia," I responded.

"They have no business doing that."

Pru smiled indulgently. "Jim is real conservative."

"Rock-ribbed," he said proudly but with some hint of self-mockery.

We talked some more, and when they left Jim said again how pleased he was to have me in the neighborhood. A short time later, Greg and Mark came over—handsome, athletic-looking boys, polite and taciturn. They invited Dan and Mike to come out to play. It was a curious start. The Eads family certainly seemed friendly and pleased to have us as neighbors, but I wondered how long it would last. Did they know we were Jewish? Would they still be so friendly when they discovered that we were not religious and that our political views were far different from theirs? During the next few weeks, Pru frequently came over for coffee. Bobby found her quick, interesting, intelligent, and perceptive. Bobby was deeply disappointed when Pru said that she found it difficult to overcome her early Louisiana-bred prejudices against blacks.

Despite their unenlightened views, the Eadses turned out to be good neighbors. Once toward the end of the summer, Jim cut a swathe in my lawn as a way of hinting that "it wanted trimming." I did not get a chance to mow before we left for a trip East, which upset me greatly because I thought I would be confirming all their prejudices about us. When we returned, I noticed that our lawn had been neatly cut and a box of cookies and a bottle of lemonade had been placed outside the door.

I expected to see the less pleasant side of the Eadses when a black veterinarian named Darrel Roney moved into the neighborhood. At first his children were welcomed by the other kids but about a week later they became subjected to abuse from a youngster named Gary. He called the Roney children "niggers," threw stones at them, and tried to get the other kids to exclude them. Neither Bobby nor I was sure how to respond. Should we intervene, leave the situation to the kids, or consult other parents? We were debating the alternatives when we heard Pru calling Gary in a sharp, peremptory voice from her back porch. Our window was open, and we could hear her plainly. "Gary, the Roney children are members of our church. They are our guests when they come to play on this block. Now, I hope you have been brought up to know how to treat people politely and decently, because, if you haven't, you will not be welcome on this street, and I will personally be forced to keep you from it. Am I clear?"

"Yes, ma'am," he responded meekly.

"Well, don't let me hear you doing anything like this again. God expects us to treat all people with respect, and if you ever want to play with Greg or Mark again you had better do as God expects."

Gary nodded politely and promised to change his ways. I never doubted the Eadses again, nor did I ever have reason to. They were, I realized, what people referred to when they talked of the basic, God-fearing, decent folk of middle America. I was not surprised that summer to see Pru acting as chauffeur for the dark-skinned Jamaican history professor to whom we sublet the house.

There was a rootless quality to our lives during our first months in Bloomington. I felt cut off, lonely, filled with doubts and anxiety about my future. Yet I also had by then a pleasurable sense of anticipation and a feeling that by living there I would come to understand the basic nature of America. We quickly learned that Bloomington was a more complex, interesting, and tolerant community than we had anticipated. This realization was borne out in our day-to-day dealings with neighbors. They treated us with casual friendliness, as evidenced by their pleasant greetings, small talk, and inconsequential gossip.

By the end of our first year, I realized that life in a predominantly university community can be easy and pleasant. The cultural opportunities were varied, of high quality, and inexpensive. We saw plays, operas, concerts, and ball games at a fraction of what they would have cost in New York or Boston, and they were almost always within walking distance. Faculty members invited us to dinners and to post-football-game cocktail parties. Other social activities filled our schedule: the Spaghetti Club for the wives, University Club picnics for newcomers, monthly play-readings with a local group, and regular parties and receptions sponsored by the law school.

Almost every activity in Bloomington had its social component— going to Aults' IGA, a grocery store, meant chatting with the Aults about children and running into colleagues, students, or people we had met at a party. Repairmen did not hurry in and out of the house but stopped to chat about the I.U. basketball team or what was happening in the city. Most people in Bloomington identified with the university, were proud of its stature, and rooted for its teams. My students were ubiquitous. They tended bar at the local tavern, sold clothes in the men's shop, and instructed the children in tennis and swimming.

The local newspaper frequently printed articles featuring the achievements of the faculty. It also provided a forum in which social and political issues were addressed by townspeople, faculty members, and public officials. Nobody thought it unusual that an editorial about China would set off active correspondence by experts on Southeast Asia, graduate students, and members of such diverse organizations as the John Birch Society, Young Socialists, and members of the League of Women Voters. When I wrote a letter criticizing the paper's "neutral" editorial, which condemned everyone involved at Selma, Alabama, people I hardly knew made a point of congratulating or criticizing me. It later occurred to me that my letter had received far more attention than had my scholarly writing.

When I went back East and people asked me, with evident condescension, "What's it like living in the Midwest?" I told them that my life was richer and more satisfying than I would have thought possible. My comments were invariably received either with scorn or polite disbelief.

In retrospect, the most remarkable and wonderful thing about Bloomington was that it changed me in ways for which I am still grateful. My personality slowly took on traits common to people who lived in the area. I slowed down in my walking, relaxed when I went shopping, and became involved in the community. Being a member of the law faculty made entry into community affairs easy. I was asked to talk to Baptists about biblical law and to Unitarians about labor relations. I was a founding member of the Bloomington Fair Housing Committee, made up of various ministers, a few lawyers, some townspeople, and several other academics. During my third year, I became president of the Elm Heights PTA.

The style of life and social opportunities of Bloomington made it difficult, if not impossible, to become a workaholic. The lawyers worked from 10:00 A.M. to 5:00 P.M. They met in Bender's Cafeteria for breakfast from 9:00 A.M. to 10:00 A.M., and several always were to be found in Nick's having a drink or a beer in the late afternoon. Just keeping up with my kids' swim club meetings, acrobatic lessons, and dramatic performances took up time and reminded me of the pleasures of the nonprofessional aspects of university life. Social invitations filled up a good deal of the weekends. Because of the nature of Bloomington society, friendships were not limited to the law school.

This pleasant life-style is common at other colleges and universities throughout the Midwest, in places like Iowa City, Iowa; Madison, Wisconsin; and Ann Arbor, Michigan. Austin, Texas, is archetypal. It offers cultural richness combined with an egalitarian atmosphere constantly refurbished by the influx of unknown and struggling artists, musicians, and writers.

Resolving Town-Gown Conflict

The testing time of the relation between universities and their surrounding communities came during the late 1960s and early 1970s. At many places (New Haven, Connecticut; Ithaca, New York; and Berkeley, California, among them), student activism led to a long period of bitter division. This did not happen at Bloomington, even though the level of political activity was quite high. Rallies, frequent marches in which the Viet Cong flag was carried, and regular confrontations between students and university police took place. A Bloomington-Berkeley radical axis existed which included Emily and Bill Harris, the young couple who were involved in the abduction of Patty Hearst. The students elected Keith Parker, a member of the Black Panthers, as student-body president. He was at the time the only popularly elected Black Panther official in the country. Inevitably, many of the townspeople were stunned and angry. Yet, remarkably, the basic connections between the university and the town remained strong and positive.

A variety of factors kept the enmity from being greater. Many of the townspeople had relatives or friends who were part of the student movement. There were many crossover figures like Warren Henegar, a farmer who was highly regarded both by students and conservative farmers. The young Republican prosecutor, Tom Berry, was a graduate of I.U. and the law school, and he was a great fan of its teams. All of the student events were open to the townspeople, some of whom came and spoke up. During all this time, the normal friendly meetings and opportunities continued at Nick's, at ball games, at the Faculty Club, and at the college mall. Probably most significantly, Bloomington was and still is a tolerant community in which most people were unhappy with the students but most never ceased to think of them as "our kids." Archetypal was my sons' warm, encouraging gymnastics coach, the politically reactionary Otto Reyser, who bitterly opposed the student movement. Even he had a son who was loosely connected to the radical student movement.

The students eventually began to realize that their only chance to become politically effective was to form coalitions with the townspeople. During the early 1970s, the I.U. voters' union was formed and quickly became a potent political force. Frank McCloskey, now a U.S. congressman but then a recent law school graduate from New York, was elected mayor; Marilyn Schultz, a recently arrived graduate student from Texas, was elected to the state senate. Many of the liberal people who became involved in Bloomington politics during the 1960s and 1970s are still politically involved and effective.

Community and Ideology

Those of us who teach and write about significant aspects of American society do so from a perspective at least partly shaped by our experiences, which are, in turn, shaped by the communities in which we live. Being in Bloomington gave me a new vision of American society and government, one in which access was available and in which people knew their political leaders and called cops by their first name. All of these attributes seemed remarkable to me. Growing up in the Bronx, it was "us versus them." Those who had money and power chased us out of Moshalu Park, broke up our stickball games, imposed foolish rules on us, treated us with contempt, and were not available if we called for help unless we could make contact through some important person who was known by some distant relative or acquaintance. But in Bloomington I felt a part of the community, capable of affecting things through my personal intervention. I did not see this as a special status accorded to me because I was a law professor but as something available to anyone who cared to become involved.

During my time at Yale, I realized that my political and social views had been shaped by Bloomington in ways that made me different from many of my colleagues whose lives had been spent almost entirely at elite institutions and on one coast or the other. Many of them had never met people like the Farises or Henegars, had never spent time at a midwestern PTA meeting, had never settled a case with a small-town prosecutor. They did not understand the diversity, complexity, basic friendliness, or commitment to education of middle America. Some seemed to see rural midwestern and southern communities as filled with stereotypical bigots and proto-Fascists. I might have felt the same way had I never lived there. I believe that a narrow, stereotypical view of most of America is not uncommon among academics whose experiences have been limited to large coastal cities and elite academic institutions.

Living in Austin has also provided me with unexpected insights into American society and politics. In Bloomington, the insights were about decency and continuity; in Texas, they are about change. When I was in the U.S. Army and stationed in Texas from 1953 to 1955, the culture seemed monolithic, unenlightened, and racist. People dressed alike and spoke alike. Commerce was backward, industry nonexistent. The governor and other high elected state officials were pledged to resist desegregation. Today all that is changed. The society is integrated, multicultural, progressive. Austin is a major center of research concerning computer technology. Active groups exist for every progressive and environmental cause. A liberal, prounion, strongly feminist Austin woman, Ann Richards, currently serves as governor after beating out a more liberal attorney general in the primary and a conservative, nonracist businessman in the general election. The attorney general, Dan Morales, is Chicano. The inner circles of both parties include blacks, Hispanics, and women. The University of Texas actively seeks minority students and faculty. All of this takes place with only a fraction of the racial and ethnic tension noticeable in Boston and other Eastern cities.[3]

Special Features of Academic Life

At one time I had an opportunity to visit Cornell as a prelude to joining the faculty. I was at first delighted with its physical beauty. When I returned to Bloomington from Cornell, I realized that I did not want to go to Ithaca. The tall, mountainous hills and great gorges that separated Cornell from the town of Ithaca conveyed unmistakably a sense of the university's removal from the life of the community. I contrasted it unfavorably with Bloomington. There was no obvious meeting place, no Nick's, which on Fridays was filled with professors, university officials, local politicians, students, and townspeople, all drinking beer and eating pizza together in an atmosphere of shared pleasure.

When I read Allan Bloom's discussion of the 1960s (one of the few chapters in *The Closing of the American Mind* which I thought effective), I was struck by the fact that the type of issues and attitudes which he describes at Cornell were present at Bloomington, but their resolution was far different.[4] Bloomington never experienced either the violence or the capitulation to student demands that Bloom describes. The black students stayed more connected to the students generally. Neither the black students nor the students who thought of themselves as radicals at Indiana ever separated themselves as fully as the black students did at Cornell. They were ultimately persuaded that they could have an impact on the general community. The one action that the black students at Indiana undertook on their own ended peacefully. The criminal charges that resulted from the action ended with some acquittals and mild penalties. In short, all sides in Bloomington seemed better able to compromise and work out accommodations. I believe that the resolution of issues at Cornell was made far more difficult because of the absence of regular contact between races, including the lack of places in which students, townspeople, and university administrators might meet in an atmosphere conducive to settlement and compromise. Cornell in this regard typified the social and intellectual isolation of elite eastern institutions generally and of Ivy League schools in particular. Bloom makes the mistake of treating the Ivy League as representative of higher education in general—a mode of thinking not uncommon at elite institutions.

Elite versus Nonelite Academic Communities

Elite institutions are either in modern, high-priced settings, like Stanford, physically separated from their communities, like Cornell, or living in states of tension with their outside communities, like Harvard, Yale, and Brown University. Yale is in the middle of things, being located right in the heart of downtown New Haven and surrounded by all of the inner-city problems of crime and poverty which go with an urban area. Yet Yale is a separate community, quite removed from the lives of the people in New Haven. It is surrounded by private eating clubs. I recall that on those rare occasions when the faculty would go out for lunch together to social-ize, we went to Morey's, whose membership is limited to people connected with the university. The Graduate Club, the New Haven Lawn Club, and several other places managed by different devices to keep contact with the town to a minimum. Non-Yale people sometimes attended functions at the Yale Repertory Theater or some of the concerts, but they were invari-ably well-educated upper-class professionals.

Midwestern and southwestern college campuses offer the possibility of different groups coming together socially, politically, and educationally: in short, community. This experience of community is far different from the great coastal and Ivy League universities, where separation and mutual resentment are the rule. When I attended Harvard, Cambridge residents were seen as corrupt, anti-intellectual, and antagonistic. Chicago, when I was there, had almost a siege mentality. In New Haven, great loyalty to Yale is powerful and constant, while contempt for the city and most of its residents is equally common within the university community. An echo of this was heard in the Supreme Court confirmation hearings of my one-time colleague, Robert Bork, who explained to the committee that he wrote his antitrust book in England because the alternative was to write it in New Haven.

Conclusion

The nature of the surrounding community affects the nature of the edu-cational experience. In part, this occurs because the nature of the com-munity affects the life-styles, personalities, and cultural views of the fac-ulty. In addition, one of the topics always dealt with, although sometimes indirectly, in any university is, "What does it mean to be educated?" Are educated people different from or superior to other people? The nature of the answers supplied by any university or college is inevitably shaped by its relation to the surrounding community.

The Ivy League institutions typically convey a message of separation and superiority. I do not think that this message is intentionally given, but at both Harvard and Yale it was delivered in countless small ways. At schools such as Indiana and Texas, this message, while still present, is muted by the positive interaction of the university and the community.

Conferences and International Travel and Programs

Academic Conferences

Academics frequently have the chance to travel, both within the United States and to foreign countries. The most common form of travel is to scholarly meetings, where professors from different institutions meet to discuss common scholarly issues. Such meetings help to establish a common academic language and a shared research agenda for professors throughout the world. They also serve more mundane purposes. Professors find jobs, collaborators, and sometimes publishers at such meetings. Meetings occasionally provide younger scholars with the special pleasure that comes from learning that one's articles have been read and appreciated by senior scholars in the field.

Unfortunately, conferences, travel, and meetings in glamorous places also have the capacity to reinforce the worst aspects of academic life and personality. Travel provides an opportunity to escape from responsibilities—to dine, visit, and play at other people's expense. It helps professors to feel important, successful, and superior.

The lure of conferences and travel frequently has nothing to do with teaching or research. This point is made by David Lodge in the prologue to his academic novel, *Small World*, where he satirically compares modern academic travel with the pilgrimages to the Holy Land described by Chaucer in *The Canterbury Tales*: "The modern conference resembles the pilgrimages of medieval Christendom in that it allows the participants to indulge themselves in all the pleasures and diversions of travel while appearing to be austerely bent on self-improvement. To be sure, there are certain penitential exercises to be performed—the presentation of a paper, perhaps, and certainly listening to the papers of others. . . . Today's conferees have an additional advantage over the pilgrims of old in that their expenses are usually paid . . ."[5]

The environment of academic conferences described by Lodge is self-indulgent, pleasure-seeking, corrupt, and intellectually deadening. Its participants, with minor exceptions, have either given up on being, or never were, serious academics. Morris Zapp, one of the more likeable characters in the book, is typical of those who have given up the search for meaning that first led them to academic life: "There comes a moment when the individual has to yield to the *Zeitgeist* or drop out of the ball game . . . For me it came in '75, when I kept getting invitations to Jane Austen centenary conferences in the most improbable places: Poznan, Delhi, Lagos, Honolulu—and half the speakers turned out to be guys I knew in graduate school. The world is a global campus . . . The American Express card has replaced the library pass. . . . Food and accommodations are the most important things about any conference."[6]

The world that Lodge describes is exaggerated, but it corresponds to the lives of a few—and the fantasies of many—academics. Almost all academics, even those who resist the temptation, are likely to find an invitation to an international conference tempting. For those involved in creative scholarship, conferences are an interruption, but they also occasionally provide an opportunity to meet people interested in similar issues located on remote campuses. They give those who have abandoned any serious effort at scholarship a substitute for the excitement that once came from discovery and creation. They give the nonscholar a chance to appropriate the manner and language of serious academics. To the academically well known, the professors from the Ivy League, Oxford, Cambridge, and the like, conferences provide the chance to bask in envy and constant reminders of their own exalted status in the academic world. And for the bored, the incompetent, those who are depressed by a constant feeling of failure, they provide hope, often illusory, of escape, a chance to become revitalized. In real life, as in Lodge's novels, almost everyone in attendance at an academic conference is on the make.

My own experience at academic conferences supports most of Lodge's conclusions. The papers are generally pretentious, the people competitive. Special honors are awarded to manipulators and operators at least as often as to important scholars. I have one major disagreement with Lodge's portrayal. Lodge's characters are motivated by the desire for luxury and sex. My experience suggests that the main focus of behavior at academic conferences is prestige and recognition. Much of the point is to revel in the pleasure of one's distinction.

I can still remember the first meeting of the American Association of Law Schools that I attended in 1962. The convention was held at the Edgewater Beach Hotel in Chicago, an imposing, old-fashioned, high-ceilinged building with slightly faded, once-elegant carpets. The lobby was crowded with distinguished-looking men in dark-colored suits and striped ties, some earnestly conversing with others or moving about with an air of importance. I felt an instant surge of envy and excitement, and a strong desire to belong. How I admired those who seemed at ease in this impressive gathering and those whose name tags identified them as professors from first-rate schools. I walked over to a group of Harvard faculty members who were stationed prominently in the lobby. They seemed to be holding court. Former students and professors from other schools approached them tentatively, vying for their attention. When the Harvard faculty members spoke, the others would listen intently, sometimes unconsciously nodding approval.

Each year that I taught at Indiana, I attended the annual convention of the American Association of Law Schools, seeking recognition and job offers from more prestigious schools. I thought of the convention as the arena in which my standing in the academic world would be measured and in which casual conversations could sow the seeds for future interest. The conventions were invariably unpleasant. People would look at me with mild curiosity, read my name tag, and look away with indifference. The Harvard people I knew greeted me as they greeted scores of other Harvard-trained law professors of the second or third echelon—in a friendly fashion, but without cordiality or personal interest. I circulated frantically, hoping that, somehow, at the next cocktail party or reception or meeting I would find the acceptance and approval for which I longed. I tried to impress the people I met with suggestions of my success at Indiana, but it was fruitless. Discussions with important faculty members were likely to be terminated when the person I was talking to saw someone "I just have to see for a few minutes."

I attended receptions, cocktail parties, and meetings; drank great quantities of liquor; tried constantly to meet with professors in my field, deans of good law schools, and people prominent in legal education; wandered around the city in which the convention was held; and invariably returned exhausted, feeling empty and defeated, with a strong sense of having demeaned myself. As Whitlock writes, "[T]he annual meetings are first and foremost rituals of prestige competition. Professors strut around on the soft carpets of hotel lobbies with the assiduousness of Birds of Paradise in their display dance, but without even the excuse of a tangible reward, such as the favors of females. Unknown young scholars attend conventions to court the favor of the nationally known ones, and the latter in order to receive the homage of the nonentities, to bask in the sunshine and the glory, and to defend their territory against challengers."[7]

International Travel

International programs have great capacities to enlighten and even to inspire. Academics who had the opportunity to visit Poland during the initial period of Solidarity, between 1980 and 1982, invariably came back excited by the thought of democratic change sweeping the country and by the vision of workers and intellectuals, academics and politicians, combining in a single movement. The writing about Solidarity that followed helped people to anticipate some of the reforms that have since occurred in Eastern Europe, and it provoked efforts to develop similar alliances in the United States.

When I visited China in 1985 to teach about dispute resolution and attended one of the many pro forma banquets thrown by our Chinese hosts, I sat next to a Chinese law professor who was, like me, an afficionado of Russian literature. He described why he enjoyed Turgenev better than Tolstoy: "I always feel that Tolstoy is lecturing to me but that Turgenev wants to share his experiences with me." As he spoke I became elated by the thought that somehow he, I, Tolstoy, and Turgenev were all joined together across time, distance, and national boundaries in a common effort to understand the connection among art, study, and the solution of social issues.

Sometimes international travel is undertaken for research purposes (for example, to compare institutions, relationships, and attitudes in the United States with those in other countries). Such comparative research is extremely difficult to do well because good comparative scholarship almost always requires an understanding of how the institution being studied fits into the culture in each country. Very few people are capable of complex understanding of different societies. As a result, comparative scholarship varies enormously in quality. The best of it is careful, informative, and insightful. It helps us to understand how different societies deal with similar problems.

Serious scholars travel to other countries because they want to learn more about something there. Harry Powers, an ethnomusicologist from Princeton who specializes in Indian music, has made repeated trips to various unglamorous regions of India to learn the oral traditions of Indian classical music. His work has helped to stimulate interest in and teaching and research about Indian music in the United States.

My former colleague Jerry Mintz, an anthropologist, lived for years in Casas Viejas, a small village in Andalusia, becoming part of the community, learning its mores and subtleties, and developing friendships with the survivors and descendants of the Spanish anarchists. He visited the homes of the Andalusian peasants, shared their holidays, and learned to play local card games for cheap wine. He went out into the field with the cork workers. He spent many afternoons meeting and talking about educational reform with aging radicals who had taken part in a small uprising many years ago. Using this information, Jerry wrote an excellent book,

The Anarchists of Casas Viejas,[8] and made a series of first-rate documentary films. His work introduces the reader to people they would not otherwise meet and explains something of their culture, attitudes, and lives.

Much comparative scholarship, however, is pompous and filled with misleading generalizations. A fair percentage of those working in this area are lured to it as much by the chance to travel and visit other countries as by any particularly scholarly impulse. Once a noted comparative law scholar, after drinking a good deal of wine at dinner, assured me that comparative studies was "a travel agency, not an academic discipline."

Sometimes international travel is undertaken for the purpose of advising governments or companies in other countries about how things are done in the United States or otherwise aiding them to solve the problems of their societies. Such aid from American academics, which is often administered by U.S. foundations, is subject to both the problems of comparative scholarship and the abuses typically attendant upon international conferences. Such aid also has special problems of its own, some related to the nature of foundations and foundation-run programs. I learned this early in my career when I spent academic year 1967–1968 in India. While the experience, which is related here in some detail, was obviously unique, conversations with academics who have taken part in other foundation-run international programs convince me that the problems and the benefits were both typical in many respects.

In the mid-1960s, a program to aid Indian legal education was developed by the Ford Foundation at the urging of Professor Arthur Von Mehren of Harvard. A major goal of the program was to develop two law colleges, Benares Hindu University and New Delhi University, as centers of excellence in Indian legal education. Part of the program involved the use of American law professors. I was recruited to take part in the program at Benares during academic year 1967–1968. The terms were beyond my expectations. Ford provided a high salary, fringe benefits, vacation facilities, a large house, servants, private schooling for our boys, first-class travel around the world, and various extras, such as free vacations in the Himalayas.

Initially, everything about dealing with the foundation appealed to me. I liked the elegant offices, the small and posh New York hotel at which they put me up, the air of quiet authority that the program officers and directors affected, the sense that they conveyed of being familiar and powerful people who dealt with important issues all over the world.

The chief program officer in law was vague about my duties. I would have the title of visiting professor at Benares Hindu University, Law College, but I was not expected to teach regular courses. I was to work with the faculty, not the students, and my specific assignments were to be worked out with the dean. "You are to be a wholesaler, not a retailer, of legal education," the chief program officer kept saying. I wasn't quite sure what this meant, but I took it to be an assertion of my importance. Merely teaching Indian law students would not be worthy of me.

Indian legal education had a reputation for poor quality in almost every respect. But I was told that Dean Anandji of Benares Hindu University, who had studied at Yale, was the main hope for significant change. He was committed to adopting the methods that had made legal education in the United States so successful, and he had won the loyalty and support of his faculty. An internal Ford memo stated, "The energy and talents of Dean Anandji persuaded the Foundation that the Benares efforts deserved support."[9]

My first dealing with Anandji suggested that he was indeed a committed educator. I wrote a letter in which I told him that personal problems made it desirable for me to postpone my coming until late summer. He responded graciously but firmly. My arrival could be delayed until July 21, 1967, but no longer. Disappointed as I was, I was favorably impressed by Dean Anandji's seriousness of purpose and the importance which he attached to my presence.

My family and I arrived in India on July 11, 1967, and spent the next few days in New Delhi being briefed at the Ford Foundation office on Ferozah Road, an impressive building with tastefully decorated offices and people moving about with an air of quiet importance. I met Doug Ensminger, the chief of mission, and John Masland, who was in charge of the educational programs.

The impression I received at the foundation office was that the Benares program was off to an excellent start. There had been two American professors there the previous year: one was A. Kenneth Pye, now president of Southern Methodist University. Pye's report of his activities was full of descriptions of new courses devised, research projects started, talks given, contacts made. The report suggested that the law school was an enclave of creativity in an academic wasteland. I hardly noticed that there was little mention of completed action—no materials ready for use, no courses newly placed in the curriculum, no research published.

The foundation officers talked casually of meetings with ambassadors, cabinet ministers, Supreme Court justices, even the prime minister. I would meet most of the important people in legal education, and I was encouraged to think about conferences and seminars that I wanted to or-

Special Features of Academic Life

ganize and talks that I might give at various law schools. I enjoyed this sense of closeness to power, but I deeply regretted that I was being sent to live in dangerous isolation at Benares when it was clear that the important decisions were made in Delhi.

I did not find Delhi frightening. The sense of chaos and disorder that I expected was not apparent. I witnessed its poverty only casually while being driven from one part of the western enclave to another.

After a week in Delhi, my family and I flew to Benares. To travel the twenty miles from the airport to Benares Hindu University was to enter a strange world of poverty, ignorance, and desolation. There was almost no grass or shrubbery visible. The earth had been baked sandy by two years of drought and was crisscrossed with long, narrow cracks. We drove by village after village made up of small huts and simple adobe houses with thatched roofs crowded together about a well. Cows, donkeys, and dogs wandered aimlessly through the narrow, unpaved streets, which were filled with people, many standing or squatting listlessly, some washing clothes, some getting dressed, some picking lice from children's heads, and some patting cow manure into patties. Along the road, we passed people pedaling slowly on large, old bicycles, groups of women and men carrying bundles on their heads, and small, incredibly thin herds of animals that were being driven to pasture or market. Only rarely did we meet or pass another car. When we met one coming the other way, both cars would head straight at each other until an accident seemed imminent, and then both would give way slightly at the last moment, barely avoiding each other.

With each passing mile, the landscape seemed more desolate and the life that I witnessed more removed from my experience. I felt alternately intrigued, baffled, and depressed. I could not have articulated it, but part of my depression was based on the realization that I was observing an ancient and powerful culture that I did not understand and was unlikely to affect.

The next afternoon, I had my driver take me to the law school. I wanted to ask Dean Anandji about my duties and seek his help in getting established. As we approached, I noticed that there were signs posted at various places, some in Hindi, some in English. A huge banner written in English hung across the road. When I was able to read it, I noted with horror that it stated, "Why do Dean Anand[10] and his American friends want to change Indian education?" That banner was followed almost immediately by one which said, "We don't need Ford Foundation money and advisors." Two or three similar signs had been posted on trees between our house and the law school, which was almost a mile away. The law building, which had just been built with Ford Foundation money, was gray and undistinguished-looking. Even in my fear, I was struck by how dirty it had become in the month since it had been dedicated.

A group of poorly dressed people lolled about in front. I tried to explain who I was, but they did not understand me. Finally, someone pointed me toward a small office in which a young, broad-faced man with a moustache was working. A small typed card over the door identified him as "V. J. Bhardwaj, Instructor."

I introduced myself. "I'm Jack Getman. I am going to be a visiting professor."

He rose to his feet, smiling pleasantly, and we shook hands. "Professor Getman, it's wonderful to meet you. I know that Dean Anandji will be very eager to talk to you when he gets back."

"When he gets back?"

Bhardwaj looked embarrassed. "Ah. Well, you see, Dean Anandji is in the United States just now as a guest of the State Department. Evidently he forgot to have someone notify you. But he will be back when school opens in August."

I was incredulous. "He told me I needed to be here now because school began July 1."

"Yes, that is true. Officially school should have begun July 1."

"But unofficially?"

He smiled cynically. "Maybe sometime in August. Just now it is much too hot, as you can see."

"Did Dean Anandji leave a message for me?" I asked in a strained, demanding voice.

"Ah, perhaps so. We will just look in your office." Bhardwaj smiled at me in a conciliatory manner and snapped his fingers at a man who was lounging on the law school steps. "You will kindly show Professor Getman to his office."

My office, which was large, contained a desk and a single blank pad. There was no note from Dean Anandji. When I managed to locate the dean's secretary, she shook hands with me formally. She said that the dean had left no message, but she knew that he was looking forward with great enthusiasm to my arrival. She spoke without conviction, as though repeating a formula.

"I rushed here in the middle of the summer with my whole family because Dean Anandji said it was necessary. What am I supposed to do now?" I asked angrily.

"Perhaps one of the other people will know whether Dean Anandji had any plans. I will talk to them when they arrive. Just now very few people are in the station."

The incident was typical of my relations with Anandji and of my experiences with important figures in Indian legal education. The situation was frustrating and disappointing and demonstrated that my role in the complex reality of the Indian educational system was to be limited and largely ceremonial. The Ford Foundation had wealth and influence, but its officers were at the mercy of Indian educators like the dean, who had a powerful investment in the existing system and who saw in the foundation a source of revenue and prestige, not an opportunity for reform. Significant change is difficult to promote without allying oneself with those forces fundamentally opposed to the existing system, and those seeking profound change viewed the Ford Foundation with great suspicion, as the sign that had greeted me showed.

The academics I have talked to report that this has been their experience with international programs. The trappings of prestige and importance are always present, but the ability to change things and influence events often turns out to be missing.

I returned home from the law college feeling angry, frightened, and inadequate. During the next few weeks, we rarely left the house. There was no place to go but the park or the law school; the heat, which reached more than 115 degrees every day, made walking outside or driving intensely unpleasant and brought activity at the university to a standstill. We spent time reading, arranging our rooms, eating, writing letters home, and slowly working out our relationship to the servants.

During our first weeks in Benares, we were almost totally disconnected from the world. We had no friends, no phone, little to do, and nowhere to go. Television was unavailable, and radio programs and movies were in Hindi. Our period of isolation lasted three weeks. It ended unexpectedly one afternoon when we were visited by an oddly assorted group of young people: three young women, two Americans and one French, all in saris; a young Englishman with long hair and a short beard; an African in a dashiki; and an Indian wearing loose white pajamas. They undertook to tell us about Benares, the university, and the special problems of Westerners in this environment.

At one point, one of the Americans asked, "Did you notice the anti-American signs between here and the law school?" When I nodded, she pointed to the young Indian and said almost proudly, "Deepak was responsible for them. He's the SRS [Radical Socialist Party] leader on campus."

Deepak smiled at me in a friendly, serious manner. He had a round, handsome face, sharp, intelligent eyes, and a generous but neatly trimmed beard. "I hope I did not frighten you, but I am opposed to Dean Anand and to the Ford project. He is power hungry, and the foundation leaders are cultural imperialists. We Indians will never become self-sufficient until we get rid of our corrupt leaders and our deference to foreigners." He started speaking calmly, but quickly became passionate and spoke as though addressing a meeting.

I tried to explain that my desire was to help.

He was surprisingly good-natured in his response, although he continued to express strong opposition to the foundation's efforts in India.

During this conversation one of the students asked us whether we had seen the Ganges River at twilight; when we said no, they invited us to go for a boat ride with them, and we accepted eagerly. The students hailed several bicycle rickshaws, and we went to the Ganges. The near side of the river was crowded with people. Washermen pounded clothes on huge stones, people walked about aimlessly, and small groups bathed according to Hindu ritual, their bodies weaving in the rapid current. High up on the bank in terraced rows were the burning *ghats* in which devout Hindus were cremated.

We traveled in two boats. I was with Deepak, together with Mary and Sue, the two young American women. While we were on the river, Deepak and I talked about his political philosophy, which was a perplexing blend of idealism, naïveté, and shrewdness. He considered himself a Marxist but he despised the Russians and most European Communists. His idol was Mao, even though China had just humiliated India in their brief border war. "Mao is not corrupt. He has suffered with the peasantry. He has weeded out corruption. He has caused the society to change," Deepak said.

"But the cost is human freedom," I protested.

He looked at me as though amazed by my lack of understanding. "In India we have political democracy but people are degraded by hunger, poverty, ignorance, and caste, all of which make freedom a mockery." He paused, then said to me, "You live in a great society. America doesn't need a revolution. India does."

"If you agree that America is a great society, why do you oppose my being here?" I asked.

"You personally are most welcome, but the organization you represent is spreading the wrong message and you are helping the wrong people to achieve power in the country and in the university. Dean Anand has no concern for the people. He is interested only in himself. He wants money, a fine building, and a chance to visit his friends in the United States."

At one point I asked him who his political heroes were. After thinking for a while he answered, "Lenin, Mao, Lincoln, Nehru, and Kennedy."

Deepak and I argued with each other constantly throughout the trip, but without anger. I found him likeable. His Marxism seemed to me to be based not on ideology or admiration for the Soviet Union but on his strong concern for the terrible state of the poor, uneducated masses of Indian society.

After the trip we invited them all to dinner. They accepted promptly, ate heartily, Deepak in particular, and stayed until past midnight. When the day ended I was not sure whether Deepak was friend or opponent, agent of needed change or unthinking radical.

Before long, our house was a meeting place for the small Western community in Benares which was composed mainly of young people in their early twenties. Deepak was among the most regular of our visitors. Whenever he came over, the servants would clamor for his attention. He became a means of communicating with them.

One evening I asked him if he would talk to Gunga Jali, the ayah, and find out what was troubling her. When he approached her, she burst into tears and began speaking rapidly in Hindi. His eyes moved sympathetically from her to me. When she finished, his appearance was almost as miserable as hers. "She has gone to a moneylender for money to build a house, but the money is gone and she cannot finish it. She has three girls and her husband says he will leave her. Her life has been a tragedy of exploitation. She doesn't know where to turn."

My wife and I exchanged glances. "We have to do something," she whispered.

"How much does she need?" I asked Deepak.

His face brightened. He spoke to her gravely. She responded at some length. "She is a very impressive and reasonable person. Only 500 rupees."

It was four months' salary for her, but only seventy dollars in American money. We could easily afford it. "Tell her we will buy the house."

"Oh, Doctor Sahib, this is a wonderful thing. She will always be grateful."

"But tell her not to mention it to the others. We are already in trouble about how much we pay them."

Gunga Jali's face was joyous, and for the next several weeks she worked with great enthusiasm. We received a series of optimistic reports about the state of the house, and when the construction was complete, Gunga Jali proudly invited us to see it. She took my wife Bobby through the small village to the site on which the house stood. Bobby came back totally depressed. She reported that excavation of mud for mortar was being conducted immediately next to the building site and that the house would probably soon crumble into the pit. A month later the house was destroyed by the heavy rains. It was yet another example of our ostensible power and ultimate lack of ability to shape events as we would have wished.

The incident convinced me that Deepak was someone who identified with the exploited and the helpless. It also suggested that the forces seeking fundamental and necessary changes in Indian society were the very ones that opposed Anandji, the Ford Foundation, and the privileged position of naïve American visitors, such as myself.

One morning an emaciated and bedraggled Indian student came to the door pleading for work. He told me that unless he could earn some money he would be forced to drop out of school. Since he spoke English well, I offered him a job teaching me Hindi for five rupees a day, a huge salary by Benares standards. He accepted with alacrity. He appeared overcome by his good fortune and assured me repeatedly that I would not be sorry. He came every day that I was home for the next four months, and he turned out to be a fine teacher: patient, understanding, and well prepared. Under his guidance, I learned with surprising speed. After a week or so, I tried speaking Hindi to the servants. Bechen, the cook, and Shanti, the sweeper, were confused; Lal, the driver, quickly took to correcting me; and Gunga Jali giggled happily at my incompetence. But they all began to understand me, and I felt excited at the prospect of communicating with people in their own language.

I spoke Hindi whenever possible—with the servants, merchants, western students, and people at the law school. Indians invariably responded with pleasure. From the moment I started speaking in Hindi, my fear of living in Benares began to disappear. I started to explore the university grounds and the relatively fashionable shopping areas nearby. The university had several colorful, exotic museums and a fascinating, ornate temple in which I witnessed the elaborate religious rituals and listened to the musical chanting of Hindu prayers.

Buoyed by feelings of success, I purchased Indian clothing and a bicycle so I could travel by myself to the downtown areas of Benares, where I discovered an exotic world that had initially terrified me—dirty, incredibly poor, and teeming with life. The streets were as narrow as cow paths: noisy, filthy, and packed with people shoving, arguing, bargaining about small purchases and tending to their bodily needs along the tiny gutters. Bicycle riders traveled through the crowded streets at great speed, barely noticing the pedestrians and merchants, whom they seemed constantly on the verge of bowling over. Somehow, serious confrontations and acts of violence were rare, although any unusual incident would attract a great crowd of onlookers and sometimes create an atmosphere of tension that seemed about to erupt into large-scale violence, but which never did during the times I was there.

In the midst of all this, the famous sacred cows of Benares wandered untouched, looking in vain for food, their skin darkened by filth, their ribs showing pitifully through their sagging skin. And constantly through the streets came the funeral processions—the bodies held aloft in sitting positions followed by small lines of people mostly dressed in rags and accompanied by the beating of drums and the ceaseless solemn chanting *Ram Nam Satja Hay* ("The name of God is truth").

In Benares, I regularly witnessed the most appalling aspects of human life—disease, poverty, and injustice. Most of the people who crowded into the center of the city looked undernourished and were dressed in tattered clothes. They walked barefoot through streets that reeked of urine and littered cow dung. Only the vaguest connection existed between them and the corpulent merchants and smug-looking tourists in elegant silk saris and suits who sauntered through the shopping areas in search of bargains. Much of the hard manual labor was done by children, some barely in their teens, some even younger. It was not uncommon to see an angry merchant slap a child's face as people passed by indifferently.

A street set aside for prostitution was filled with desperate, angry-looking women who leaned aggressively out of windows or stood in vulgar poses in the narrow doorways calling out noisily to the passersby. The center of the city also had a proscribed area for beggars, who squatted patiently in rows beside their tin begging cups, which rarely contained more than a few pitiful coins, their eyes cast downward, their features almost inanimate, showing neither interest nor hope.

To be part of this scene on a regular basis was to feel the poverty and injustice of India in an immediate, personal, and disturbing way that was far different from anything I had experienced before. This recognition did not help me to contribute anything significant to Indian legal education. It did reinforce my growing feeling that Indian society was more complex and powerfully controlled than it first appeared to be. I began to realize that I could not contribute to the development of legal education in a society that I did not understand. I became increasingly aware that understanding required prolonged first-hand exposure to the lives of the people I was ostensibly trying to help. This awareness has been the source of all of my best research.

I was invited to give a series of talks about American labor relations at an institute in Calcutta to which I traveled by train. The trip turned out to be a nightmare. The train started late. The air-conditioning broke down, making the first-class compartment unbearably hot. The only car in which windows opened was a second-class car that reeked of urine. Along the route protestors lay down on the tracks and were roughly dragged away by soldiers. The scene in the train station in Calcutta made the center of Benares look almost affluent. Most of the huge station had become a makeshift living area filled with miserable refugees from West Bengal and the poorest, most backward areas of Calcutta. People were sleeping on straw mats, washing from small bowls, and shaving. The station reeked of feces and illness.

The drive to the Ford Foundation office was a further ordeal, even though in most ways Calcutta was far more like a Western city than Benares. It had broad boulevards, tall buildings, and traffic lights. British influence was evident in the private clubs, homes with manicured tennis courts, elegant hotels, a large number of automobiles, and many people in Western dress. But a little way from the boulevard I saw the tiny, makeshift refugee villages, known as *bhustis*, in which people lived packed together in tiny mud huts, obviously lacking the most basic attributes of civilized communities, such as water, sewerage, or electricity. Children played without joy in the dirt and mud while the adults stood expressionless. When we came to the downtown areas, the *bhustis* were no longer visible, but whenever the car stopped at traffic lights we were instantly accosted by beggars, almost all crippled, some hideously deformed. Unlike the beggars of Benares, they were aggressive, angry, and malevolent, demanding money as the price for permitting me to escape from the sight of their wretchedness. This was a level of misery with which I could not identify or even sympathize. It was too deep and widespread to comprehend. I felt hopelessly battered by the time we arrived at the foundation office in Calcutta.

The house was large and elegant, with massive stone walls all around it and a huge gate in front. I entered with the immense relief of someone escaping from a nightmare. I later discovered a description from another academic, William Van Til, that summarized my feeling at the time:

"Hell—my only descriptive word that comes close to describing Calcutta. Yes, I've seen the Victoria Memorial and the art galleries and mansions, too, but my pervading memory of Calcutta is the unimaginably dense-packed streets. Incredible numbers of human beings are born, live, and die on the squalid streets. Naked babies lie in the dust and the sacred white cows drop their loads beside the little heads. The old sit and wait for death. Outside the Department of Education of the University of Calcutta is a vast garbage dump in which the ravaged bodies of what once were human beings compete with the sacred cows for a morsel of food.[11]

When he returned to India in August, Dean Anandji was immediately caught up in internal university politics and was rarely at the law school. It was early October before I could talk to him. He had not done any thinking about how I might be used, and he agreed without enthusiasm when I volunteered to work with some of the junior faculty to develop a legal process course. I no longer recall precisely why I thought such a course desirable.

In mid-October, Anandji finally designated two junior faculty members and an aging instructor to work with me on the legal process course. They were a curiously mixed group. The ablest was Bhardwaj, the person I met on my first day at BHU. He was intelligent, ambitious, articulate, and friendly. Gupta, the senior lecturer, was stolid and dull. He seemed bored by the enterprise. The most ambitious was Aggarwall, who had just returned from a year studying at Yale. He had a broad face, a long, fleshy nose, and dark, smoldering eyes. He taught courses in jurisprudence and constitutional law, and he spoke about law in a curious jargon partly derived from the famous Law and Social Policy course at Yale and partly from the typically ornate style of Indian jurisprudential writing. He was very difficult to understand. He seemed resentful of me and contemptuous of everyone else.

Each of the men had a variety of commitments that made regular meetings impossible. We finally met at my home. I hoped this would make the atmosphere less formal, but the Indians seemed uniformly uncomfortable. They sat stiffly on the couch, rose whenever I got up, and addressed me as Professor Getman, although I had asked them to call me Jack. Since they did not do so, I felt compelled to refer to them by surname as well. When I asked them at the start whether they were interested in working with me to develop a legal process course based on Indian materials, they said "certainly," but without enthusiasm. We discussed what might be achieved by such a course. Aggarwall spoke in grandiose language about demonstrating the sociological considerations that a decision maker must consider. Gupta talked about the wisdom of legal rules. Bhardwaj expressed confusion.

I suggested that such a course could demonstrate why Indian courts needed to break away from following British cases. Bhardwaj asked me what sort of cases I had in mind. I answered rather generally that each person might try to find cases in his own area in which English precedent was inappropriate. We would later put them all together to form a single body of materials. They promised to do so, but I sensed some feeling of annoyance at the vagueness of the task. None of the Indians really wanted to put in time on this project. Bhardwaj was doing his own work. Gupta had long since given up the idea of doing any work, and Aggarwall found the task unworthy of his talents.

They were right to be wary. I had little idea of how an Indian-oriented legal process course might be structured. I did not know which issues were most significant, most typical, or most amenable to legal solution. I did not know and had not thought of how such a course would fit in with the rest of the curriculum. The legal process course was never developed beyond the outline stage, and none of the faculty involved learned anything of value from it beyond the need to be cautious in dealing with inexperienced Americans.

I never developed good working relationships with Aggarwall or Gupta. I later learned that Aggarwall believed that I was reporting to the dean about him. I did become friendly with Bhardwaj and finally helped him somewhat by encouraging him to continue the work he had been doing before I arrived.

I fared no better in my efforts to improve teaching. I sat in on two classes, one taught by Aggarwall and one by Tripathi. They were much worse than I had expected. They lectured in English with little fluency, focusing uncritically on doctrine. The students sat as though in a trance. Hardly a flicker of interest was noticeable until a general expression of relief signaled the class's end.

I decided to demonstrate at the next class meeting how contracts were taught in the United States. I prepared a typical, slightly simplified class utilizing the basic Socratic style.

I began the class by asking, "Why did the Indian court use English precedent?" No response or interest. "What was the rule that the court applied?" Still no sign of animation. I realized gradually that the lack of animation was because the students did not understand my question.

I decided to speak to them in my halting Hindi. "Why," I asked, "did the poor person have to pay when he didn't get what he expected?"

Special Features of Academic Life

I expressed even simple ideas with difficulty in Hindi. The process of communicating took a long time, but, when I looked over at the students, I noticed looks of surprised delight and even interest. When I finished, several students applauded my efforts, a few hands went up, and I called on someone who spoke rapidly in Hindi that I could not follow. I asked Aggarwall to translate and we spent the rest of the hour communicating in a kind of pidgin Hindi. The students seemed much livelier than I had expected. I left the class thoroughly confused about the value of the Ford program. It seemed ridiculous for teachers who did not speak English well to use it to teach students who could not understand it at all. The idea of a sophisticated legal process course for these students seemed worthless. I wondered whether Socratic dialogue made any sense in this setting. The Ford program, which represented a commitment to American techniques and to the use of English, might be an impediment rather than a help to Indian legal education.

During the final months of my stay, I wrote an article in which I argued that law teaching in India should be conducted in language understandable by the people in the community. I also argued that the language of law could not be separated from the language of the people without doing both harm. Ford Foundation officers and officials of the newly created International Center tried to convince me not to publish the article. They felt certain that I did not understand the delicacy of the language problem, and I felt equally certain that they did not understand the educational issues in a community like Benares.

My efforts to improve the administration of the law college by utilizing American concepts of faculty governance also proved to be futile. Once I suggested to Dean Anandji that his almost continual absence from the law school was creating a serious problem, since he alone decided on such things as curriculum and only he was authorized to spend some of the Ford money for research or other programs.

"Clearly you are right," he said. "But I have no other choice. You don't know how vicious are the attacks on me from those who are jealous and from those who fear that I am controlled by you Americans." He looked depressed and frustrated and I felt a surge of sympathy. "I know that right now nothing is happening at the law school, but by the end of the day, I am exhausted from everything and I can't really think about what's happening at the school. Besides, nobody really tells me anything and I need to know the people I can trust. What do you think of Aggarwall? He is supposed to be working with you."

I tried to evade the question. "Well, we haven't really started working very much. I have talked to him a few times."

"You watched him teach. What did you think of the class?"

"It was a little rigid, but it's difficult to tell from one class."

Anandji seemed lost in thought. "I believe that he is very much a protégé of Shukla [one of the senior professors] and would like to see me ousted. Has he ever spoken to you about this?"

I felt trapped. We both knew that for me to be effective in any way, I needed his support. He was making it plain that in order to obtain his support, I had to become his ally in internal politics and act as his informant.

I tried to finesse the issue. "I think you can win the loyalty of the younger faculty by giving them a greater sense of participation."

He smiled politely. "That is the very thing I am trying to do. But, in India, it is very difficult. The sense of distrust is so great.

"Why don't you establish faculty committees to help you administer the school? You might have one for curriculum, one to deal with students, one to deal with appointments. Of course, you yourself would be a member of the most important ones. It would also give the faculty a greater awareness of your problems."

Anandji looked annoyed. "It would be quite impossible. Things are different here in India. People would have to be appointed according to rank. The two full professors would control everything. They are opposed to what I am doing. There is no other choice."

I realized at that moment that I would accomplish nothing at Benares. Anandji did not want to share power, and I did not want to become his confidant. Thereafter, our meetings became less frequent and more formal. Anandji rarely came to my office, and he showed little interest in the development of the legal process course that I was supposedly helping to establish.

The more I observed Anandji in action, the clearer it became that he was neither a scholar nor an educator. How had someone whose flaws seemed so obvious managed to convince the Ford Foundation that his leadership made the Benares law school worthy of support? I realized during my stay in India that his central position was not an isolated mistake. Indeed, when I left Benares and was assigned to the Indian Law Institute (an institution established and controlled by the foundation), I discovered that the director of the organization, much like Anandji, was capable of talking eloquently about the need for empirical study and academic reform when he spoke to Americans. However, again like Anandji, he was old-fashioned and dictatorial with his Indian subordinates. He discouraged empirical or innovative research. He insisted upon rigid adherence to traditional protocol. One promising young scholar was dismissed for not getting to his feet quickly enough when the director entered a room.

The Difficulty of Contributing to Other Cultures

My relations with the faculty were complex. I visited classes and spent as much time conversing with them as I could. They responded to conversational initiatives with elegant clichés and vague generalizations. They neither openly disagreed with me nor openly defended Indian legal education, which most were willing, indeed eager, to criticize as too conceptualistic and rigid.

They treated me more like an emissary from a powerful foreign government than a colleague. I was associated with the Ford Foundation, which had created the Indian Law Institute, supplied its funds, and selected the director and principal researchers. It could make dreams come true—bestowing trips to the United States, positions in international agencies, and support for academic research or programs—and it could make a native scholar important in India.

My status did not translate into reform, however. It did not convince the dean or faculty members of the wisdom of my ideas. Indeed, my status was one of the things which motivated them to resent me. Moreover, I had no significant ideas about how to improve Indian legal education. The more I learned about it, the more difficult I realized the problem was. My effectiveness was also limited by the realization that I would be leaving at the end of the academic year, to be replaced by another American, almost certain to be equally unsophisticated about Indian legal education.

The Naïveté and Arrogance of Foundations

Foundation officials are pampered and treated with special consideration by faculty everywhere. This frequently gives them the ability to shape research, even when they are not particularly knowledgeable. They are especially powerful in poor countries that have few resources of their own. I witnessed a particularly egregious example of this power in action at a meeting in New Delhi in which a group of Americans (some were neophytes like myself and two were foundation experts on a quick trip from the United States) made decisions about legal education in India. At one point, we discussed the work of the Indian Law Institute, which everyone agreed was deplorable. One law scholar said, "They are addressing themselves to the wrong project. Their research is sterile and traditional and their involvement with developing casebooks seems silly." The constitutional law casebook developed by M. P. Jain, one of the two professors at Benares, was pointed to as a particularly silly waste. Students couldn't afford it, professors didn't assign it, it would soon be outdated, it wasn't really directed to the right problems, and no one could see any point to it. The group agreed that the Indian Law Institute was squandering its money publishing casebooks and that the practice should be stopped. I agreed with the conclusions, but I felt uncomfortable. I had learned enough about India to realize that sometimes Indian counterparts of American institutions functioned in ways quite strange to Americans but nonetheless sensible for India.

"It troubles me that we are evaluating the impact of Ford programs on Indian legal education with no Indian law professors present. We haven't even talked to them about this," I said.

One of the participants, a distinguished professor from Columbia visiting at Delhi, smiled benignly. "Jack makes an excellent point. I wish we had the time to involve them more, but our visiting experts are not going to be here long." He paused and smiled again. "The truth is, we can talk more freely among ourselves when we don't have to worry about Indian sensibilities."

The decision to stop publishing casebooks was recommended to the chief justice of India, who was the ex officio head of the law institute, who promptly ratified the decision. When I returned to Benares about a week later, I told M. P. Jain, who wrote the casebook, about the decision. He was dismayed. He told me angrily that the casebook had been a great success. He insisted that it had been intended not for students but for lawyers, that it provided a common body of precedent for use in constitutional litigation, and that many Indian lawyers had told him how useful it was. Jain might have exaggerated, but his basic point was probably correct. His contention was never investigated. By the time I mentioned his comment to Ford officials in Delhi, the decision had been formally announced.

The BHU campus shut down in December and did not reopen again until mid-January, when the semester that was supposed to end in November was just beginning. Not a single week of uninterrupted classes had been conducted. School had been closed by strikes, riots, holidays, and natural disasters. One particularly ugly incident occurred when the stu-

Special Features of Academic Life

dents caught a "thief" and marched him from dorm to dorm, beating him with sticks while he howled with pain and fear. I tried to get the law faculty to intervene, but I was told this was a "customary form of rough justice." The next day, I learned that he had been beaten to death.

Even without violence, the atmosphere was made depressing by the apathy of the students, their lack of understanding, and the intrigue and unhappiness of the faculty. The idea that the Benares law school would become a model of excellence seemed absurd, a vision concocted by Americans under the blandishments of Dean Anandji, who saw in the program an opportunity to achieve the political influence that was his only genuine ambition.

Riots broke out just before we were due in Delhi once again for midwinter meetings. While I was there, I wrote a memo to the Ford Foundation in which I evaluated the situation in Benares as clearly and honestly as I could. I was certain that Ford officials in Delhi would resent my memo, as would the academic consultants at Harvard and Columbia who helped originate the program and felt that they would conclude that my report was different from Ken Pye's because I was less able to function in the hurly-burly of India than he was, less imaginative and resourceful, and less able to serve as a model or a source for acceptable ideas and programs. The ambition that I still nurtured to be selected for future Ford assignments would be far less likely to be attained. But I was angry, I wanted to be heard, and I wanted something meaningful to come from my experience.

The memo I wrote was five typewritten pages. It had little diplomatic padding and began with my overall conclusion concerning the program:

> The Benares law school has not become a center of excellence for Indian legal education, and it is most unlikely that it will do so in the near future—the Benares law school student body is especially poor. It draws from BHU undergraduates who are among the worst in India—the students are almost completely incompetent in English—all four of the best faculty members are likely to leave shortly. I have observed most of the faculty in their teaching; with some notable exceptions, the level is very poor; it is unimaginative, conceptualistic and doctrinaire. It gives a rigid and mechanical picture of the legal system—the informal bull sessions so common to American legal education are nonexistent. Very little thinking is done by the faculty about the future of the school.
>
> The administration of existing programs is chaotic. Dean Anandji has delegated very little authority and he has been involved in university affairs and largely unavailable himself. He has only rarely been in his

office this semester. When he arrived in August I suggested . . . that a committee should be appointed to work with the students in a variety of ways. He accepted the idea but the committee has not yet been appointed. The plans to recruit good students have not been implemented.

There have been no efforts to develop new materials—no efforts have been made to formulate a coherent approach to the language problem. . . .

The Dean does not appreciate [the] significance of research (he has done none himself) and I am told that at previous faculty meetings he has insisted that research is not a matter of immediate concern.[12]

This remains one of the very few memos that I have written in my academic career that I am proud of. I felt that in taking a position that the Ford Foundation did not want to acknowledge, I gave up the chance of being used by the foundation in future overseas programs. This signified the beginning of my disillusionment with academic hierarchy.

A few months later I learned about Robert Kennedy's assassination. The news reinforced a feeling of dissatisfaction with my academic emphasis, which had grown quite powerful during my period in India. I felt increasingly that the law review articles on which I had labored so hard were too technical, too erudite, and too pedantic, removed from the concerns of workers and the important issues of labor relations with which the society had to deal. I did not, at the time, understand the origins of the feeling or even which of my experiences gave it the sense of urgency that it developed. Perhaps the great problems of life and death that surrounded me and the timeless quality of life in Benares gave me a more demanding scale against which to weigh my contributions; perhaps the excitement of dealing with high-level issues in my talks and discussions with Indian leaders prompted the strong feelings. The constant exposure to suffering, poverty, and injustice brought me to the realization that none of my work was relevant to the solution of any of these problems. When Michael was ill and we took him to Holy Family Hospital in New Delhi, I noticed on a plaque the dedication to "the glory of God and the cause of suffering humanity." I found the statement stirring and disquieting, a criticism of my life and values.

Conclusion

Travel, particularly international travel, expresses the best and the worst aspects of academic life. At its best, it demonstrates the universality of thought and inquiry. It reveals and makes closer the ties that connect teaching and scholarship in different societies. It shows the power of scholarship to illuminate and enrich our lives. At its worst, it demonstrates the pervasiveness and destructiveness of hierarchy in academic life. It reveals the arrogance of the wealthy and the selfishness of the poor.

The phenomenon of academic travel is closely tied to the wealth and power of foundations. The role of foundations in the world of higher education is a mixed one, at best. Foundations contribute money and have provided first-rate scholars with time for research, but they have also diverted energy to wasteful issues and in other ways illustrate the wisdom of Lord Acton's observation: "Power tends to corrupt; absolute power corrupts absolutely."

Travel abroad is exciting and interesting for the great majority of academics, but most of us lack the training and background to aid educators in other countries or do valuable comparative research. For most of us, travel can be enlightening. We can acquire from it a greater sense that the forms of our institutions are not preordained; realization of the common struggle, problems, and joys of educators; and a sense of being allied with honorable people all over the world.

Hierarchy

The Complex Relationship between Status and Meaning

People who become professors are rarely indifferent to the title and status that come with the role. It would be difficult to overstate the role of hierarchy in academic life. Its power is manifest at every point, its impact felt on every issue. In Kazuo Ishiguro's book *The Remains of the Day*,[13] the narrator, a butler deeply committed to his profession, describes how the top butlers would engage in long discussions of the attributes necessary for greatness in the profession, deciding who had those attributes and which of the contemporary butlers could properly be described as great. Similar discussions take place in almost any faculty lounge. Who are the great scholars? Who among us are truly brilliant? Which are the great departments or schools? How do Yale, Harvard, and Stanford compare? What are the attributes of true academic greatness?

The desire for status—a higher place in the academic hierarchy—shapes both personal and institutional goals and decisions. It can have a positive impact in fueling effort, but it can be destructive, as well, interfering with effective teaching and scholarship and leading institutions and professors away from useful or enjoyable endeavors toward those thought to be more prestigious.

The equally powerful desire for meaning often conflicts with and limits the pursuit of status. That is why good scholars or teachers on occasion turn down honorific opportunities to continue pursuing something they care about. Val Nolan, a first-rate law professor at Indiana University, would have been a very effective dean and was offered deanships on many occasions, but he always turned them down because he thought his research in another field, ornithology, was far more interesting and meaningful. Often, however, academics make the mistake of assuming that status and meaning go together. This confusion affects selection of subject matter for teaching and research, a preference for students whom professors want to have in their classes, and the choice of colleagues. The desire for and impact of status is particularly powerful with respect to the school at which one teaches.

Professors almost always want to teach at highly rated institutions. One reason is that ideas from professors at top schools are automatically treated with respect. That is not true for those who teach at nonprestigious schools. Fledgling academics also assume that at more prestigious schools one's life is spent with more interesting colleagues, teaching brighter students, and in more pleasant circumstances. When I entered teaching, I naturally equated success with the caliber of the school at which I taught. I would have liked to begin at one of the first-rate law schools, but I knew that this was impossible since I had mediocre grades for someone who wanted to enter law teaching.

The Confusion of Grades and Intelligence

My efforts to obtain a teaching position were a powerful illustration of how unpleasant the academic enterprise can be for someone who lacks adequate credentials. When I initially wrote Harvard Law School indicating my desire to enter teaching, I was informed quickly that I would be of interest only to schools of modest status and little ambition. I wrote back that I would be happy to begin teaching at such a school, but it turned out that none of those institutions to which my name was sent wanted even to interview me. I became a teaching fellow at Harvard to make up for the fact that my law school grades were not outstanding. As a teaching fellow, I had almost no status and was essentially treated as a nonperson by most of the regular faculty, some of the students, and much of the permanent staff. I learned that gradations of status existed within the regular faculty based on such things as rank, subject matter taught, styles of argument, and reputations for brilliance. I also learned that a reputation for brilliance remained tied to student grades long after far more sensible measures of intellectual achievement were available. I attended a faculty meeting at which a visiting professor from Berkeley was being considered for a senior appointment. Several people objected to his faculty appointment on the grounds that his scholarship was shallow. The dean responded by first listing his grades at a midwestern law school and then as an LL.M. candidate several years before. He boomed them out in a loud voice, "82 in Federal Procedure, 81 in Copyright, 83 in Advanced Property, and 84 on his LL.M. paper. If any of you can do better, you're welcome to try," he concluded. This seemed to satisfy the critics and an offer was promptly voted. Whenever the faculty discussed eminent former students, their grades and their performances on exams would be analyzed. At the time, only one person on the faculty, the constitutional law professor Mark De Wolfe Howe, had not made law review as a student. He was a great friend of Louis Jaffe's, and Jaffe told me that Howe was so apologetic about not having made law review that it substantially reduced his effectiveness in faculty discussions. Years later when Howe died, Erwin Griswold's eulogy for Howe, which was published in the *Harvard Law Review*, pointed out that he had not made law review. I concluded that in legal education, mediocre grades were like original sin in Calvinist doctrine— something which could not be overcome by future good works. I wondered whether anything corresponding to grace exists in the theology of legal education. I did not at that time, however, question the use of law school grades to measure academic potential. I considered it protection against judging people by their background, manners, or appearance.

When I first went into law teaching, I was pleased to be associated with a group of people almost all of whom had been outstanding academic successes. I felt somehow retroactively elevated by being associated with them, as though my inclusion in such a group was proof that I had the intellectual ability to have succeeded in school even as they did. I did my best in faculty recruitment to make sure that we hired people with academic records far better than my own.

In general, academics equate intelligence with grades and teaching qualification with success as a student. This is particularly true in legal education, where it is unduly assumed that no one who was at the top of the class at Yale or who made law review at Harvard could be intellectually inadequate. And that, whatever the paths of their careers, people who "made review" are almost by definition smarter than those who did not.

But just as I came over the years to see that many of my weaknesses as a student could be strengths as a professor, so I came to appreciate that for most of my colleagues their strengths as students would often lead to weaknesses as teachers and scholars.

Many who are able to construct intellectual frameworks are quite poor at connecting them with reality. Frequently in their research, these people limit themselves to topics calling for the same type of reasoning at which they excelled as students. As teachers, they assume that all students should approach learning as they did. Many of them as professors assume the usefulness of anxiety as a pedagogical technique. They have little sympathy for those who find the process demeaning. They often continue the practice of equating grades with intelligence, an assumption that pervades their dealings with students and inevitably shapes the self-perception of both.

Status, Grades, and Job Hunting

Almost anyone seeking a first academic position quickly learns about the importance of both grades and hierarchy. I was no exception.

I attended the annual meeting of the American Association of Law Schools for the first time in 1961 to seek a tenure-track position. I was nervous but mildly optimistic because I had received a complimentary letter from Dean Victor Kramer of George Washington University Law School, expressing great interest in me and inviting me to a cocktail party. The letter urged me to introduce myself to any members of the George Washington faculty whom I might meet.

While going to check my mailbag for messages, something I did about every forty minutes, I met two members of the George Washington faculty. Remembering the letter from Dean Kramer, I introduced myself. It was clear from their manner they had never heard of me. I mentioned the letter from Dean Kramer. "I'm very interested in George Washington," I told them. "Nice to hear that," one said in a voice expressing total lack of interest. "See you at the cocktail party."

Neither was present when I showed up at the appointed time. There seemed to be about thirty job candidates present, all of whom had received letters similar to mine, but only four or five members of the George Washington faculty. I realized with a sinking feeling that even to be considered I would have to compete fiercely. I took a drink and joined five or six applicants who had grouped around one of the faculty members present. The professor glanced at my name tag. An expression of recognition seemed to pass over his face. He turned to me. "How are you enjoying Harvard?"

"Very much. I'm really learning to teach by observing the masters."

He looked more interested. "What are your teaching preferences?"

"Labor law."

His face fell. I remembered too late that potential labor law professors were a glut on the market. He turned and asked the same question of someone else.

"I'm very flexible. I could teach anything," the candidate said.

"Do you have any ideas about teaching civil procedure? We are short-handed since one of our procedure people has just taken a high-level position in the Justice Department."

"I would focus on the Federal Rules of Civil Procedure so the students would learn a single system."

At that point, another applicant interrupted. "I have a great deal of litigation experience. I could teach civil procedure from actual cases."

"Really? Can you give me an example?" the interviewer asked.

The applicant was midway through his example when yet another prospective teacher challenged him on the appropriateness of one of his cases. I stood about uncertainly. I did not want to compete, but I also did not want to give up on the one school that had seen fit to contact me. I remained there, sullen and depressed. When I spoke, my remarks were either angry or bland. When I finally left about an hour later, I knew that I would not be joining the faculty at the George Washington University Law School. When I later received a letter telling me that I was rejected "after careful consideration of your excellent record," I was far more surprised at the letter than the rejection.

I did not have another interview until the next day, when an associate dean at Harvard managed to convince someone on the faculty of the Rutgers University Law School in Camden, New Jersey, to interview me. As I was being seated, I noted a member of the hiring committee reading my résumé.

"There is nothing here about law review," he commented, his tone of voice suggesting that the omission was possibly inadvertent or due to an inappropriate sense of modesty.

"I wasn't on the law review," I said.

He smiled benignly, then asked, "How do you explain that?"

"This may be an admission against interest, but I didn't work very hard during my first year in law school."

"The admission against interest is your résumé. Your statement just now is an explanation," he responded cheerfully, and I realized that for all practical purposes the interview had just ended. After a few minutes of dreary, insulting discussion, I left, thinking seriously of giving up and going home.

I had several other interviews before the convention ended. None were enjoyable or fruitful except for a chance meeting with the associate dean at Georgetown University Law School, which was the only school that had invited me to come out for an interview. I traveled to Washington early in January to meet with the Georgetown faculty. For the most part I was interviewed by people in the privacy of their offices. The tone and content of the interviews varied. Some of the faculty tried to sell me on the school and the pleasures of living in the Washington area. Some grilled me about my reasons for entering law teaching and my approach to legal scholarship, as though I were a law student seeking admission to their classes. Some spent the time trying to convince me that their contribution to the school was not adequately appreciated by their colleagues. Some seemed interested almost entirely in trading gossip about Harvard. Some seemed to be concerned with my positions on legal education, wondering with whom I would side on the issues that were currently dividing the faculty. I did not understand the issues that were explained to me, but I got a sense of the strong feelings they aroused. Several of the people with whom I spoke asked me about my performance as a student. Although they did not say so, it seemed clear that they were upset by the fact that I had not been on law review. Several seemed most interested in letting me know that the most prominent of their colleagues were vastly overrated.

The associate dean, Kenneth Pye, whom I later dealt with during my year in India, convinced me that I was lucky to be seriously considered by so prestigious a school. He assured me that, among those who really knew legal education, Georgetown currently stood "somewhere between ninth and twelfth among all American law schools." There was something so definitive in his tone that I accepted that evaluation instantly and believed it unquestioningly for many years thereafter. Only very late in my career did I realize that about fifteen schools claim to be rated eleventh or twelfth.

I had difficulty figuring out how I was doing. There were so many people and approaches that I felt increasingly confused as the interviews progressed. The low point seemed to come on my final day, when I was brought to the faculty lounge for coffee. I had expected relaxed conversation, but I suddenly found myself surrounded by members of the Georgetown faculty intent on probing my views on law teaching. A heavyset constitutional law professor took the lead in questioning me: "Well, Mr. Getman, I understand you have been a successful teacher at Harvard. How would you go about teaching the less gifted and somewhat older students of the type we have here?"

"I think it's important to gear your teaching to the best members in the class. If they become interested, they'll stimulate the others. Intellectual excitement tends to filter down from the top." I could see smiles of approval.

"What basic approaches would you take in teaching contracts?"

"I would try to get students to understand the ambiguities of doctrine and how rarely doctrine decides cases. Also, I would try to get the students to wrestle actively with the problems. I believe learning law is like learning to swim. You can only achieve so much watching someone else do it. You have to thrash around for yourself." More smiles.

"You talk about the ambiguity of doctrine, but surely it's important to help the students realize what's fixed and what's settled in the law."

"I agree fully, but contract law has many fewer settled principles than most other fields. Lon Fuller and I were discussing that just the other day." I mentioned Fuller's name to let them know that I was having regular conversations with the top legal thinkers of the period. It seemed to work.

A thin, pompous-looking man with a long nose, who had been staring severely at me, suddenly smiled. "You must be considering quite a few schools. I wonder if you would be willing to tell us the identity of our competition."

"Nobody else is interested in me at the moment," I replied. I noticed his smile slowly disappear, and I quickly added, "I haven't been actively pursuing the available opportunities. This faculty is the one I would like to join. I think Georgetown is an excellent law school, and I would be proud to teach here." They smiled again, but I could sense that my eagerness for the position struck several of them as unseemly and that several others were disturbed by the fact that I was not being pursued by other schools. It seemed clear that my value as a prize was as important as the contribution I might make to the educational process. Despite these concerns, I felt that I had acquitted myself well. When I returned to Harvard, I was hopeful. I knew the faculty would meet on the following Friday, and, when the day came, I hung around the phone shared by the teaching fellows, feeling nervous and excited. Toward the end of the day, a telegram was placed under my door describing in detail the outstanding academic record of the person chosen. It expressed regret that I, too, could not have been made an offer.

Looking back now on the hiring process that I went through, I am struck by the fact that so much of it was geared to gratify the egos of the people already in teaching at the expense of the applicants. Why else would the dean of the George Washington University Law School have set up so many people to be disappointed and humiliated by writing letters suggesting that they were under serious consideration and then inviting them to a cocktail party at which serious consideration was impossible? Why should the faculty at Rutgers-Camden turn me down before even making an effort to find out about me? Only by chance had I been considered by Georgetown; I was rejected there for displaying some of the traits, such as enthusiasm and forthrightness, that have made me a good teacher and a competent scholar. I was subsequently rejected for jobs because of my lack of religious observance, because of my poor undergraduate grades, and because I offended the dean at Wisconsin University Law School at a time when we were both under the influence of liquor.

While the entire process was notable for its pomposity, it was mild compared to the way candidates were interviewed at Yale during my time there in the late 1970s and early 1980s. Applicants presented papers and were grilled mercilessly. They were required to demonstrate learning in a variety of fields, have ideas for original scholarship, and show familiarity with and appreciation of the writings of whomever they talked to. More sensible systems are to be found only at less prestigious schools. For example, Elizabeth Warren described interviewing at the University of Houston Law School: "They were funny interviews. You just told stories and had a good time and talked a little bit about law but not a lot."

Although not as crucial to hiring as it once was, the use of grades as the measure of a person's potential and of his or her "smartness" continues. Despite abundant evidence to the contrary, faculties continue to believe that the best single measure of a young person's potential as a teacher and scholar is performance as a student at a first-rate graduate school. My former colleague at Stanford, Lawrence Friedman, once commented to me after a faculty appointments meeting, "If only we were hiring them to be students, our system would make perfect sense." At schools that have considerable choices in hiring, the emphasis on grades is often supplemented by other criteria, which are more subjective and even more troubling. One characteristic that helps a candidate is intellectual arrogance, the willingness to paint in broad conceptual strokes regardless of accuracy.

When I was at Yale, I discovered that the appointments committee was considering a person whose only writing was in my field. The article that drew him to the attention of the committee was filled with overstatement, exaggeration, and obvious error. His categories were confused and misleading. I told this to one of the people on the appointments committee. The committee had already been told this by someone else, but the faculty member's enthusiasm was unabated. "I know his article is all wrong, but it's so intellectually ambitious and challenging that it's bound to be important. Besides, imagine the work that he will do once he learns the field." The ability to sparkle at interviews is invaluable in getting hired at a good law school, but it is unconnected to scholarship and irrelevant to good teaching. The process is further corrupted at the major schools where faculty members are seeking not only people of comparable backgrounds but also disciples.

Today less importance is attached to grades, but the process is as irrational and as demeaning to most of the applicants as it ever was. Candidates are supposed to have an established research agenda before they even begin teaching. This puts a premium on the theoretical, the glib, and those capable of speaking in the scholarly clichés of the day. It puts teaching applicants like a former student of mine—who had ten years of excellent experience in the labor field but who had been out of law school without significant publication in that same decade—at a disadvantage. Hiring processes in fields other than law, according to people I have interviewed, are even less rational and more demeaning. Sometimes people are chosen by their allegiances to one or another currently fashionable academic movement, sometimes by their willingness to collaborate or support a senior colleague.

The Desire for Recognition

Young academics yearn for recognition. They spend inordinate amounts of time around the mailbox hoping for letters that will certify their significance—requests for reprints, invitations to present papers, or letters from publishers. I was typical in this regard. I would go to the mailbox each day, and if I found a request from a law review for an article, an invitation to join a bar committee, or a letter from an academic referring to my work, I would feel momentarily elated and reassured. When the phone rang and I could tell that it was a long-distance call, I would experience a surge of excitement. I hoped that the caller would be a professor from another school asking my opinion about a scholarly topic, a scholar inviting me to give a talk at one of the many labor law conferences held each month, or, most wonderful of all, a dean calling to find out if I were interested in joining a faculty. Any call or letter that helped to establish my status as a successful academic would give me a sense of elation, but there were never enough of them, and for many years I felt inadequately recognized and envious of other people's successes. Observing my young colleagues, I get the impression that things have gotten worse rather than better.

Many faculty at less prestigious schools spend much of their lives waiting for "the call"—an invitation to teach at one of the top schools in their disciplines. In this, too, I was typical. When I received a call from Harry Wellington, dean of the Yale Law School, inviting me to visit the following year with the likelihood that if things went well Yale would make me a permanent offer, I could hardly sleep that night, thinking how pleased my father would have been. I thought of how he would have smiled with embarrassed pleasure while telling his friends that his son was teaching at Yale and how he would have enjoyed visiting me there. He admired Yale enormously, dating back to his days as a pattern maker in the New Haven garment industry. The university symbolized power, academic leadership, and intellectual tradition.

Professors who are offered an opportunity to teach at one of the top schools rarely say no, even when the acceptance means disrupting a satisfying life or separating from their families for a year. People do not make these sacrifices for nothing. Institutions with reputations for greatness have special, ego-gratifying characteristics. This was certainly true at Yale, which illustrates the advantages offered by some institutions with a tradition of scholarly excellence.

High-level intellectual exchange was a constant feature of the school. I got to read and make suggestions to colleagues who were writing the articles that shaped legal scholarship. I got to attend the famous legal theory workshops, at which professors from other schools gave papers. Beforehand were dinners with about half a dozen especially invited people at Morey's, where good wine was served, academic gossip was shared, and serious intellectual discussion took place in an atmosphere of ostentatious good fellowship. The seminar itself was held in the faculty lounge, a darkly imposing room that gave off the scent of old books, coffee, and comfortable leather chairs. It was adorned with imposing pictures of some of the school's former faculty, such as Justices Douglas and Taft, and the great contracts teacher, Arthur Linton Corbin. The discussions were earnest, learned, spirited, and intense.

The speaker had responsibility for defending a paper that had been distributed a few days before the meeting and carefully read by most of the participants. Discussion generally started with someone innocuously questioning a sentence, a citation, or a line of argument. Explanation would lead to further questions, then to counterarguments, and gradually to a set of recommendations for change. When the faculty members got really involved, they would interrupt the speaker and each other in their zest to expose error and confusion. Only the most secure academics were able to keep their composure and respond effectively. Others would become flustered, hesitant, inarticulate, or shrill. Often, after the speaker had left, discussion would continue. New approaches were developed and an evaluation of the speaker's performance was shared and refined. What was impressive was how seriously the faculty took the enterprise and how committed they were to unearthing the proper subjects for academic research and coherent approaches to law.

Yale students were diverse, accomplished, scholastically superb, and academically oriented. The student body included professors, business leaders, politicians, and writers. At Yale, the faculty made clear its pride in the scholarly achievements of the students. At many schools, however, members of the faculty acted as though the students were unworthy of them. This was true at Indiana and even at Chicago, where the students were academically gifted.

Almost everyone on the Yale faculty feels like a success. Many reminders were present that the status which I had long sought came automatically with membership on the Yale faculty. I received invitations to deliver papers, write law review articles, address meetings, and take part in scholarly programs. I was asked to evaluate the work of young faculty members at other law schools and to give my opinions of Yale students being considered for teaching positions elsewhere.

That my sense of satisfaction at being on the Yale faculty became less powerful over the years is partly idiosyncratic. I am, thanks to a stubborn anti-intellectual streak that I acquired from my mother, the sort of person who is bound to have trouble with large, prestigious organizations. But Yale also has many of the defects that I have come to associate with academic elitism. The pervasive recognition of its great tradition is at best a short step from arrogance: the assumption that ideas are important when and because we announce them, a defect often accompanied by the ostentatious presentation of unoriginal ideas. Even the faculty appointment process is frequently corrupted by the desire to maintain greatness. The process favors those whose scholarship seems to have the greatest sweep and ambition, those who formulate principles over those who investigate reality.

The Relationship between Recognition and Achievement

For almost everyone in academic life, success has two aspects: professional recognition and meaningful achievement. The former, like success in most other fields, is identified through promotions, raises, job offers, and similar status indicators; it is powerfully related to the school at which one teaches. The latter refers to impact on students, the importance of one's scholarship, and contribution to thinking about education.

Throughout my career I have sought professional recognition. It still pleases me to receive deanship inquiries or overtures to join other faculties, to see favorable citations of my writings, and to receive requests to present papers. All these indicate that I am considered important in my field. They give me a rush of reassurance and a secret glow of pleasure, even if I turn them down. Like runs scored in baseball, they have little independent meaning; they are simply a way of measuring how one compares with the competition. Not surprisingly, conversations in which academics discuss aspects of professional recognition (and they are frequent) are often competitive exercises to prove that one is better known and recognized than one's colleagues. At schools like Indiana, the competition centers about the law reviews in which one's articles are published and the schools at which one has been asked to visit. In more prestigious schools, the faculty members compete about the importance of their named professorships, the impact of their work, the prestige of their lectureships, or the importance of the governmental appointments that they have been offered. When I visited at the University of Chicago, I had lunch one day with a group of senior faculty who were talking about phone calls from the White House. One of the brilliant young professors complained of the White House staff's tendency to call at dinnertime. Each person at the table but me had a complaint in this regard, each one suggesting more White House contacts and more personal indifference than the previous speaker.

A degree of status is achieved automatically by anyone who develops a reputation for brilliance. Consequently, some people expend a great deal of effort in achieving such a reputation. Not infrequently, this quest distorts not only research and teaching but also relationships. Some seek reputations for brilliance not through their teaching or research but

Special Features of Academic Life

through regular debates with colleagues. These debates may take place in colloquia and seminars, or in the lunchrooms and faculty lounges where the line between play and fierce academic combat often disappears. Outsiders and young academics are frequently surprised at the amount of intellectual effort and emotion expended in such settings. I learned this early in my career. As a teaching fellow at Harvard, I was eligible to attend the regular afternoon faculty teas. The setting was genteel but the discussions were not. They were hierarchical, competitive, and angry. Noted professors would stalk out of the lounge barely nodding to colleagues after discussion of some seemingly minor issue of school policy.

At Indiana University, the coffee hour played a crucial role for several of my colleagues in the effort to establish their brilliance. The coffee lounge served simultaneously as a forum for the exchange of ideas, a platform from which one might demonstrate wit and intelligence, and an arena in which professors battled with colleagues for intellectual superiority.

Most academics are also moved by a deeper desire to contribute something meaningful, but meaning in academic life is notoriously difficult to measure. Neither for teaching nor research is there any agreed standard. The most obvious ways of defining success in teaching are through student performance and achievement. If one teaches at a prestigious school, it is easy to get the sense that one's ideas are being carried forward in important ways by one's students.

Similarly, meaningful scholarship is difficult to define and in most fields even more difficult to measure. In the sciences, significance sometimes announces itself and everyone recognizes that an experiment, theory, or discovery is important. Such moments are rare, however, even at the highest levels. In the social sciences, including law, the task of identifying meaningful research in terms of its quality or impact upon future thinking is almost impossible. Certain indicators serve as surrogate measures of significance. These include the extent to which a work is used, discussed, cited, and responded to in other scholarly articles or books. All of these reactions are facilitated by its author teaching at a prestigious school. It is easier to have work published in prestigious journals if the author is associated with a prestigious school. In addition, the top schools are richer and can provide smaller teaching loads and more time off for faculty. At Yale, a triennial leave system assures tenure-track professors a semester off after each 2½ years of teaching. Not surprisingly, members of the Yale faculty have been highly productive, their works have been recognized with prizes for scholarship, and the faculty members have received all of the other forms of recognition which are available.

Hierarchy

What conflicts with the conclusion that meaning and quality of school are related? In teaching, the opportunity to awaken people to their intellectual potential, which is the most satisfying of academic experiences, is only rarely present.

At Harvard, Stanford, and Yale, the students almost always come well aware of their intellectual abilities. At one point in the 1992 presidential campaign, the three remaining Democratic contenders were Bill Clinton, Jerry Brown, and Paul Tsongas—all graduates of Yale Law School. They are archetypal Yale law graduates in several ways: each is bright, socially conscious, and believes that the country would be improved if he were running things. In scholarship, the problem partly arises from the premature attention accorded to one's early writing. This often impels young faculty to strive for greatness before they have anything significant to say. The presence of distinguished senior colleagues is as much a problem as a blessing. Inevitably, distinguished scholars will have ideas about the way a junior colleague's work should progress. These ideas will often reflect the senior person's path more than a vision of what makes sense for the younger person. The ideas of different senior colleagues are likely to conflict. Such conflicts occur frequently in institutions in which many faculty are willing or even eager to play the role of mentor. The natural pressure brought upon the younger person by such conflicts is exacerbated by the fact that those with strong views about what the beginner should be doing will read and criticize the completed work and will eventually evaluate the beginners' fitness for tenure. At less prestigious institutions, one is more apt to be left alone to find one's own voice, as happened to me at Indiana University. After my first article, I discovered that I enjoyed scholarship. I do not think this would have happened had I begun at Yale. In such cases, the pressures (both internal and external) to do something great are both powerful and pernicious. This leads young people to do pretentious scholarship filled with sweeping generalizations rather than work focused on the exploration of reality. Both the pressures and opportunities that come with membership on a major faculty discourage the painstaking investigation of reality, which is the type of scholarship most needed but least present.

Ultimately, any scholar, wherever located, must recognize that professional recognition and status are different from and often in conflict with meaningful achievement either as a scholar or as a teacher, and that while membership on a distinguished faculty brings the former, it may actually discourage the latter.

Community, Continuity, and Polarization

Academics like the idea of community. The term's use is ubiquitous. Professors often refer to the "academic community," which includes all who teach at the college level. Each institution is also referred to as a community. There are departmental and professional school communities, the community of scholars, and the community of those who teach a particular subject matter. Thus, I am a member of the academic, University of Texas, law school, labor law, and industrial relations communities.

The regular use of the term "community" is a recognition of the capacity of academic life to bring people together in a common intellectual enterprise. It is when this capacity is realized that academic life is most rewarding. Unfortunately, however, such experiences are rare and tend to be ephemeral. The majority of academics with whom I have spoken mentioned alienation and disappointment at the absence of community feeling. Several said that relations with colleagues and administrators are the worst feature of academic life.

The subcommunities represent divisions as well as positive groupings. There are ego-related differences between hard and soft scientists, classical and monetary economists, and experimental and theoretical psychologists. Although mathematicians may seem alike from the outside, considerable difference and often mutual disdain may exist between theoretical mathematicians, who investigate patterns and speak of the beauty and elegance of numbers, and applied mathematicians, who try to resolve immediate problems. Applied mathematicians see little need or use for great numbers of theoreticians, and many theoreticians consider applied math as a lower order of intellectual endeavor.

A number of divisions within academic life are based on differences in political or academic philosophies and various scholarly movements. Straussian and mainstream political scientists barely tolerate each other at some institutions. A few traditional legal scholars have suggested that critical legal theorists have no proper role in law schools. Marxists see liberal thinkers as apologists for a corrupt system, others think of Marxists as hopeless romantics, fools, or unconscious agents for tyranny.[14]

One of the most complex and significant divisions is that based on age. Relationships among young and old reflect the best and the worst features of academic life. Each group needs the other. Young professors require the approval of their seniors to achieve tenure, promotion, and recognition. Senior colleagues need the respect of their younger colleagues to feel that their lives' work has meaning and that they remain vital and important to their institutions. As a result of this mutual dependence, seniors and juniors often come together and discover ties that surmount the differences based on their backgrounds and experiences. Yet powerful psychological and practical forces also lead to divisions.

Senior professors—I among them—are very often jealous of younger colleagues. We resent the special privileges that they have, the attention lavished on them by administrators, the ease of their relationships with students, their sense of discovery in dealing with old ideas, the fact that their lives and accomplishments are before them—in short, that they are young. When senior professors get together and talk about younger colleagues, we are likely to compare them unfavorably to our own and preceding generations. They are pampered. Their approach to scholarship is inadequate. They publish too much, think too little, are not dedicated teachers, and are sadly unaware of previous contributions in their own fields.

Younger faculty in turn often feel that they are being evaluated by, and are expected to be deferential toward, incompetent senior faculty. They may feel pressured to adopt outmoded approaches, feel lectured to, and conclude that discourse with seniors is not a real exchange of ideas.

Something valuable exists in such generational differences. Older scholars can help younger scholars to find their own voices. When I was at Yale I suggested to one of my younger colleagues, Don Elliot, that he begin his scholarly career with a short, unambitious article directed to a technical issue. When I finished explaining the benefits of such an approach, he looked confused. "What you say makes sense but it's the exact opposite of what Owen Fiss told me, and what he said made sense also. In fact, everyone on the faculty seems to know exactly what I should do." His anguish was real and understandable, and I realized that he needed to ignore all of us and do what he wanted. As this story suggests, being a younger faculty member at a prestigious school where the seniors are likely to have firm ideas about scholarship is not always a blessing. At such schools the junior faculty often live uneasily in the shadow of their illustrious predecessors.

At Yale I realized how lucky I was to begin my career at Indiana University at a time when the school had many able young people, few seniors seeking to influence our work, and little prestige among elite law schools. The younger members of the faculty quickly formed their own scholarly community. I can still picture a group of us, all in our early thirties, sitting around a coffee table, laughing contemptuously while my young colleague Alan Schwartz read aloud from the lead article in the *Harvard Law Review*, written by a well-known member of the Harvard Law School faculty. In the maddeningly certain style of the times, it simply declared the nature of reality without citation or even acknowledgement that the author's assumptions might be wrong.

In our laughter was the unstated commitment that we would approach scholarship differently from our teachers and seniors, that we would deal more honorably and respectfully with the underlying reality on which legal doctrine must be based. Several of those present later did valuable work along those lines.

We were, unfortunately, as arrogant as those we mocked, dismissing, without any real basis, styles of scholarship and modes of discourse we thought of as old-fashioned. We ignored the important work of our senior colleague Jerome Hall and most of us had little idea of the great contributions of Ralph Fuchs to scholarship and academic life.

Some years later, when I was a senior member of the Yale Law School faculty, we considered making an offer to a well-known authority on contracts, a man in his midfifties who taught at Berkeley. He was coauthor of a leading casebook and had written many law review articles. His appointment was bitterly opposed by several of the younger faculty who disparaged the old-fashioned, balancing-of-interests approach of his articles as well as the absence of economic analysis and philosophic insight. I left the faculty lounge, where the meeting had taken place, with Harry Wellington, then dean of the law school. As the meeting had been fairly tame in comparison with other meetings in which appointments were discussed, I was surprised to see that his expression was morose.

"What's troubling you?" I asked. "You didn't expect the offer to be voted without opposition, did you?"

"No, but I realized that everything that the younger people were critical of in his work could have been said about mine," he replied frankly.

In 1991, a group of younger faculty at the University of Texas Law School, including one of my former students, and I interviewed a teaching candidate who had recently graduated from Yale. Everyone but me became involved in a lively discussion of standards of interpretation, a currently hot academic topic. They discussed whether critical legal theorists and feminist thinkers differed and analyzed the writings of various young academics. The work they discussed so avidly was work that I found pretentious, difficult to understand, and not very important.

At a later point in the interview, I asked about a labor law case that had come before the Supreme Court while the candidate was clerking there. The candidate answered perfunctorily and the discussion quickly changed to something I knew little about. My young colleagues found him interesting and promising. I not only differed as to his promise but I felt profoundly disconnected from all of my colleagues and from the current trends in legal scholarship. New scholarly movements arise in almost every decade, which help make the younger faculty feel that their work is pathbreaking and important. Because of these movements, a few senior academics feel vindicated, while many feel bypassed.

Although conflict among academic generations is quite common, many positive personal relationships cross generational lines. The best young scholars and teachers are the ones most likely to acknowledge the influence of senior colleagues and teachers in their work. The most satisfied seniors are those who see their own influence in the work of the younger generation.

In addition, most professors have been significantly influenced by mentors who personify the values that make academic life meaningful. Their achievements provide goals to strive for and standards against which the young person measures his or her progress. It is when academics speak about their mentors that expressions of caring, affection, and love are most clearly stated. In such conversations one can understand the values and dreams that have led people into academic life.

Matthew Straud, who teaches Spanish at Trinity University in San Antonio, described his mentor as "a luminous, spellbinding figure." Elizabeth Warren described her mentor, John Mixon, professor of law at the University of Houston Law School: "I was very lucky. John Mixon took me under his wing. . . . He just talked to me. He was calming, like the first stage of a mantra, or like psychotherapy. He was like that, calming and loving and yet very intense about teaching. . . . I would tell a story about an exchange I had with a student and how I felt so badly about how I hadn't done the right thing. And John would keep questioning me about it until finally it would become clear what the dynamics were. . . . Usually the student was trying to shift the responsibility of learning difficult material over to me."

Herbert Marks, who now teaches comparative literature at Indiana University, had a series of mentors when he did graduate work at Yale. One was Professor Geoffrey Hartman, of whom Marks said:

> He handled our relationship with a sparkle, a twinkle. It was a game of serenity. He was tremendously quick . . . one never had to force an insight. He started a train of thought and then knew what you were saying instantly and could always suggest a step further. And he had a prac-

tical sense about how to pursue scholarship. There are certain people who have the gift. I have it myself in certain moments when I feel very little anxiety and am open and alert, invariably turning to the important page, reading the central paragraph, leafing through the book and knowing what the work is about.

Ray Marshall, a distinguished scholar and successful cabinet member in the Carter administration, told me of a great teacher who handed back a paper to him when he was in fourth grade saying, "Your name is a very important possession. Never degrade it by putting it on something this bad again." Marshall told me that he recalls that statement every time he writes something. Bruce Mann, professor of law at the University of Pennsylvania Law School, told me of the great Yale historian, Ed Morgan, whose impact on his students was of "such extraordinary respect and affection that you truly loved the man, that the thought of disappointing him was not something any of us could face."

Sometimes relationships evolve, as they did for Melvin Schwartz. His first mentor was Jack Steinberger of Columbia University, who started as his undergraduate teacher and "great hero," then became his graduate advisor and ultimately his senior colleague and collaborator. In 1989 they shared the Nobel Prize in Physics.

The most satisfying aspects of my own career have included my relationships with senior colleagues when I was starting out and with younger colleagues today. My first mentor was John P. Dawson, a distinguished legal scholar at Harvard Law School. When I was a teaching fellow, I took a seminar with him that paved the way for a new first-year course on the development of legal institutions. We discussed materials Dawson had prepared that described ancient conflicts whose resolution shaped the law's development. The issues all seemed to have contemporary significance—controlling bureaucracies, limiting executive discretion, and protecting individual rights. Dawson was personally engaged with the material. He expressed anger at some of the old judges, was tolerant of some, and enthusiastic toward others. We discussed an ancient meeting in which Lord Coke, the Chief Justice of the King's Bench, refused to tell King James in advance how he would decide an issue in which the royal prerogative was implicated. He told the king that he would give his opinion "when the case should be." It was a great moment in legal history—the assertion of judicial independence against the claim of overriding sovereign authority. When Dawson read the report to us, his face beaming with delight, I felt proud to be connected to so illustrious a tradition. I could recognize the concepts that joined Lord Coke with John Minor Wisdom, Elbert Parr Tuttle, and James Skelly Wright, the great judges then on the United States Court of Appeals for the Fifth Circuit who were developing the civil rights laws to achieve racial integration.

In Dawson's class, I experienced most directly one of the great joys of academic life: the realization that seemingly esoteric material provides an important way of learning about the current world. At times like that, the elitist and egalitarian aspects of academic life merge.

During the semester, Dawson asked me to research the development of the requirement that jury verdicts be unanimous. I spent what seemed to be a great deal of time reading reports of common-law cases decided during the sixteenth and seventeenth centuries and reading other historical accounts of the period. It occurred to me that the requirement of jury unanimity arose naturally from the cooperative experiences of people in sixteenth- and seventeenth-century England. This was different from the traditional historical explanations that focused much more on the role of judges.

I stopped by Dawson's office one Friday afternoon to discuss my theory. He was sitting at his desk, which was stacked high with huge, dusty volumes. Three opened yearbooks, ponderous old leather-bound volumes of medieval legal cases, took up all the desk's center. He was leaning back in his chair reading a fourth volume intently. His face reflected total concentration, excitement, and pleasure. A paper cup half-filled with whiskey was placed on the typewriter stand.

He poured out a cup for me, and we sipped whiskey and talked for more than an hour about the relationship between research on group dynamics undertaken during World War II and the issue I was researching for him. Dawson's views about this, as about everything, were a mixture of scholarly passion for accuracy and intellectual boldness. I felt a deep sense of satisfaction, certain that no one had ever addressed the issue in this way before. I recognized for the first time the appeal of scholarship, its combination of excitement, collaboration, and contentment.

My second mentor, Louis Jaffe, changed my view of intellectual life. He exemplified its pleasures and its pains: the sense of alienation from students and colleagues that frequently marks gifted academics. I was at the time a teaching fellow, a minor academic functionary with no status and little role at the Harvard Law School. Jaffe was one of the most prolific scholars on the faculty. In his books and articles he articulated better than anyone else the concepts that should govern the relationships between courts and administrative agencies. He was, however, cut from a different mold than the rest of the faculty. He was less a teacher with a defined pedagogic style than a thinker who scattered insights about law and society in a rambling, unconnected fashion during his classes.

When I first met him, he had just seen Maurice Evans' television portrayal of Macbeth, and he spoke of it excitedly in a high-pitched voice: "I never realized before how neurotic Macbeth was. When the character says, 'Macbeth has murdered sleep, Macbeth shall sleep no more,' he is speaking literally. He will never have a peaceful night's sleep again."

I could sense that Jaffe, who had been on medical leave during my senior year because of emotional problems, identified with Macbeth in this regard, that he knew the terrors of sleepless nights and living with powerful feelings of guilt. Still, it surprised me that he was so favorable to Evans' performance, which I thought was too histrionic. When Jaffe paused for a moment, I said so. He looked surprised, as though the table had suddenly asked to join the conversation.

"Too histrionic? I didn't think it was too histrionic. I thought he was playing Macbeth as he was meant to be played—full of passion, anger, guilt, and poetry. You're probably one of those people who finds the open expression of emotion embarrassing. How would you prefer it to be played?" I told him that my idea of good Shakespearian acting was exemplified by the British Broadcasting Corporation production of the historical plays, entitled "An Age of Kings," and that part of *Henry IV, Part II* would be seen that evening. He snorted, mumbled something unintelligible, and left. The next afternoon, I was surprised to find him outside my office.

"I have watched 'An Age of Kings,' and I have the following to report," Jaffe said. (I was struck by his word *report*.) "You are right that the acting is quite good. Falstaff and Hal were both played excellently and there was pace and intelligent restraint in the production, but this is a different play than *Macbeth*, and it calls for different acting."

We argued for a while. It surprised me that he took the ideas of a mere teaching fellow seriously. I told him that I particularly enjoyed the confrontation between Prince Hal and Falstaff in the Boar's Head Tavern when a dialogue that began in jest and evident good humor ends with Hal solemnly responding to Falstaff's entreaty that he not be banished by stating, "I do. I will," thereby clearly announcing the impending end of their relationship.

"I liked the way the characters conveyed that barroom banter is often a hidden form of hostility," I said.

He became thoughtful. "What struck me about that scene was how dangerous it is to play games with kings."

"That's it," I said, suddenly excited by his insight, which seemed to state my reaction more clearly than I had been able to do myself. I realized that this theme was not only central to the scene, but also that it helped to explain my feeling of discomfort in social situations with people whose approval I considered crucial to my ambitions, such as Harvard faculty members. For me, a great message became clear in this anecdote. My explanation was a restatement of conventional wisdom, something that I knew to be a safe conclusion. Jaffe's statement was based solely on his own reaction to the material.

Jaffe could articulate the subtle themes of literature, the intricacies of films, and the complexity of public issues better than anyone I have ever known. He did it casually, as though this was a common skill of educated people, but I never heard anyone at the Harvard Law School or any of the other places at which I have taught come close to matching him.

Jaffe's influence upon me was profound. He recommended books that I read and films that I made it a point to see. He pointed out subtle flaws in works that I admired and thereby slowly changed my standards for judging them. He awakened my interest in larger issues of social policy outside of law. In this way, he reversed some of the narrowing impact of law school.

I received great pleasure from observing Jaffe's interactions with his colleagues. I admired his acuteness in recognizing when one of his colleagues unfairly characterized a position, his boldness in challenging generally accepted premises. I can still hear him demanding of one of his colleagues, "Why do you put it that way? Wouldn't it be just as accurate to state . . . ," and he would then characterize the other person's position in a manner just the opposite of the way it had just been stated. His colleagues would attempt to point out the unfairness in Jaffe's characterizations, but they never succeeded. When the occasion called for it, Jaffe could be eloquent. I was present at a debate among the Harvard Law School faculty about whether a person who had been an organizer for the Labor Youth League (which was considered a Communist-front organization) and had not revealed this on his résumé should be appointed as a teaching fellow. The debate was emotional and the faculty closely divided until Jaffe recast the issue, making it less a question of principle and more a matter of giving someone the opportunity to demonstrate his commitment to academic integrity. When Jaffe concluded, it was obvious that the appointment would be voted overwhelmingly. When I congratulated him afterward on his eloquence, he was surprised. "I thought I was merely restating what everyone knows."

Had it not been for Jaffe, I would not have attempted to write a law review article during the summer of 1962 after my first year as a teaching fellow. Scholarship was not expected of teaching fellows in those days. My article was entitled "The Use of the Writ of Mandamus as an Instrument of Judicial Review in California." Many of its forty pages were taken up by a long (and, I thought, erudite) discussion of the development of cases. In the final five pages, I pointed out that California law was irrationally based on a meaningless distinction between property rights and professional interests.

When Jaffe returned from his summer home on Martha's Vineyard at the end of August, I eagerly gave him a copy and we scheduled an appointment for the following week. When we met, he wasted little time in preliminaries. "It's amazing that someone teaching at the Harvard Law School would refer to cases without telling the reader what they decided. Your writing style is awkward and verbose. Your criticism is probably sound but presented unfairly. You neither suggest how the courts could have done a better job nor point out how much of the problem is attributable to the legislature." He went on in this matter-of-fact manner for about twenty minutes, seemingly unaware of my feelings. I was surprised at first, then resentful, and finally overwhelmed by the accuracy of his criticism.

I do not remember a single favorable comment. I felt that his opinion of me had been substantially lowered and doubted that I could ever write anything that would meet his standards. It was a humiliating experience that left me depressed and bewildered. Yet it has since proven to be enormously helpful. When I wrote my first article as a law professor, one constant concern was to gain Jaffe's approval. I read over each paragraph trying to anticipate how he might criticize it. Even when it was accepted for publication by the *University of Chicago Law Review,* my joy was tempered by concern about his response. I sent him the first reprint. When his return letter began, "Yes, I think well of your article; it is well reasoned and constructive," I felt as though I had successfully completed a rite of passage. To this day, I have never written an article without, at some point, hearing him ask in his singsong voice, "Why do you say that? Why couldn't someone just as plausibly take the opposite position?"

Mentors and Meaning

Probably the most satisfying relationship of my career was with Ralph Fuchs, who was a friend, mentor, and inspiration to me until his death in 1984. Ralph was a first-rate scholar and teacher, but what he most exemplified was the importance of nonacademic values—friendship, caring, fairness, and family—to the achievement of a decent life as a professor. His life was built around service to the community, but his sense of community did not have the narrow institutional focus so common among academics. Instead, it extended to the profession generally and beyond to the broader national and international society.

When I first arrived at Indiana University, Ralph was near retirement age. I knew from Louis Jaffe that he was highly thought of as a scholar and that he had been an influential lawyer working with the solicitor general's office. I was pleased to have someone so distinguished as a colleague, but the idea of becoming friends seemed out of the question. When we had occasion to speak, Ralph was friendly but in an impersonal way. He did not fit my vision of what an open person should be. Everything about him seemed too formal and correct—his three-piece suit, his courtly manner, his perfectly grammatical and erudite way of speaking, his unwillingness to engage in gossip. I thought him unexciting, overly controlled, and basically unfriendly. Scott Daily had told me that Ralph was considered by the students to be someone who could even make the most exciting cases seem dull, and I found the criticism easy to believe.

There was, at that time, considerable ferment on campus over what was called the YSA case. The local prosecutor had brought charges of sedition against three students based on their membership in the Young Socialist Alliance and the use of heated rhetoric, which soon seemed tame on college campuses.

Ralph invited me to go with him to Indianapolis, where he was to give a talk to the Indiana Civil Liberties Union about the case. The meeting was held in a crowded high school auditorium. The audience, young and intense, convinced of the threatening and unconstitutional nature of the prosecutor's actions, was ready to be outraged. But Ralph's discussion was so unemotional, precise, and technical that the mood of the group became noticeably calmer. He explained the theory that the state would probably use and then set forth the competing arguments which seemed to him "on balance, preferable." I was astonished by his bland tone, his careful phrasing, his lack of passion, the absence of outrage. I thought contemptuously: "Now I understand why he is not considered an exciting teacher." But, as he continued, I realized that I had not previously understood the issue.

It struck me, finally, that he was using the occasion to teach, to inform people about how the constitutional issues related to our federal system, rather than to exploit the emotions of fear and outrage which most of the audience felt. A sense of admiration and pride that this man was my colleague replaced my earlier disappointment.

As we left the hall to go to Ralph's car, a tall, arrogant-looking blond man approached us. "Frank Richards, *Indianapolis Star*," he said. Then, turning to me, he said in an unpleasant tone, "Take a walk for a few minutes, will you, buddy? I wanna ask Dr. Fuchs a few questions."

I started to leave, but Ralph put his hand on my arm. "This man is my colleague," he said with evident but controlled anger. "If you want to talk to me, you will have to show basic courtesy toward us both. If you have any legitimate questions to ask, you can ask them in his presence."

"I want to know if you were ever a member of the Young Socialist League and ever supported Communist candidates."

Suddenly Ralph moved forward so that his jaw was next to the reporter's face. "I resent this harassment. You have no basis for asking such a question. If you were really interested in knowing the answer, you would have discovered that I have answered those questions on public record. Now, please get out of my way."

The reporter seemed stunned. "It's nothing personal. Don't get so angry," he said rather lamely.

"That's all I'm going to say. Good evening." The reporter started to say something, then stopped, perhaps deterred by the firm, indignant set of Ralph's features. I realized that I had underrated the fire that lay just beneath Ralph's calm exterior.

The next week, when Ralph suggested that I join the American Association of University Professors, I did so. After that we slowly became friends. The Fuchs often entertained and almost always invited an interesting and diverse group of people. At first, I simply felt pleased to have him as a colleague, someone whose judgment I could seek on questions of fairness or academic principle. Gradually, almost imperceptibly, our conversations became more personal and meaningful, marked by a continually greater sense of warmth. We became friends during the 1960s, when the great civil rights confrontations were taking place. At that time I feared that American society might take a great swing to the right, abandoning its commitment to civil rights and equality. Ralph, who left Washington University of Saint Louis to protest the university president's lack of commitment to integration, would reassure me. He was an incurable optimist who always thought that the world was getting better, more civil, more caring, more committed to equality, and that, in whatever issue he faced, rational discourse would ultimately prevail.

We talked much about our children. Ralph's son Hollis, who had recently returned from the Korean War in which he had lost a leg, had, to Ralph's dismay, rejected the idea of law school. He had instead moved out west to become a cowboy. Ralph, after much turmoil, decided that his task was to support Hollis in whatever way he could. When we first began speaking of it, Ralph was worried that he had made a mistake, but he lived to see this decision abundantly vindicated. Hollis became a successful rancher who raised champion quarter horses and then became a well-known sculptor of western scenes.

Eventually, the formality that had initially put me off began to take on a different aspect, illustrative of Ralph's steadfast commitment to an old-fashioned but appealing style of academic life. I came to admire him for not changing, for never trying to be trendy, and for constantly struggling to live up to a personal inner vision of decency. Once, at a party where everyone else was dressed in the casual style of the early 1970s, a woman told Ralph she could not understand why he continued to wear suits on all occasions. "You are the stiffest person I know," she said with some severity. Ralph responded calmly, "I believe that people should dress the way they are the most comfortable. For me, that means wearing a suit."

Ralph had no trouble accepting his granddaughter's African husband and was delighted when they both chose to study law at I.U. But when his grandson-in-law planned to accept an additional diploma from the Black Law Students' Association, Ralph, whose commitment to racial equality had caused him to leave Washington University of Saint Louis, was surprised and hurt that the law school's regular diploma was not sufficient. He told this to his grandson-in-law politely. They discussed the issue and each came to understand the other's position. Not surprisingly, Ralph's grandson-in-law, now a successful lawyer, became one of his ardent admirers.

Ralph never boasted about his contributions to the university or to the broader community. Yet they were widely recognized, as was the special quality of his life. Ralph played the role of mentor and friend for so many of us that when he died at the age of eighty-five, the memorial services held in packed auditoriums were more celebrations of his life than mourning for his death.

Mentors, like great teachers, remain forever in one's memory. The continuing power of the mentor relationship is best illustrated for me by the lasting bond between Max Rheinstein, a comparative law scholar who taught at the University of Chicago, and Mary Ann Glendon, his former student, now a distinguished comparative law professor at Harvard. He was a German-Jewish refugee, an old-world scholar with great intellectual sweep. When their collaboration began, she was a young woman of both Yankee and Catholic background, unformed as a scholar but interested in ideas. The affection and caring that they felt for each other was regularly manifested by the pleasure evident in their constant earnest discussions of law, scholarship, and life. Mary Ann was aware that, in her relationship with Max, she was able to transcend the limits of her own background and experiences. When she was appointed to the Harvard faculty, she saw it as an opportunity to carry forward the work she had begun under Max's tutelage. She describes the evolution of their relationship in the dedication to *The Transformation of Family Law*, a revised edition of *State, Law, and Family*, which was dedicated to Max:

> The contributions of Max Rheinstein to that book were substantial. I would have to say they began long ago when, as his student at the University of Chicago, I was first exposed to his contagious fascination with the complex interaction of law and society and to the remarkable example set by his habits of work and thought. Later, as his coauthor, I had the extraordinary privilege of being able to observe closely a master at work on the technical intricacies as well as the grand design of an enterprise. While I was writing *State, Law, and Family*, Max in his characteristically generous way found time to read and comment on every chapter. Although he died in the summer of 1977, shortly before the book appeared, he was the first and most attentive reader of the manuscript. In the course of preparing this successor volume, I have been conscious of continuing, in some way, our happy collaboration. Thus, it has seemed fitting to me to dedicate this book to the memory of my beloved friend and teacher.[15]

Few passages in the extensive literature about academic life so clearly reveal its promise or so compellingly testify to the possibility of its fulfillment. The passage captures the inspiration of great teaching, the joys of scholarly collaboration, and the potential of academic life to join together people of diverse backgrounds in the common pursuit of truth. The dedication illustrates the continuity of the academic enterprise across time. No one who talks with Mary Ann to this day can fail to notice the extent to which her professional activity continues to be shaped by Max's teaching. Beyond all these themes and adding to them is the love and affection that our best teachers and scholars inspire in their students and colleagues.

Notes

1. The Attraction of Academic Life

1. I do not know if that is still true; I get mixed reports from friends who teach there.

2. The Basic Academic Processes and the Search for Meaning: The Conflict between Elitist and Egalitarian Values

1. Elizabeth Forsythe Hailey, "A Fellow Conspirator," in *An Apple for My Teacher*, ed. Louis Rubin, Jr. (Chapel Hill, N.C.: Algonquin Books, 1987), pp. 52–53.

2. Max Wise, "Who Teaches the Teachers?" in *Improving College Teaching*, ed. Calvin B. Lee (Washington, D.C.: American Council on Education, 1967), pp. 78, 79, 81. As Max Wise reports, teaching assistants "get little help from senior faculty members on the teaching problems they encounter." He also notes that "they report feeling that they are treated as individuals of low status" (p. 81). Wise also points out that "in most programs of study the graduate student develops very limited perspectives of teaching" (p. 78). The final result is that "having uncritically assimilated limited perspectives of teaching, the typical young teacher is prepared to spend his professional life replicating these experiences" (p. 79).

3. Baird W. Whitlock, *Educational Myths I Have Known and Loved* (New York: Schocken Books, 1986), pp. 49–50.

4. Houston A. Baker, Jr., "What Charles Knew," in *An Apple for My Teacher*, ed. Rubin, pp. 123–131.

5. Ibid., p. 127. Given the immediate elitist impact of Professor Watkins, it is interesting that Houston Baker has emerged as one of the leading exponents of egalitarian multiculturalism, one of those accused of "animus to the traditional values of Western thought and culture" by Roger Kimball in *Tenured Radicals* (New York: Harper & Row, 1990), p. xi. Kimball accuses Baker of being the voice of those who "deliberately blur the distinction between high culture and popular

culture," quoting Baker as stating, "I am one whose career is dedicated to the day when we have a disappearance of these standards." Ibid., p. xiii. Baker is also attacked for his antielitist attitudes in Fred Siegal's "The Cult of Multiculturalism," *The New Republic* 204, no. 7 (February 18, 1991): 36.

6. As of this writing, Carol Moseley Braun had won the Democratic primary in Illinois as a candidate for the U.S. Senate, the first black woman in any state ever selected by statewide primary balloting as a nominee for a Senate seat.

7. *Hoyt v. State of Florida*, 83 S.Ct. 159, 162 (1961).

8. *Reed v. Reed*, 92 St. Ct. 251 (1971).

9. Brief for Sally M. Reed in *Reed v. Reed*.

10. See Julius G. Getman, "The Emerging Constitutional Principle of Sexual Equality," in *The Supreme Court Review 1972*, ed. Philip Kurland (Chicago: University of Chicago Press, 1973), pp. 157–180.

11. *Reed v. Reed*, p. 68n9.

12. Ibid.

13. Ibid., p. 68n5.

14. Christopher Jencks and David Riesman, *The Academic Revolution* (New York: Doubleday, 1968), p. 531.

15. Howard R. Bowen and Jack H. Schuster, "The Faculty at Risk," *Change*, September–October 1985, pp. 15–16.

16. The doctrine gets its name from an early case, *Midwest Piping and Supply Co. Inc.*, 63 NLRB 1060 (1945).

17. Julius G. Getman, "The Midwest Piping Doctrine: An Example of the Need to Reconsider Labor Board Dogma," *University of Chicago Law Review* 31, no. 1 (1964): 292–322.

18. Jencks and Riesman, *The Academic Revolution*, p. 532.

19. Howard R. Bowen and Jack H. Schuster, *American Professors* (New York: Oxford University Press, 1986), p. 147.

20. Jencks and Riesman, *The Academic Revolution*, p. 533.

21. Bowen and Schuster, *American Professors*, pp. 149–150.

22. Ralph Fuchs, "The Prerequisites to Judicial Review," *Indiana Law Journal* 51 (1976): 817.

23. Julius G. Getman, Stephen B. Goldberg, and Jeanne B. Herman, *Union Representation Elections: Law and Reality* (New York: Russell Sage, 1976).

24. For a review of the criticism, see Archibald Cox et al., *Labor Law Cases and Materials* (New York: Westbury Foundation Press, 1991), pp. 193–198. The book has also received a modicum of sophisticated criticism that used our database as the starting point for independent analysis and arrived at different conclusions. Such criticism is interesting and even flattering. I regret how little of it there is and how often academics have rejected our findings on the basis of commitment to traditional ways of looking at things.

25. Jerome R. Mintz, *The Anarchists of Casas Viejas* (Chicago: University of Chicago Press, 1982).

26. Michael Riordan, *The Hunting of the Quark*, (New York: Simon & Schuster, 1987), p. 211.

27. Electromagnetism, gravity, the strong interaction that binds subatomic particles, and the weak interaction.

28. The experiment involved an accelerated proton beam striking a mass of beryllium that created a pion beam which disintegrated into muons and neutrinos. This beam collided with an iron wall 13 meters thick that stopped everything but the neutrinos. The neutrinos passed into a huge spark chamber. Every time a neutrino was absorbed by a proton or neutrino, a charged particle would be emitted and a trail of sparks was formed in the charge chamber. The experiment is described in Yuval Ne'eman and Yoram Hirsh, *The Particle Hunters* (Cambridge: Cambridge University Press, 1983), p. 206.

29. I learned this from Federal District Judge Jose Cabranes, a former student of Mel Schwartz.

30. Riordan, *The Hunting of the Quark*, p. 206.

31. Ibid., pp. 209–210.

3. The Relationship of Faculty to Academic Institutions

1. Minutes of the meeting for the organization of the American Association of University Professors, January 1, 1915.

2. "American Association of University Professors, Declaration of Principles (1915)," reprinted in *Academe* 75, no. 3 (May–June 1989): 9.

3. Ibid.

4. Walter P. Metzger, "Origins of the Association," *AAUP Bulletin* 54 (Summer 1965): 237.

5. John Silber, *Straight Shooting* (New York: Harper & Row, 1989), p. 100.

6. American Association of University Professors and Association of American Colleges, "Statement of Principles on Academic Freedom and Tenure (1940)," reprinted in *Law and Contemporary Problems* 53, no. 3 (Summer 1990).

7. Metzger, "Origins of the Association," p. 237.

8. Walter P. Metzger, "A Note on the AAUP in the McCarthy Period," *Academe* 72 (November–December 1986): 29–30.

9. The facts as set forth are contained in Terry Doran's "Two Lives," an unpublished manuscript in the author's possession. The facts relevant to the legal proceeding are set forth in the opinion by Judge Lowdermilk in the decision of the Court of Appeals of Indiana, First District, in *Doran v. the Board of Education of Western Boone County*, Cause no. 1271-A-266, issued June 5, 1972. The charges against Doran were set forth in a Statement of Reason for Consideration of the Cancellation of the teaching contract of Terrence Doran by the Board of Education of Western Boone County Community School Corporation (undated memo, James P. Fritch, superintendent, Western Boone County Community School Corporation to Terrence Doran).

10. "Students Demonstrate at Wells over Teacher Dismissal," *Lebanon Reporter*, December 12, 1968.

11. Cases such as Terry's made the NEA far more militant; schoolteachers

282 · · 282 · ·

are now typically provided greater protection through collective agreements between the NEA and local school boards.

12. Unless otherwise indicated, the essential facts and quotes in the Allen Miller case are contained in the transcript (hereafter cited as transcript) of the hearing conducted on January 12–15, 1970, by an ad hoc hearing board whose members were chosen from the Associate Instructors Implementation Committee. A copy of the transcript is in the author's possession. The confrontation with Colonel Jones appears on p. 14 of the transcript and has been emended to reflect the pseudonym Allen Miller. Other pseudonyms are Rod Smith and Randy Baker. All other names are real. Additional information on the case may be found in issues of the *Indiana Daily Student*, the *Bloomington Herald Telephone*, and the *Louisville Courier Journal* from the fall of 1969 and January of 1970.

13. Statement issued in October of 1969 by the Indiana University chapter of the AAUP, as reported in "Reinstate Allen, Professors Urge," *Bloomington Herald Telephone*, October 29, 1969.

14. Letter, James B. Christoph, chairman of the political science department, Indiana University, to Chancellor Byrum Carter, October 24, 1969. The letter was distributed to the faculty; a copy is in the author's possession.

15. Connie Haas, "TA Association Supports [Allen]," *Indiana Daily Student*, October 28, 1969.

16. "Eng TAs Oppose Suspension," *Indiana Daily Student*, October 29, 1969.

17. On direct examination, Remak testified that he had urged a less drastic approach than that actually taken (transcript, p. 75). On cross examination, Remak stated that he was "in touch with several members of the Executive Committee of the AAUP and relayed to the chancellor the feeling that . . . it might be desirable to have a hearing . . . before possible suspension" (transcript, p. 76).

18. Transcript, p. 84.

19. Transcript, p. 89.

20. Transcript, pp. 39, 132.

21. Recommendation of the hearing board in the case of Allen Miller, May 1970. On May 28, 1970, the chancellor sent a copy of the recommendation and a brief note to all departmental chairmen and deans explaining that "the most persuasive aspect of the Committee Report to me was their concern with the absence of prior warning."

22. Burton R. Clark, *The Academic Life: Small Worlds, Different Worlds* (Princeton: The Carnegie Foundation, 1987), p. 139. Even John Silber, the controversial, academically conservative president of Boston University who fought the AAUP on his own campus, has recognized the importance and "high mindedness" of the early AAUP and the "righteousness" of its approach to academic freedom (Silber, *Straight Shooting*, p. 100).

23. The antiacademic freedom activities of left-wing groups has received considerable publicity. See, for example, Fred Siegel, "The Cult of Multiculturalism," pp. 34–47. The claim that multiculturalism and political correctness pose a major threat to academic freedom is denied in Cathy N. Davidson, "P.H. Stands

for Political Hypocrisy," *Academe* 75, no. 5 (September–October 1991): pp. 8–14. See also materials cited in Chapter 4.

24. For a discussion of the interplay of different forces in college and graduate school admissions, see David Owen, *None of the Above* (Boston: Houghton Mifflin, 1985). See also Dwight Lang, "Equality, Prestige and Controlled Mobility in the Academic Hierarchy," *American Journal of Education* 95, no. 3 (May 1987): 141 and 467, and articles cited therein.

25. *Catalogue, Indiana University School of Law* (Bloomington: Indiana University, 1969).

26. Lewis Cosner, "Academic Intellectuals," in *The Professors: Work and Life Styles among Academicians*, ed. Charles H. Anderson and John D. Murray (Cambridge, Mass.: Schenkman, 1971), p. 79.

27. See *Faculty Bargaining in Public Higher Education: Report of the Carnegie Council on Policy Studies in Higher Education* (San Francisco: Josey Bass, 1977), p. 2; see also David Rabban, "Can American Labor Law Accommodate Collective Bargaining by Professional Employees?" *Yale Law Journal* 689 (1990).

28. *NLRB v. Yeshiva University*, 444 U.S. 672 (1980).

29. Silber, *Straight Shooting*, pp. 100–101.

30. The general counsel is a part-time position held by a person who is otherwise a full-time faculty member. The AAUP also has two full-time staff attorneys. They, of course, do the vast majority of its legal business.

31. At the most prestigious schools, it is often understood that very few junior faculty in most departments will be tenured. New Ph.D.'s and others entering academic life often accept positions as assistant professors at schools like Harvard, Yale, or Princeton knowing that even if they do very well they are unlikely to be tenured. The prestige and opportunities for research that affiliation with such schools brings, together with the opportunity to work with and obtain sponsorship from important faculty members in one's field, make the assistant professorships desirable, even if the untenured professors have very little chance to remain on the permanent faculty. No stigma is attached to the refusal to grant tenure to assistant professors at such schools. However, at most academic institutions, an appointment as a regular or tenure-track faculty member is understood to imply that he or she will be granted tenure if the teaching and scholarship are good.

32. Service refers to an amorphous group of factors: work on university committees, public appearances, talks to alumni groups, and collegiality, which means friendliness and sometimes willingness to aid other faculty members with their research and teaching. Service is a very minor factor in the typical tenure consideration. It is occasionally used to justify the grant of tenure to a well-liked person whose scholarship and teaching would otherwise be inadequate. The absence of service is only very rarely mentioned as a reason for denying tenure to someone who is generally disliked but whose teaching and scholarship are adequate.

33. When I joined the faculty at Yale Law School, one of the deans told me that the faculty was divided on how much weight to assign teaching. He said, "Attitudes range all the way from those who give it only marginal weight in close

cases to those who give it no weight at all." While the story is not quite fair, it is nonetheless true that Yale Law School tenure decisions during the period that I was on the faculty focused primarily and sometimes exclusively on scholarship.

34. Sometimes elite schools have the ability to make their own determinations as to tenure. At Yale Law School, for example, only the law faculty vote on the grant of tenure.

35. Janet Lever, *Soccer Madness* (Chicago: University of Chicago Press, 1983).

36. Rick Telander, as quoted on the *Soccer Madness* dust jacket.

37. James F. Short, Jr., as quoted on the *Soccer Madness* dust jacket.

38. Ian Taylor, *Bulletin, International Committee for the Sociology of Sports*, as quoted on the *Soccer Madness* dust jacket.

39. As later described by U. S. Magistrate Bernard Weisberg, the process is as follows: "The Dean . . . decides whether to recommend to the Provost, the chief academic officer of Northwestern, that the candidate receive tenure. . . . the Provost's recommendation is required for a grant of tenure . . . Occasionally the Provost disagrees with the Dean's recommendation and does not recommend tenure, and occasionally he recommends for tenure someone not recommended by the Dean.

"If the Provost recommends a grant of tenure, that recommendation is passed through the president's office for action by the Board of Trustees. Approval by the trustees is only a formal step. . . . [the current Provost] had never known the trustees to reject his recommendation." *Special Master's Report, Lever v. Northwestern University et al.*, No. 84c11025 (June 11, 1991), p. 3.

40. *Special Master's Report*, p. 4.

41. Copies of the letters, which are in my possession, came from noted sociologists who do not wish to be identified.

42. *Report of the Ad Hoc Committee to Consider the Appeal of Professor Janet Lever*, February 6, 1982, pp. 3–4.

43. Ibid., p. 20.

44. Memorandum opinion and order, *Lever v. Northwestern University et al.*, October 4, 1991.

45. "I anticipated being a teacher and a community activist because that kind of activity was supported by the department. People had gotten involved in writing up cases on local plant closings and in local community education. I went [to Bucknell] because I could combine regular classroom teaching with regular activities in the community that were related to my research and that would be counted as academic scholarship. According to a departmental document, you could write articles if you wanted, or you could do other types of things, including consulting work. . . . All of that was perfectly acceptable," Adrienne Birecree said.

46. "I had very good experiences there. I loved . . . my students. I had made a good decision in terms of wanting to teach, and I did get involved in a lot of different projects, including the Popular Studies Institute with Charles Zachary, who was an assistant professor at Bucknell at the time. He and another temporary fellow had started a free economics class for adults at night in the community. The idea behind that was to use the university's resources to enrich the community, to bring people on campus, to get them to use our library, to get them to take advan-

tage of the fact that the university was theirs. So from 1983 to 1987, we codirected the Bucknell Popular Studies Institute and offered economics classes for adults. A lot of those people turned out to be members of different unions, . . . very interesting people from all different socioeconomic backgrounds. We usually had about twenty to twenty-five students per class and usually offered one class per semester," Adrienne Birecree said.

47. Letter, Robert H. Chambers to Adrienne Birecree, December 14, 1983.

48. Letter, Larry D. Shinn to Adrienne Birecree, December 14, 1985.

49. The other locations were Jay, Maine; De Pere, Wisconsin; and Mobile, Alabama. These strikes have been the focus of much testimony at Congressional hearings on the bill to outlaw the hiring of permanent strike replacements, currently HR-5. They have been studied by researchers at MIT and by various labor law professors, including myself. My own study had focused on the strike at Jay. I first learned about Adrienne Birecree when I read a draft of one of her articles dealing with International Paper Company. I considered it a first-rate piece of work.

50. Letter, URC to Adrienne Birecree, December 15, 1988.

51. Judy Dunn, "Bucknell Students Plan Speakout for Tuesday," *Lewisburg (PA) Daily Journal,* May 9, 1988.

52. Report of Committee on Academic Freedom and Tenure, May 13, 1988.

53. Adrienne's scholarship arose out of her earlier community involvement. In 1986 a bitter labor dispute erupted in the nearby town of Lewisburg, Pennsylvania. The dispute involved the International Paper Company and a local of the United Paperworkers International Union. The situation was similar to a strike in Clinton, Iowa, that Adrienne had studied in preparing her thesis. For scholarly and ideological reasons, Adrienne found the strike at Lewisburg interesting and stirring. Adrienne and her colleague Charles Zachary sought to help the strikers. "We had the Popular Studies Institute available, so we tailored a couple of courses to the interest of some of the union people who were involved in that dispute," Adrienne Birecree said.

4. The Struggle for Change

1. Maxine C. Hairston and John J. Ruszkiewicz, *The Scott, Foresman Handbook for Writers* (Glenview, Ill.: Scott Foresman, 1988).

2. Paula S. Rothenberg, *Racism and Sexism: An Integrated Study* (New York: St. Martin's Press, 1988).

3. Memorandum, Linda Brodkey, director of the LDEPC, to English Department faculty, May 1990.

4. Alan W. Friedman, "English 306 at the University of Texas at Austin," *Texas Academe,* n.s. 1, 2 (Spring 1991): p. 22.

5. Ibid.

6. Advertisement, "Statement of Concern," *Daily Texan,* July 24, 1990.

7. Professor Daniel A. Bonevac on the PBS television program "Austin at Issue," July 26, 1990.

8. Alan Gribben also described himself in the letter as "a dedicated teacher, a producing scholar with a national reputation, and a principled person oriented toward stability." Alan Gribben, "Alan Gribben Pushes Receivership for English Department," *Daily Texan*, August 6, 1990.

9. George Will, "Radical English," *Washington Post*, September 16, 1990.

10. Maxine C. Hairston, "Required Writing Courses Should Not Focus on Politically Charged Social Issues," *Chronicle of Higher Education* 37, no. 19 (January 23, 1991).

11. See Candice Driver, "Gribben Asks Faculty Senate to Screen E 306," *Daily Texan*, July 20, 1990; Gribben, "Alan Gribben Pushes Receivership for English Department"; Brian Builta, "Gribben Defends Stance on E 306 Professor: I'm Doing the Correct Thing," *Daily Texan*, August 10, 1990; and Kevin McHargue, "Confusion Reigns in the World According to Gribben," *Daily Texan*, July 20, 1990. While these articles were by no means all favorable to Gribben's position, they did all serve to make his views known. Other articles and editorials set forth the views of Professor Brodkey and those of other supporters of the course. See, e.g., Christopher Anderson, "Faculty Supports New E 306 Theme," *Daily Texan*, September 17, 1990; and Chris Barton, "Dean Postpones E 306 Revision. Meacham Says Delay Necessary," *Daily Texan*, July 24, 1990.

12. See, e.g., McHargue, "Confusion Reigns in the World According to Gribben," and Sara Diamond, "Readin', Writin', and Repressin'," *Z Magazine*, February 1991, p. 45.

13. Rothenberg, *Racism and Sexism.*

14. Ibid., p. 6.

15. Gregory Curtis, "Behind the Lines: The Bring-something-Texan-that-you-want-to-burn Party," *Texas Monthly*, May 1990, p. 5.

16. Barton, "Dean Postpones E 306 Revision. Meacham Says Delay Necessary."

17. Christopher Anderson, "E 306 Questions Go Unanswered," *Daily Texan*, September 18, 1990.

18. David Loy, "E 306 Controversy Called Sobering," *Daily Texan*, February 7, 1991.

19. See, e.g., John Taylor, "Are You Politically Correct?" *New York Magazine* 24:3 (January 21, 1991): 33.

20. Letter, Douglas Laycock to Barbara Bergmann, September 17, 1990.

21. Letter, Kurt Heinzelman to Douglas Laycock, October 30, 1990.

22. Francine Bosco, "New 306 Syllabus Able to Unite Divided Department," *Daily Texan*, June 4, 1991.

23. An excellent defense of the pedagogical reasons for the course was contained in a whimsically titled but serious article, "E 306; or, How I Spent My Summer Vacation," by Linda Brodkey and John Slatin, which appeared in the *Daily Texan*, September 4 and 5, 1990.

24. According to Linda Brodkey in a telephone interview on February 2, 1991, a version of E 306 using the same assignments has been taught successfully

at the University of Rhode Island in a collaborative effort of two faculty members, one conservative and one liberal.

25. "Not Just a Matter of Course: Lillian S. Robinson Talks with Linda Brodkey," *The Women's Review of Books* 9, no. 5 (February 1992): 23.

26. See, e.g., E. D. Hirsch, Jr., *Cultural Literacy: What Every American Needs to Know* (Boston: Houghton Mifflin, 1987); Allan Bloom, *The Closing of the American Mind: How Higher Education Has Failed Democracy and Impoverished the Souls of Today's Students* (New York: Simon & Schuster, 1987); Kimball, *Tenured Radicals*; and Einesh D'Souza, "Illiberal Education," *The Atlantic*, March 1991, p. 51.

27. Kimball, *Tenured Radicals*, pp. xii–xiii.

28. On the other end of the cultural spectrum is Paul Simon, whose *Graceland* (Warner Brothers Records, 1986) and *The Rhythm of the Saints* (Warner Brothers Records, 1990) albums bring together rhythms, images, and language of musicians from the different cultures in a musical poetic form. Simon has been dismissed by snobs and attacked by some multiculturalists as being insufficiently authentic.

29. Transcript, Allen Miller hearing, p. 193.

30. Transcript, pp. 118–119.

31. Allan Bloom is particularly critical of this aspect of the student movement and the mood of the campuses during the 1960s. He found the challenge to the "King's English" most disturbing, "more important than the bad teachers and the self-indulgent doctrines." His reason for condemning it seems less than overpowering: "The awareness of the highest is what points the lower upward" (*The Closing of the American Mind*, p. 321).

32. I saw this approach in action twice—once, briefly, when I visited Poland during the early Solidarity period, and again during the organization drive and strike by the clerical workers at Yale. Yale's union had by far the best group of organizers I had ever seen in action. A high percentage of the organizers were former student activists who had put in time doing community work. The organizing drive and successful strike that followed were among labor's few successes during the period.

The success of Local 34 contains an important message for liberal academics and labor leaders. It is possible to forge the alliance that the student movement talked about but, because of its own arrogance, never really attempted. If such an effort is made, many of those shaped by the 1960s are likely to reemerge within the academy, perhaps to express in a more mature form the impulse that led them to see themselves briefly as revolutionaries.

33. Jencks and Riesman, *The Academic Revolution*. This is not to say the authors were unaware of the changes underway. Their chapter "Feminism, Masculinism, and Coeducation" (pp. 291–311) foresees and favors greater gender integration in higher education.

34. See *Fact Book on Women in Higher Education*, comp., Judith G. Touchtan and Lynne Davis (New York: Ace McMillan, 1991); and *Women in Academe: Progress and Prospects* (New York: Russell Sage, 1984), Chapter 2.

35. Memorandum, Dean Wilford Baine to Central Administration, July 1972.

36. Taped recording of testimony of dean of music school, in Ethel Merker's hearing before the Faculty Board of Review in March and April of 1974.

37. Report of the Faculty Board of Review in the matter of Ethel Merker, April 24, 1974.

38. Carol Gilligan, *In a Different Voice* (Cambridge: Harvard University Press, 1982). Gilligan's work has also been criticized from a feminist perspective; see James C. Walker, "In a Diffident Voice: Crypto Separatist Analysis of Female Moral Development" *Social Research* 50 (1983): 665.

39. See Carrie Menkel-Meadow, "The Comparative Sociology of Women Lawyers: The Feminization of the Legal Profession," *Osgoode Hall Law Journal* 24, no. 4 (1986): 897; and Phyllis Goldfarb, "A Theory-Practice Spiral: The Ethics of Feminism and Clinical Education," *Minnesota Law Review* 75, no. 6 (1991): 1599.

40. Evelyn Fox Keller and Helen Mogler, "Competition and Feminism: Conflicts For Academic Women," *Signs: Journal of Women in Culture and Society* 12, no. 3 (Spring 1987): 493.

41. See Owen, *None of the Above*, pp. 216–217; see also William E. Coffman, "The Scholastic Aptitude Test: An Historical Perspective," *The College Board Review*, no. 117 (Fall 1980): p. A8, and articles cited therein.

42. Owen, *None of the Above*, pp. 216–229.

43. Similar arguments were made on each side earlier in the century when Jewish students generally performed poorly on IQ tests.

44. Owen, *None of the Above*, pp. 200–229.

45. Donald K. Hill, "Myth, Law, and Linguistic Thought," *Multicultural Law Review* 1 (1988): 10.

46. From Franklyn Ajaye's album, *I'm a Comedian, Seriously*. A&M Records, 1974.

47. Everette J. Freeman and Dale G. Brickner, "Labor Education: A Growth Sector in a Stagnant Industry," in *The Re-education of the American Working Class*, ed. Steven H. London, Elvira R. Tarr, and Joseph F. Wilson, (New York: Greenwood Press, 1990), pp. 4–5.

48. Ibid., p. 5.

49. Ibid., p. 7.

50. Taylorism refers to the theories of Frederick Taylor, an industrialist who believes that scientific management dictated that jobs should be kept as simple as possible and not require creative thinking.

51. Freeman and Brickner, "Labor Education," p. 9.

52. Memorandum, A. A. Liveright, Notes on a Day Spent at Indiana University, December 6, 1963.

53. Letter, J. Frederick Truitt to Ford Foundation, February 18, 1964.

54. Evaluation of 1962–1964 fellows by staff member, n.d.

55. Memorandum, Preliminary Report on Resident Labor Education Program at Indiana University, Center for Study of Liberal Education for Adults, Chicago, December 29, 1963.

56. Ibid.

57. Ibid.

58. Fellows' statements are from program evaluation forms, December 4, 1963.

59. Tom Mboya, *Freedom and After* (London: Andrew Deutsch, 1946), p. 580, as cited in Al Nash, *Ruskin College: A Challenge to Adult and Labor Education* (Ithaca, N.Y.: New York State School of Industrial and Labor Relations, Cornell University, 1981), pp. 46, 55.

60. Nash, *Ruskin College*, p. 46.

61. Leonard Kriegel, *Workers' Education. Kaleidoscope*, Fall 1986, p. 23.

5. *Special Features of Academic Life*

1. Bowen and Schuster, *American Professors*, p. 28.

2. Harry Shulman, "Reason, Contract, and Law in Labor Relations," *Harvard Law Review* 68 (1955): 99.

3. I have come to realize the wisdom of Dr. Kenneth Clark, my psychology professor at CCNY. After he appeared as a witness in the famous *Brown v. Board of Education of Topeka* desegregation case, he stunned our class of New York liberals by predicting that racism and segregation would end first in the South.

4. Bloom, *The Closing of the American Mind*, pp. 313–335.

5. David Lodge, *Small World* (New York: Warner Books, 1989), prologue.

6. Ibid., pp. 72–73.

7. Whitlock, *Educational Myths I Have Known and Loved*, p. 5.

8. Mintz, *The Anarchists of Casas Viejas*.

9. Memorandum, Ford Foundation, concerning India program.

10. The *ji* suffix, which signifies affection or respect, was deliberately left off his name.

11. William Van Til, *My Way of Looking at It* (Terre Haute, Ind.: Lake Shore Press, 1983), pp. 261–262.

12. Memorandum, Julius Getman to Douglas Ensminger, Ford Foundation, New Delhi, India, Winter 1968.

13. Kazuo Ishiguro, *The Remains of the Day* (New York: Knopf, 1989).

14. In general, little division based on ethnicity or religion exists in academic life. Increasingly, however, tensions are appearing between women and men and between minority group members and white Anglos. In each case, however, the relationship is complex and the tensions are less than those present in the general nonacademic society.

15. Mary Ann Glendon, *The Transformation of Family Law* (Chicago: University of Chicago Press, 1989), pp. ix–x.

Index